THE ANGLICAN EVANGELICAL CRISIS

THE ANGLICAN EVANGELICAL CRISIS

Edited by Melvin Tinker

Christian Focus Publications

Acknowledgements
In addition to all those who have contributed essays to this volume I would like to express my appreciation to Tina Bowers and Sheila Waller for typing the manuscripts and also to John Weetman for his assistance. Last but not least my deepest gratitude goes to my wife Heather for her patience and support during the long period covered in seeing the project through to completion.

Melvin Tinker
St John's Newland,
1995

Cover design by Donna Macleod

Published by
Christian Focus Publications Ltd.
Geanies House, Fearn, Ross-shire,
IV20 1TW, Scotland, Great Britain.

CONTENTS

Contributors

David Holloway is Vicar of Jesmond Parish Church in Newcastle upon Tyne, one of the largest churches in the north of England. Formerly on the staff of Wycliffe Hall, he has been a member of the General Synod of the Church of England and of its Standing Committee.

Mark Thompson taught doctrine and church history at Moore College Sydney and is at present engaged in research for a D. Phil. at Oxford University on the Doctrine of Scripture in the theology of Martin Luther.

Melvin Tinker is Vicar of St. John's Newland in Hull. He has written on a wide variety of subjects relating to doctrine and ethics and is the editor of *Restoring the Vision - 'Anglicans Speak Out'* (Monarch).

Dr Gerald Bray is Professor of Anglican Studies at Samford University, Birmingham, Alabama. He is the General Editor of the 'Contours of Christian Theology' series, published by IVP and author of the widely acclaimed *The Doctrine of God* which appears in the same series.

Dr Douglas Spanner is a non-stipendiary minister in the Oxford Diocese and retired Professor of Biophysics at the University of London and the author of several articles on theology and science.

Dr James I Packer is Professor of Systematic and Historical Theology at Regent College, Vancouver. A major speaker at the first two National Anglican Congresses, he edited 'Guidelines'. A prolific writer and international speaker, amongst his writings are *Knowing God, Keep in Step with the Spirit* and *A Passion for Holiness*.

Dr Peter Adam is Vicar of St. Jude's, Melbourne, and a teacher of Theology and Preaching at Ridley College, Melbourne, Australia.

Dr John Woodhouse is Rector of Christ Church, St. Ives, Sydney, formerly lecturer in Old Testament at Moore Theological College. He is a member of the Diocese of Sydney's Doctrine Commission and was largely responsible for steering through the legislation adopted by

Sydney Diocese which enables deacons and lay people, in appropriate circumstances, to administer the Lord's Supper.

Rachel Tingle is the Director of the Christian Studies Centre in London and author of *Another Gospel?* and *Revolution or Reconciliation*, both published by the Centre.

Dr Os Guinness is a well known international speaker and writer and Director of the 'Trinity Forum' in the United States. Author of the best selling *Dust of Death*, his recent titles include *Dining with the Devil* (Baker) and *The American Hour*, 'a time of reckoning and the once and future role of faith' (Macmillan).

David Field is a member of staff at the Church Pastoral Aid Society and former tutor in ethics at Oak Hill theological college. He is the author of *Homosexuality - a Christian option?* published by Grove books, Bramcote.

Dr Don Carson is Research Professor of New Testament, Trinity Evangelical Divinity School, Illinois. A popular speaker at Word Alive, he is the author and editor of several major theological works, including a masterly commentary on *John*, published by IVP.

PREFACE

1967 was a significant year. Not only was it the year of 'flower power', 'Sergeant Pepper' and other notable developments which marked the rising 'counter culture', it was the year when Anglican Evangelicals decided to break out of their cosy parochialism and enter into the structures of the established church. It was the year of the Keele Congress. Nearly thirty years later many are now wondering to what extent has the established church entered into Evangelicalism, thus generating its present crisis of identity, theology and purpose.

Of course there are many who, like a former British Prime Minister at the height of the so called 'winter of discontent', when asked 'What is your response to the present crises?' would reply, 'Crisis, what crisis?' They would point to the tremendous gains of the Keele experiment – the numerical strength of the 'Evangelical' theological colleges and the sizable number of Evangelical bishops and archdeacons. It is now fashionable to court Evangelicals instead of ignoring them or dismissing them as troublesome fundamentalists. It is 'OK' to be evangelical now, after all, in a relativistic age like ours what is wrong in having one more theological brand name on the ecclesiastical shelf?

Such upbeat, evangelicals-now-come-of-age attitude marked the collection of essays published in 1993 entitled 'Evangelical Anglicans' edited by the former and present Principals of Wycliffe Hall, Oxford – Dr Dick France and Dr Alistair McGrath. The title of the book itself spoke volumes, for unlike as earlier generation of Evangelicals in the Church of England (including Dr John Stott), the new Evangelicals see the term 'Evangelical' functioning simply as an adjective, describing the type of Anglicans they are, rather than the primacy being given to Evangelicalism in defining their theological outlook and practice.

However, that there is a crisis is evidenced in several ways.

The increasing influence of the newly formed REFORM group cannot be ignored. Many people on the ground, both clergy and laity instinctively feel something is wrong and many have turned to RE-FORM to be the clear voice of mainline Evangelicalism within the Church of England. With increasing perplexity, people are asking where is the distinctive evangelical voice from the bench of bishops? Which one has raised his voice not only in urging caution regarding the ordination of woman, but against a report on human sexuality which effectively undercuts the clear vote of the General Synod against validating homosexual practice?

The frantic efforts of the Anglican Evangelical Assembly and its steering committee, the Church of England Evangelical Council, to try and hold the increasingly precarious alliance together as at the 1995 AEA further points to a looming crisis.

Neither can it be doubted that the so called 'Anglican leaders Conference' held in London in January 1995 was largely convened because some of those in the establishment hierarchy felt that too much thunder was being stolen by the likes of REFORM and who better to take the lead than Evangelical bishops? Nonetheless a most uncertain sound was heard at that conference only to be followed by the resignation of one of its leading Bishops from the Church Pastoral Aid Society because of a more than ambiguous stance that he had taken over the issue of ordaining practising homosexuals. Could one have imagined Evangelical bishops even contemplating this as a possibility say ten years ago?

A crisis there most certainly is.

First there is a crisis of identity.

How are Anglican Evangelicals to be identified, by others and by themselves? For many the term 'Evangelical' has become merely a label of convenience, a sociological cypher denoting those who have had a similar past – maybe converted at a Billy Graham meeting, members of the IVF (now UCCF) in their university days, folk who are keen on evangelism and having a taste for modern hymnody. This is a far cry for the theological confessional identification which marked our forbears. Although primarily writing of the American scene, David F. Wells observations have a certain poignancy which applies much more widely:

> As evangelicalism has continued to grow numerically, it has seeped through its older structures and now spills out in all directions, producing a family of hybrids whose theological connections are quite baffling: evangelical Catholics, evangelicals who are catholic, evangelical liberationists, evangelical feminists, evangelical ecumenists, young evangelicals, orthodox evangelicals, radical evangelicals, liberal evangelicals, Liberals who are evangelical and charismatic evangelical. The word evangelical, precisely because it has lost its confessional dimension, has become descriptively anemic. To say that someone is an evangelical says little about what they believe. And so the term is forced to compensate for

its theological weakness by borrowing meaning from adjectives the very presence of which signals the fragmentation and disintegration of the movement. [1]

Are we observing a similar demise here? This leads to the second element of crisis, a crisis of theology. This may sound strange given the number of 'Evangelical' theologians gaining academic prominence today. But two things need to be said. First, how is the adjective 'Evangelical' functioning with some of these theologians, is it really Evangelical theology they are promoting or some other theology with an Evangelical gloss? Secondly, who is reading their books? Usually only a small part of the church, often other theologians, little percolates down to the pulpit or the pews. The theological diet of many Evangelicals is very weak indeed if the Christian best-sellers lists are anything to go by.

Even to point to some doctrinal basis of faith as a sign that Evangelical theology is alive and well is not sufficient. We are all aware of the danger of notional assent, a faith without works, this is no less a danger in the evangelical world. It is this lack of theological vision that has been most noticeable since the third National Anglican Evangelical Celebration at Caister. Whatever cohesion existed at the Leaders Conference in January 1995 was largely tactical but not theological. We are being pragmatically driven, not theologically driven. The great sin in the mind of the older Fundamentalism was to compromise, the great sin in the mind of the new Evangelicalism is to be narrow.

Third, there is a crisis of purpose. This naturally follows from the last two. Without a clear identity arising out of a coherent theology, purpose is going to be unfocused. For those who have risen to leadership positions within the established Church the pressures of administration, together with the natural tendency to maintain the status quo, will make the adoption of a distinctive evangelical theology and its consequent radical practical outworking less and less attractive. The 'Pauls' who have the courage to publicly challenge even a Peter face to face (Galatians 2:11) will give way to the 'Barnabases'. We need both of course. But the Paul's are notably absent from our present bench of Bishops.

Accordingly, this collection of essays seeks to draw out a different path than that traced by the France/McGrath volume. Although this

---

1. David F. Wells, *No Place for Truth*, Eerdmans, 1994, p.134.

book is not strictly a response to that collection, at points it does engage with it, most notably the final essay by Don Carson, not himself an Anglican, but an observer and Evangelical friend.

Those who have written here are would say that they are first evangelical before they are Anglican, this being a matter of conviction and theology, rather than temperament. Issues are considered which lie at the heart of much of the present day confusion and crisis. Here is a call not merely to be Evangelical by association but by conviction. It is also a call to allow that conviction shaped and guided by Evangelical theology founded upon Scripture, to determine Evangelical behaviour and practice. This position sees Evangelicalism not simply as one tradition amongst many, but as representing authentic Christianity, because it is Christianity which is one with, and arises out, of the New Testament. It is also believed that what is represented here in principle lies at the heart of historic Anglicanism as defined by the Church's Articles. Far from Evangelicals being the cuckoos in the Anglican nest, we do humbly believe the nest to be ours and invite others to receive and enjoy its riches.

It is hoped that this book will help clarify issues of concern and positively indicate the way forward. It is also hoped that it will be read by Anglicans and non-Anglicans, Evangelicals and non-Evangelicals alike thus stimulating thoughtful and gracious discussion amongst all of those who wish to see the cause of Christ promoted in an increasingly needy world.

Soli Deo Gloria
Melvin Tinker, St John's Newland, Hull.
July 1995

1

Semper Reformanda

David Holloway

Introduction

'Semper Reformanda' – 'always to be reformed' – is a motto which is needed in the Church of England today. I believe that there is something radically wrong with the Anglican Church, and something must be done, under God, soon. In short there must be a new Reformation. It was Malcolm Muggeridge at that remarkable International Congress on World Evangelisation in 1974 at Lausanne, Switzerland in his paper entitled *Living Through an Apocalypse*, who said this:

> I was reading the other day about a distasteful but significant experiment conducted in some laboratory or other. A number of frogs were put into a bowl of water, and the water very gradually raised to the boiling point, with the result that they all expired without making any serious effort to jump out of the bowl. The frogs are us, the water is our habitat, and the media, by accustoming us to the gradual deterioration of our values and our circumstances, ensure that the boiling point comes upon us unawares. It is my own emphatic opinion that the boiling point is upon us *now*, and that as a matter of urgency Christians must decide how they should conduct themselves in the face of so apocalyptic a situation.[1]

In fact we can apply that picture of the frogs to our own experience in the Anglican Church at large and the Church of England in particular.

Here is an example from the USA, but such a situation could easily be encountered before long in this country if something is not done. I quote from Richard Neuhaus. He is referring to (Artificial Insemination by Donor) AID:

> A recently publicized example was the case of an Episcopalian priest who wanted a baby but definitely not a husband. She invited three friends over (two of them priests) to masturbate for her, and she then impregnated herself with the mixture of their sperm. The purpose of having several sperm

---

1. *Let the Earth Hear his Voice*, ed. J. D. Douglas (Worldwide Publications, Minneapolis, 1975), p 449.

sources, she explained on national television, was to avoid knowing who the father was, and thus to make sure that the child would have an intimate bond to no one but herself. The child is now three years old, and the mother has declared that she intends to have another baby by the same procedure. The *Washington Post* described her as the first artificially inseminated priest in history, which is probably true. Her bishop, Paul Moore of New York, appeared with her on television and gave his unqualified blessing to this undertaking, citing the need for the church to come to terms with the modern world.[2]

Richard Neuhaus elsewhere has reported on a 'multi-faith' course in USA seminaries entitled 'Making Cakes for the Queen of Heaven.' And these sorts of things are happening in our Anglican Communion. The problem is that Evangelicals are in danger of getting immune to some of the appalling things that are going on around us.

Nor should we be surprised at the moral, spiritual and consequent numerical decline of the church. Paul predicted to Timothy that he would see people turning away from the truth.

For the time is coming when people will not endure sound teaching, but having itching ears they will accumulate for themselves teachers to suit their own likings, and will turn away from listening to the truth (2 Tim. 4:3).

And what is to be the response of Timothy in such a situation?

First, he is to 'preach the word' and that is defined as 'convincing' (or arguing); 'rebuking' (or saying things are wrong when they are wrong); and 'exhorting' (or encouraging – encouraging what is good). Timothy is to be 'unfailing in patience' (he won't achieve all his goals overnight – most people overestimate what they can achieve in one year, and underestimate what they can achieve in five years); and, says Paul, Timothy must also be 'unfailing in teaching' (Paul implies the fundamental battle to be won is in the mind). But Paul concludes this little section in 2 Timothy 4:5 with these words:

As for you, always be steady, endure suffering, do the work of an evangelist, fulfil your ministry.

'Be steady' – the word means literally, 'be sober'. Don't get heady; keep alert; keep rational; don't under-react and don't over-react. 'Endure suffering' – you will be opposed if you seek to reform the church; you will be attacked, abused, defamed, and action will be taken against

2. R. J. Neuhaus *Guaranteeing the Good Life* (Eerdmans, Grand Rapids, 1990), p 3.

you. So Paul says, 'endure suffering'. But, and this is the big 'but', 'do the work of an evangelist, fulfil your ministry.' The work of evangelism can't wait until the Anglican Church, the Church of England, or any church is properly reformed. Of course we must not rename the Decade of Evangelism 'a Decade of Renewal'. The Church will never be totally reformed or renewed this side of heaven. So Paul says to Timothy, 'Yes, there has to be some negativity, and saying things are wrong; but be positive as well, "do the work of an evangelist, fulfil your ministry."' Work for the growth of the church. It is a simple fact that if people get converted and are built up in the faith and your church grows, people who want 'new teachings' will find it harder and harder to argue against you.

Yet, perhaps someone will still say: 'but do we really need to be reformed in the Church of England?'

Let me give two reasons why, I believe, the answer must be 'yes'.

First, it is a question of numbers. During the 1980s Anglican Church membership declined by 15 per cent. There is a crisis in many quarters over money and over manpower. True, these are only symptoms; but they are symptoms of something wrong somewhere.

Secondly, to reform is to be true to our Anglican tradition. The Reformation in the 16th century in England is vital for our self-understanding. So let us remind ourselves of what happened then.

The English Reformation

There were, of course, two phases to the English Reformation. First there was the phase under Henry VIII. The aim then was simply to deny the supremacy of the Pope and to reduce superstition in the church; but the authority of the visible church remained. You still needed the church to interpret the Bible. The Bible couldn't stand on its own; and so the Bible was not really set free to challenge the church.

But the Archbishop of Canterbury, Thomas Cranmer, wanted to go further. He thought that the church led us to the Bible; but when the Bible was reached, it did stand on its own and it didn't need to be propped up by the church.

This is how J. S. Marshall describes Cranmer's position:

> ... for Cranmer the authority of the Bible is different from the authority of the church. *The Bible is from God, the church here on earth is of men*. The Bible does exist in the church and is related to the church, but the security of truth lies with the Bible rather than the church.[3]

---

3. J. S. Marshall *Hooker and the Anglican Tradition* (A & C Black, London, 1963) p 12.

The second phase of the English Reformation was to put into effect Cranmer's position. In the Thirty Nine Articles, the Book of Common Prayer and the Ordinal, you have just that. That position, accepted by men such as Jewel and Hooker, is what we mean by Anglicanism. Simply put, it said this: the Bible is the supreme authority; yes, the Bible is to be read through the lens of the first four General Councils and the interpretation of the early Fathers; but if such a reading challenged those early Fathers, the Scriptural truth rather than the patristic truth was to be accepted; the church is to be subordinate to the Bible and the Bible has to be interpreted as a whole. So Article XX, for example, says that:

> It is not lawful for the church to ordain any thing that is contrary to God's Word written, neither may it so expound one place of Scripture, that it be repugnant to another.

This is all very important for today. For this is the doctrine and the basis of the Church of England constitutionally. We have it in Canon A5 which in turn is enshrined in the *Worship and Doctrine Measure 1974*. This is the doctrine of the Church of England. The title of Canon A5 is 'Of the Doctrine of the Church of England'.

It says this:

> The doctrine of the Church of England is grounded in the Holy Scriptures, and in such teachings of the ancient Fathers and Councils of the church as are agreeable to the said Scriptures. In particular such doctrine is to be found in the Thirty-nine Articles of Religion, the Book of Common Prayer, and the Ordinal.[4]

That is Cranmer. That is Hooker. But that is not what you get so often in Deanery Synods, or as the received wisdom from the General Synod and the House of Bishops.

What has gone wrong?

We have had, and are still having to battle for the Bible as the Reformers had to. But there is another battle that touches on that one, which, when we loose, we automatically lose the battle for the Bible. Because it concerns what to us, as to our Anglican Reformers, is a

---

4. *The Canons of the Church of England - Canons Ecclesiastical promulged by the Convocations of Canterbury and York in 1964 and 1969 and the General Synod of the Church of England from 1970* can be obtained from Church House Publishing, Church House, Great Smith Street, London SW1P 3NZ.

secondary matter, we fail to see the seriousness of it. I am referring, of course, to the doctrine of the church, not so much as regards its authority, but its nature. This, in historical terms, was the second battle that had to be fought by our English Reformers. And if Cranmer was the great exponent of the authority of the Bible, Hooker was the great exponent of the nature of the church.

The Doctrine of the Church

Hooker's position in short was this. We must make, he said, the vital distinction between the church of God mystical (to use his and the Book of Commin Prayer phrase) and the church visible, and then we must distinguish between the church visible sound, and the church visible, corrupt. I quote:

> For lack of diligent observing the difference, first between the church of God mystical and visible, then between the visible sound and corrupted, sometimes more, sometimes less, the oversights are neither few nor light that have been committed.[5]

This is so important. For on the one hand it contradicted the Roman Church that wanted the visible church under the Pope, with all its corruptions, to be 'the true Church' in all its glory. But on the other hand it contradicted the more radical reformers – the Presbyterians and the Anabaptists – who like some modern House Church folk wanted to reform the church into a true and perfect visible church.

Hooker said that the visible church, while God's provision and the locus of those means he has ordained for our nurture – the preaching of the Word and the administration of the sacraments – is not to be wrongly absolutized.

Add together this doctrine of Scriptural authority and this doctrine of the church mystical and we are not surprised to find what our Reformers said was the essence of Christianity. They said it was not the visible church itself, nor its ministry. No! the essence of Christianity and the unity of the church came from its Lord, its faith, and initiation into that faith.

So Hooker says:

> The unity of which visible body the church of Christ consisteth in that uniformity which all several persons thereunto belonging have, by reason of

5. Richard Hooker *Ecclesiastical Polity* Vol. 1 (J. M. Dent, London, 1907), p 289.

that *one Lord* whose servants they all profess themselves, that *one Faith* which they all acknowledge, that *one Baptism* wherewith they are all initiated.[6]

Hooker goes on to spell out that 'Faith' as credal orthodoxy. And there is no negotiation over its doctrinal implications. There is no comprehensiveness over basic doctrine.

Such comprehensiveness as he wanted and believed to be right had nothing to do with doctrine, but all to do with what, in those days, was called 'discipline'. It was the word to cover *all* questions of Church Order. Over matters of Church Order our Anglican Reformers took a relaxed, but conservative line. They said that the Bible is not prescriptive on Church Order; so let's allow anything that is useful, so long as the Bible doesn't positively forbid it. And if something is there, and it's pretty harmless, and some people like it, don't make a fuss and remove it, as there are more important things to be getting on with than having unnecessary fights with traditionalists (I paraphrase, of course!). By contrast the Presbyterians and the Anabaptists said that the Bible insisted on a certain church order; so, they said, Hooker's comprehensive view of Church Order was wrong and indulgent.

Hooker quotes with approval Gregory, Augustine and Calvin: Gregory when he says, 'Where the faith of the holy church is one, a difference in customs of the church doth no harm'; Augustine when he says, 'Let the faith of the whole church, how wide soever it have spread itself, be always one, although the unity of belief be famous for variety of certain ordinances, whereby that which is rightly believed suffereth no kind of let or impediment'; and Calvin when he says, 'As concerning rites in particular, let the sentence of Augustine take place, which leaveth it free unto all churches to receive each their own custom. Yea sometime it profiteth and is expedient that there be differences, lest men should think that religion is tied to outward ceremonies.'

When it comes to ministry, Hooker sees ministers as essential to the church, and God has set them apart (for life) for a special task. They are defined by their function. And Bishops become necessary, according to Hooker, when you have many clergy to co-ordinate. So theologically the episcopate is derived from the presbyterate and not vice-versa.

Our Reformers advocated comprehensiveness in Church Order – there you could have variety; but they never advocated comprehen-

---

6. *ibid* p 285.

siveness in doctrine. Indeed, they would be shocked by today's doctrinal comprehensiveness in the Anglican Church.

That is the Church of England according to Canon A5; the Church of England I was ordained into; and the Church of England as by Law established. But what has happened? Subtly the Cranmer Reformation has been overturned. You have in its place the religion of Henry VIII or worse. You now get people talking as though the important thing about the Church of England was 'episcopacy'; and the defining mark of the Church of England was the 'bishop in his Diocese'.

Here is R. A. Norris, the theologian and Church Historian, describing what has happened. With the Reformers, he says:

> ... episcopacy had been defined as the normative, divinely ordained or approved ordering of the church; but the one absolutely indispensable mark of a church was taken to be its continuance in apostolic and scriptural teaching. Now, however, episcopacy has come to count as a factor that grounds the identity of the church.[7]

This 'high doctrine' of ministry and episcopacy has come, of course, via the Tractarians, F. D. Maurice and Michael Ramsey. It results in the reassertion of the visibility of the mystical church. It is certainly not the doctrine of Cranmer and Hooker. But their doctrine is the only doctrine that we are canonically bound by.

So the English Reformers said that Scripture (which means the teaching of Jesus and the Apostles, not of some later deviant clergy) is to be our authority. The visible church is important, but it is to be subordinate to Scripture. But by the end of the last century all that had been reversed in much of Anglicanism. The ministry ordained in an Apostolic succession, performing the liturgy, it was now being said, guarantees the church. Of course, while you had men like Pusey who held such a doctrine together with a high doctrine of Scripture, some foolish, and we would judge, erroneous things happened; but it was not heretical. But this high doctrine of the ministry before long allowed people to let go of the Bible altogether, or at least to subordinate it almost totally to the church. The result was a liberal movement in the Church married to an inadequate Anglo-Catholic ecclesiology – the worst of all possible worlds. Men like Dennis Nineham, John Robinson, and David Jenkins, therefore emerge as a result and many others get infused with the spirit

7. R. A. Norris 'Episcopacy' in *The Study of Anglicanism* ed. Stephen Sykes and John Booty (SPCK, London, 1988) p 306.

of this deadening theology which soon becomes heretical.

This picture has been presented at length because it is essential that we know where we are starting from if we want to reform the Church of England. Too easily we can think that the trouble is *all* with 'liberal theology'. But such theology has been effective by riding on the back of a defective Anglo-Catholic theology; and it now is riding on the back of a defective Evangelical theology. Evangelicals are buying into this doctrine of the absolutism of the visible church and the fundamental necessity of bishops. The Reformers made it quite clear that Bishops were of the 'well-being' (bene esse) not the 'being' (esse) of the church.

Add to that the following: we rightly believe that matters of Church Order are secondary matters and so we are then tempted not to worry about wrong teachings over secondary matters. This I have discovered is often fatal. If someone else is teaching that a secondary matter is a primary matter, you have to intervene. We must do so on the one side, if people, for example, insist on the fundamental necessity of speaking in tongues; we must do so on the other side, if people insist on the fundamental necessity of episcopacy and an episcopally ordained priesthood. Not to do so allows the gospel to be added to; a distortion of what the church is all about; and an abnormality that is not attractive to outsiders.

So much for the past. How do we reform the visible church in the present?

The Church, as any grouping, can be analysed from four perspectives: first, its agenda; secondly, its leadership; thirdly, its structures; and fourthly, its relationship with its environment. Let us take a look at each of these but not in that order.

Reform and 'the environment'

We are at a critical point in the history of our culture. Unless we win the battle for the gospel in the next few years there could be very serious social consequences. *British Social Attitudes, the 8th Report*, tells us that a huge percentage claim they *belong* to a brand of the Christian religion – 60.3 per cent. Only 3 per cent are of the minority faiths. 36.3 per cent have no religion. But for whatever reason, we now have a society where even many of those claiming to 'belong' to a Christian denomination are, to use George Hunter's word, 'ignostics'. That is to say they have no Christian background, memory, vocabulary, or assumptions; they do not know what Christians are talking about.

Let me quote Hunter:

> Because of secularisation's massive impact upon people, the Western church needs to experience a paradigm shift that allows it to perceive that the traditional mission-sending nations of the Western world are 'mission fields' once again.
>
> To be specific, Western Christianity needs a multitude of intentional missionary congregations – churches that will abandon the Christendom model of ministry as merely nurturing the faithful – whose primary mission will be to reach and disciple people who do not yet believe.

He says the situation is similar to that of the early church. He goes on ...

> ... objectives for communicating the gospel in the church's first centuries had at least four things in common with our situation:
> (1). Because they faced a population with no knowledge of the gospel, early Christians had to *inform* people of the story of Jesus: the good news, its claims, and its offer.
> (2). As it faced hostile people and persecution from the state, the church had to *influence* people to have a positive attitude toward the movement.
> (3). As they confronted an empire with several entrenched religions, Christians had to *convince* people of the truth of Christianity, or at least of its plausibility.
> (4). Since entry into the faith involves an act of the will, Christians had to *invite* people to adopt this faith, join the Messianic community, and follow Jesus as Lord.[8]

So 'inform', 'influence', 'convince' and 'invite'. The Church of England must do that in the environment of the nineties.

Reform and 'the agenda'
Here we have massive problems. This is the reason why there must be a Reformation. No organization, or body of people, can get anywhere if there is no agreed agenda.

Let me list some of the issues people, I believe, will have to agree to if the Church of England is to move forward spiritually.

(1) There must be a return to being 'The Church of England' as intended by Cranmer, but obviously made appropriate to the 20th century. This is no nostalgia trip. Sadly for some but with relief for others, there can be no returning to the BCP – to its doctrines, yes, but not to

---

8. See George G. Hunter III *How to Reach Secular People* (Abingdon, Nashville, 1992) p 35.

its use. The culture will have to be 'Spring Harvest' or beyond.

(2) We have to realise that comprehensiveness is for Church order, *not* for doctrine. Doctrinally we must keep the general 'shape' of Biblical Christianity – that was the intention of our Reformers; and the key hermeneutic is common sense – scripture interpreted by scripture, aided by the wisdom of the first four general councils.

(3) The stance of the 'Open Letter' regarding opposition to acts of inter-faith worship is vital for our understanding of the person of Christ. There can be no threat to his uniqueness and finality.

(4) The latest offering from the House of Bishops that validates lay homosexual relationships must be roundly repudiated. There must be a clear commitment to Christian sexual morality as orthodox Protestantism understands it – no sexual intercourse outside heterosexual lifelong marriage; contraception, yes; abortion, no.

(5) The feminism that has now become an orthodoxy in much of the Church must be repudiated while affirming women and their ministry as equal but different and reversing any residual repression.

In the politics of the moment, this will mean opposing women's ordination to the presbyterate and consecration to the episcopate on the grounds that it is a de facto ordination to 'headship'. We must demand the licensing of women deacons (and lay workers) to enable them to celebrate Holy Communion.

(6) There must be a loving, but definite, commitment in England to 'make new disciples' – mostly this will be among Anglo-Saxons but if our neighbours are Jews or other ethnics of different faiths, we have a duty to seek to win them for Christ – and some groups will be called to 'target' them (as Paul targeted the Gentiles, while Peter targeted the Jews).

(7) Bishops and Clergy who openly deny or defy fundamentals in doctrine and morals must be asked to stand down. ABM (Advisory Board for Ministry) criteria must be reformed right away.

Reform and structure

The structure of the Church of England now seems to many to be a form of bureaucratic centralism. While the world at large is 'devolving from the centre'; while schools and hospitals are becoming self-governing within, of course, an over-all framework, the local churches are being, or certainly feeling, centralised. This is the result of the Synodical Government Measure and the creation of the Central Stipends Authority. These both came out of the 60's and 70's and the 'Wilson Era'. It seems that the Church of England, as so often, is behind the times – in this case in its understanding the way modern people best organise themselves.

The notion that the local Church is the 'Diocese' is now standard orthodoxy in some circles. This is certainly not the position of Cranmer or Hooker.

Article XIX is central to this discussion. It says:

> The visible Church of Christ is *a* congregation of faithful men, in the which the pure Word of God is preached, and the Sacraments be fully ministered.

Every word is chosen with care. The word 'congregation' is important. It was not used lightly. The final revision of the BCP, for example, changed the word 'congregation' into 'church' at several points, *but not everywhere*. For example in the Baptism Service the final revision of the BCP still stays:

> Regard, we beseech thee, the supplications of *this* Congregation ...

But it changed:

> Seeing now, dearly beloved brethren, that these children be regenerate and grafted into the body of Christ's congregation...

into:

> Seeing now, dearly beloved brethren, that these persons are regenerate and grafted into the body of Christ's Church

It appears that 'a' or 'this' congregation means what it means today – a visible grouping of people.

The word 'Church' referred either to the building or to 'the wider Church'.

And with regard to the Thirty-nine Articles the royal declaration 'prefixed' to them says quite unambiguously that:

> no man hereafter shall either print, or preach, to draw the Article aside any way, but shall submit to it in the plain and full meaning thereof: and shall not put his own sense or comment to be the meaning of the Article, but shall take it in the literal and grammatical sense.

Therefore, the doctrine of the Church of England must be, following Article XIX, that the *'local congregation' is the visible church.* And note, according to the BCP the minister is no longer a 'mass priest' in a vacuum, but now a minister serving *a congregation* as spiritual leader – that is the reason for his ordination. The final revision of the BCP says in the ordination service:

> Take thou authority to preach the Word of God, and to minister the holy Sacraments in the Congregation, where thou shalt be lawfully appointed thereunto.

What distinguished the 'congregationalists' from the Church of England at the time of the Reformation was this: the congregationalists rejected 'national' churches. The dichotomy for them was between the local congregation and the 'national' church (not the Diocese). The congregationalists argued that the local congregation should have the power to elect and ordain its own ministers. The Church of England thought it was necessary for there to be a national church for influencing national life; and it was better for the local congregation if there was outside input at the time of a new appointment. Acts 6 was the model, where the people selected and the Apostles validated the selection.

But the unreformed doctrine of Episcopacy that has been absorbed into Anglican thinking, means that people talk about the Diocese as though that is the ultimate spiritual reality. Not so. The Church of England is a federation of parishes that for convenience are grouped into Dioceses; and each Diocese is under and served by a Bishop. But parishes have an independent identity. For example, Jesmond Parish Church has an identity and history quite independent of the Diocese of Newcastle. It was consecrated by the Bishop of Durham and was originally in Durham Diocese! The North East Dioceses, like the old Metropolitan Counties, come and go. Unfortunately centralism, which in its synodical form is bureaucratic, is harder to move.

But it is essential, for the health of the Church, that we reject this bureaucratic centralism as being non-Anglican as well as counter-productive.

Centralism

This centralism is generating a passivity in the Church that is detrimental to its mission. Initiatives are not taken on the ground when people are for ever having to be co-ordinated with the centre. For the mission of the Church the centre must be the local congregation where the Word of God is preached and the sacraments administered. To remain part of the National Church, the clergy should generally operate within the Canons, of course. But for on-the-ground evangelism, good decisions can only be taken with a full knowledge of the facts. The facts are only known by the people who know them – the local congregation not the Diocesan office.

Please note, there is nothing in the Canons about the local congregation having to fund the work of the Diocese, much of which today we may well disagree with. All over the country this is where the structures impinge on so many – in the matter of the 'quota'. Of course, Christians should 'give'. That goes without saying. And rich churches should give away good sums outside the parish. But where should that money go to? Who is going to decide? The assumption by the bureaucrats is that some Synod has a right to decide where a local congregation gives its money – or, as the Synod sees it, spends its money. I find that unacceptable. It is unacceptable because of the doctrinal assumptions; it is also unacceptable on a purely management level. Of course, a Synod – if it is paying the stipend of a clergyman – must be reimbursed by the parish for that cost to the Synod's own budget. But after that, the determination where a Parish spends its money must be that of the Parish. The Parish must be responsible, before God, for good stewardship.

At Jesmond Parish Church we have 'capped our quota'. We are already net givers to the Diocesan budget but we believe we have other obligations to parts of the visible church that we must encourage congregational giving to fulfil, before further subsidizing the Diocese. We want to support those who are more on, to use Hooker's distinction, the 'sound' side rather than the 'corrupted' side of the visible church. For example this past year we have unilaterally helped finance a 'parish assistant' in a local UPA parish. But we decided that expenditure, not the diocese. We judged it would result in a gospel ministry.

So why has this bureaucratic centralism taken such a deep hold? Diocesan centralism, I believe, is reinforced by factors highlighted in what is called the 'New Class' thesis.

Briefly, this says that in all advanced capitalist and post-modern societies the middle class has split. This results in an 'old' middle class – producing goods and services and made up of business people and the older professions. But there is also a 'new' middle class producing 'knowledge' – through education, the electronic media and via the administration (and advocacy) of social and personal services. As Brigitte Berger claims, this new class 'controls many of the institutions central to the so-called post-industrial society ... the vast educational empire, the media ... and a seemingly boundless therapeutic apparatus, as well as increasing segments of both public and private administration.'[9]

This new class seeks to extend its power and influence. It has vested interests in increasing centralism as centralised funding often provides most of its support. Furthermore, it has acquired far greater influence than the old middle class, for the new class is essentially a 'knowledge class' and so directs and controls communal information. What is more it pervades the world of the church which then further effects the world of education in its religious aspects. But as in the wider society, so in the church. Members of the new class are never in a majority, yet they have disproportionate influence. Indeed, most of the church's leadership – many of the clergy and the central bureaucrats – are part of the new class. This is ensured by today's higher education that is coloured by new class values; and by the fact that the Church's bureaucracy tends to be a particularly effective repository for new class assumptions and attitudes.

The new class, of course, is in a linear succession from the European Enlightenment. Apart from the basic Enlightenment denial of 'sin' with the conviction that man is perfectible through education or evolution and the basic belief that God, if he exists, is distant, the main emphasis of new class values cluster around the concept of human self-fulfilment.

The new class also has a scant regard for history. In this it follows Kant in his view of 'enlightenment' as the emergence from 'immaturity', with immaturity being 'the inability to use one's own understanding without the guidance of another.' Common sense calls this 're-inventing the wheel'. New class enthusiasts call it 'exploration.' All this may help to explain why the leadership of the church is today particularly attracted to both centralism and liberalism.

Reform and leadership
Finally, *leadership*.

All I want to say here is yes, let's get rid of 'prelacy'. The ideal model for the Church of England is a federation of parishes, united in doctrine as Hooker said, but having in place 'bishops' who act as the

---

9. Brigitte Berger *Guaranteeing the Good Life* op. cit. p 199.

'catholicising' elements but their function would be that of counsellor to clergy and a teacher-consultant. They would have sufficient experience of the Christian faith, of local church management, and of the wider world to help the local parish in Godly Living, Church Growth and Changing Britain. They would not 'lord it like the Gentiles'. They would say, for example, to someone or to a congregation, 'have you thought about doing it this way? I know of another church who have had the same problem and they solved it like this; why not give them a ring?' Or they would be gifted in ministering the Word – and you would look forward to them as you do when you've booked Jim Packer or John Stott to preach – or whoever are their younger successors. As it is, quite often when dignitaries – not just bishops – go around, the parish has to be engaged in a process of damage limitation!

Conclusion

We are in a position today where the Church of England constitutionally is sound enough. The problem is that its leadership, no longer having to subscribe to the Thirty-nine Articles, is no longer required to fit in doctrinally with the church it is trying to lead. So without Hooker's unifying principle of 'one faith', what now holds the Church of England together? Ever since the consecration of David Jenkins, the former Bishop of Durham, after open doubts and denials, with the endorsement of the Archbishop of York, the credibility even of the unreformed doctrine of the Bishop as a focus of unity and the essence of the Church has effectively been destroyed. So what is left? Certainly not the Prayer Book. The cynics would say, 'the Church Commissioners computer alone is left.' I want to say that this too defeatist. *We* as main-line evangelicals are left! And we are not alone. We have the Bible. We have common sense. We have the constitution of the Church of England on our side. And remember there were over 2,000 who signed that 'Open Letter'. We just need to get back to 2 Timothy 4. We need courage, grace, unflinching firmness and above all the realisation that change will come 'not by might, nor by power, but by my Spirit, says the LORD of hosts' (Zechariah 4:6). We need to work but also to pray for a new Reformation.

2

Saving the Heart of Evangelicalism[1]

Mark Thompson

The last few years have seen a plethora of books on the subject of evangelicalism. While some writers are critical, the overwhelming majority of them present the picture of a Christian movement which is sweeping all before it, triumphing over both liberalism and ritualism.[2] Evangelical Christianity is making the church at large sit up and take notice. But the triumph is an illusion. Behind the hype, the citation of statistics and self-congratulation, many evangelicals have been confused and distracted from the critical tasks of evangelism and edification. Part of the cause of this is a new reluctance in some quarters to clarify what is genuine evangelical belief and practice.

There is no doubt that an obsession with self-definition is a recipe for disaster. It is possible to spend so much time describing what evangelicals believe and practise that no time is left to believe and practise. However, a more serious danger facing us today is an unconscious theological shift as more and more people claim the label 'evangelical' for themselves. It is that danger which makes it necessary for evangelicals to periodically call each other back to the foundations of evangelical Christianity. Only against such a call can we helpfully face the critical hard questions: Has evangelicalism sold out? Has it lost its heart?

I am convinced that genuine evangelicalism can only be defined theologically. Evangelicals are those whose beliefs and practice are shaped by the gospel of Jesus Christ. They are unavoidably cross-centred people, for the heart of the gospel is the declaration of Christ's atoning death and victorious resurrection with its summons to faith

---

1. This chapter is a development of an article which originally appeared in the *Briefing,* 1995.
2. For example: Clive Calver, *He Brings Us Together: Joining Hands Where Truth and Justice Meet* (London: Hodder & Stoughton, 1987); Alister E. McGrath, *Evangelicalism and the Future of Christianity* (London: Hodder & Stoughton, 1994); Derek J. Tidball, *Who are the Evangelicals? Tracing the Roots of Today's Movements* (London: Marshall Pickering, 1994).

and a life of discipleship. They are just as clearly Bible people, for their knowledge of the gospel arises from the pages of Holy Scripture. It is a distinctive theology which characterises evangelicalism, and for precisely this reason attempts to define it in other ways — in terms of sociology or spirituality — will always distort the picture.

The long history of the word 'evangelical' (an adjective derived from the Greek word for 'gospel') bears out such a claim. Tertullian was amongst the first to use it, around AD 200, in his defence of biblical truth against the heresies of Marcion. Martin Luther shocked the Christian church in 1519, when he described as 'altogether Christian and evangelical' some of the teaching of Jan Hus, a Bohemian theologian who had been condemned and burnt at the stake in 1415. It would later be the only label Luther would accept for his own teaching. Sir Thomas More is generally recognised as the man who brought the word into the English language. In the course of a quite vitriolic attack on William Tyndale in 1532, More spoke of 'those evangelicalles'.

This self-conscious commitment to the biblical gospel also explains why evangelicalism is not satisfied with being described as one particular brand of Christianity. John Stott put it this way in 1970: 'It is the contention of evangelicals that they are plain Bible Christians, and that in order to be a biblical Christian it is necessary to be an evangelical Christian.'[3] Such a statement raises the stakes enormously when we come to explain just what is an evangelical. We are not simply defining an interesting and distinctive group within the Christian spectrum, we are defining authentic, biblical Christianity. Evangelical theology is not simply a means of self-identification, it is God's truth for the world.

Distinctives of Evangelical Theology

Evangelical theology arises from the gospel of Jesus Christ. The grand rescue mission of God, which is the theme of both the Old Testament and the New, carries with it certain fundamental perspectives.

1. The Authority of Scripture: A Distinctive View of Revelation and Theology

Without doubt the most basic and distinctive aspect of evangelical theology is its view of the Bible. A commitment to the gospel of Jesus Christ entails a commitment to the authoritative Scripture, not only

3. John R.W. Stott, *Christ the Controversialist: A study in some essentials of the evangelical religion* (London: Tyndale, 1970), p. 32.

because the gospel is made known to us in these very pages, but primarily because this was the attitude of Christ Himself. Jesus explained himself and his work in terms of God's purposes as expressed in the Old Testament. He also anticipated the New Testament when he spoke of the Spirit enabling the apostles to remember all that he had told them (John 14:26) and when he prayed for those who would believe through the word of the apostles (John 17:20). His commission and authorization stands behind the ministry of the apostles and their writing. In the end, any attempt to separate the gospel of Jesus Christ and the Bible will distort both, for the God of the gospel is the God of the Bible (2 Corinthians 4:6), and the gospel itself is the central theme of the whole Bible (Luke 24:27).

This collection of books is not just an expression of human self-consciousness, nor is it simply a record of human religious beliefs or experiences. The Bible is the living and active Word of God. What the Bible says, God says, and those who have been rescued by God recognize his voice (1 Thessalonians 2:13; John 10:1-18).

This is clearly the Bible's own testimony about itself. An evangelical doctrine of the Word of God really begins in Genesis 1, where God speaks and the universe comes into being. The words that God speaks have a unique character. They are powerful and creative, expressing God's mind and purpose. They always accomplish what he intends (Isaiah 55:8-11). It comes as no surprise, then, that when God becomes a man he stills storms with a word (Mark 4:35-41), casts out demons with a word (Mark 5:1-20), heals the sick with a word (Mark 1:40-44) and even raises the dead with a word (Mark 5:35-43). God speaks and it is so.

It is God himself who commands that his word be written down and that it become the authoritative guide and criterion of judgement for his people. In fact, God himself is the first to present his word in written form (Exodus 31:18). In these written words God confronts his people, challenging them and comforting them as directly and effectively as when he spoke to Moses in the cloud. They are not merely a record of God's self-revelation — they are that revelation. What is more, their divine authority and reliability is in no way diminished by the fact that God uses very human writers in the process. God does not bypass the mind or personality of each writer, for those things too are his creation. Through the work of his Spirit, God enables them to write his word, not just their own (2 Peter 1:20-21). This is not only true of the

Old Testament, as is clear from the way Jesus refers to it (e.g. Matthew 19:4-5), but of the New Testament as well. Even while the apostles were still alive and writing, their words were recognised as Scripture (2 Peter 3:15-16; see also 1 Timothy 5:18, where the second Scripture quotation is not found in the Old Testament, but is a saying of Jesus recorded in Luke 10:7).

It is against this background and as part of the teaching of the entire Bible that 2 Timothy 3:14-17 is to be understood. It is the classic statement of Scripture about itself and in light of what has been said it cannot be restricted in reference to the Old Testament alone. In the context of a threat from false teaching Paul speaks of the sufficiency of Scripture. These writings are unique for they come from the mouth of God and are God's full and sufficient provision to thoroughly equip Christians for life as the rescued children of God.

The Scriptures, then, stand as the unique source of our knowledge of God. Only in the light of the Scriptures can we understand how the heavens declare the glory of God. Only in the light of the Scriptures can we understand the reason for the ambiguities of life. Only in the Scriptures can we discern the mind of God and the seriousness of his love towards us.

For this reason the Scriptures must stand above every other pronouncement on matters of faith and practice. This does not imply a refusal to think hard and creatively about the implications of the Christian gospel. Nor does it imply a presupposition that every other piece of theological writing is untrue. Even before the time of Tertullian, biblical Christians read and wrote things other than the Bible. Luther, the great champion of *sola Scriptura* (Scripture alone), regularly quoted the church fathers, especially Augustine. But Tertullian, Luther and other biblical Christians measured such writings by the teaching of Holy Scripture. Nothing has the right to bind the Christian conscience except Scripture alone. Where Christian teaching or human reason or even personal experience conflict with Scripture, they are to be rejected. The Bible settles the matter.

This must apply to evangelical theology itself, as John Stott made clear:

'Certainly it is the desire of evangelicals to be neither more nor less than biblical Christians. Their intention is not to be partisan, that is, they do not cling to certain tenets for the sake of maintaining their identity as a "party".

On the contrary, they have always expressed their readiness to modify, even abandon, any or all of their cherished beliefs if they can be shown to be unbiblical.'[4]

One important corollary of this is not particularly popular at the moment. If biblical truth matters, and if we genuinely care for our evangelical brothers and sisters, then we will be prepared to challenge them when they stray from that truth. Solomon's words are more true than we often recognize: 'faithful are the wounds of a friend; profuse are the kisses of an enemy' (Proverbs 27:6).

2. The Seriousness of Sin: A Distinctive View of Human Nature

The gospel is good news precisely because of the seriousness of the human predicament. Jesus' death and resurrection would make no sense if there was no danger from which we need to be rescued, and the cross would be a barbaric overreaction on God's part if that danger could be averted in any other way. Yet the testimony of the entire Bible is that every human being is in a very real and serious danger of his or her own making.

This greatest of all dangers facing men and women is a long-standing one, originating with the decisions of the first man and woman to disobey God and grasp the opportunity of moral independence (Genesis 3). They embraced the possibility of deciding for themselves what is right and wrong without dependence upon the word of God, and so they chose to abandon trust in God. It was a fundamentally self-centred and self-seeking decision, and as Genesis 3 and indeed the rest of the Bible makes clear, its consequences were devastating. The entire human race shares in their corruption and guilt, for from our earliest moments we are all predisposed to make the same choice, setting ourselves up as the authoritative centre of our lives (Romans 5:12). A bias towards sin characterises every man, woman and child (Romans 3:23).

The element of danger lies in the fact that our sin alienates us from God and makes us His enemies (Isaiah 59:1-2; Colossians 1:21). It provokes the coming wrath of God (Romans 1:18-32; Colossians 3:5-6). In the face of our guilt and corruption, the prospect of judgement is nothing short of terrifying (Hebrews 9:27; 10:31).

This predicament is compounded by our inability to remedy it ourselves. The Bible uses two key pictures to underline our inability to

---

4. Stott, *Christ the Controversialist,* p. 32.

save ourselves. The first is slavery: the natural human condition is slavery to sin (Romans 6). Our whole existence is conditioned by an allegiance which we are not able to repudiate. The second picture is one of death: apart from Christ we are 'dead in our sins' (Ephesians 2:1). Here there is a world of difference between 'sick' and 'dead'. The former suggests some possibility of recovery; the latter brings an end to all such hopes. If we are to be rescued from the danger pressing in upon us, it will not be by our own doing. The initiative must come from outside of us.

Evangelical theology affirms that the most basic need of men and women is for a means of forgiveness and reconciliation with God. It argues that attempts to modify this understanding of the human predicament lead in the end to a different gospel and a different ministry. Accordingly, while Evangelicals have made significant contributions in areas such as justice for the oppressed, international peace, and environmental awareness, they have steadfastly maintained that these are not the gospel and that a theological preoccupation with such goals inevitably entails a confusion about the plight of humankind. The Bible takes us beyond the symptoms to the disease.

3. The Penal Substitutionary Atonement of Christ: A Distinctive View of Salvation

As clearly as the foundation of evangelical theology is the authority of the Scripture, the heart of evangelical theology is the cross of Jesus Christ. While the incarnation is important, not least in affirming that Jesus is truly God and truly man, it is by his death that he makes the atonement which deals with our sin and restores us to God. He dies in our place, bearing the penalty for our sin, in line with God's ancient intention. Here, indeed, is the most profound demonstration of God's love for us.

This saving act of God in Christ is in prospect from the very earliest pages of the Bible. In fact, many have recognised that it is the promise of a full, final, and effective solution to the problem of sin and its consequences which holds the Bible together and propels the Old Testament into the New. This promise is unfolded gradually, beginning with barely more than the hint of a promised deliverer who will suffer in the process of rescuing God's rebellious creation (Genesis 3:15), and climaxing in the prophetic announcement of the Suffering Servant who takes upon himself 'the iniquities of us all' and bears 'the chastisement that makes us whole' (Isaiah 53). Along the way important anticipations of the atonement in and through Jesus are given in the Exodus and Passover narratives (Exodus 11-12), and amongst the Psalms (e.g. Psalm 22).

The New Testament evidence is both abundant and unambiguous. John the Baptist's critical testimony to Jesus located him against the background of the Old Testament promises. As Jesus came towards him John declared 'Behold, the Lamb of God, who takes away the sin of the world' (John 1:29). Jesus also described his mission in these terms: he came to serve and be a 'ransom for many' (Mark 10:45). He clearly embraced the mission of the Suffering Servant, explicitly applying Isaiah 53 to himself in Luke 22:37. He was the one who would accomplish at last the atonement for which the whole Old Testament had been waiting. The testimony of the apostles also stands in perfect continuity with that of Jesus himself. When they speak of the atonement effected by Jesus' death on the cross, they appeal to Old Testament images and categories to explain this great event, just as Jesus did. Jesus died in our place and bore the curse of God for us (2 Corinthians 5:21; Galatians 3:13; 1 Peter 3:18; 1 John 2:2).

Penal substitution is not, therefore, one amongst many models of the atonement, as some assert. Neither can it be described as a 'theory' arising outside of the biblical texts. Evangelical theology insists that while penal substitution does not exhaust all that can be said about the cross and resurrection of Jesus, it is the basic biblical understanding without which other perspectives are devoid of any real meaning. At the heart of the atonement is Jesus' death in our place, a death which involves bearing the penalty for our sin. Here is God's most profound answer to the human dilemma. This is what makes the gospel such good news.

4. Justification by Faith Alone: A Distinctive View of Christian Response

The gospel of Jesus Christ is both an announcement and a summons — the announcement of God's intervention to save us and a summons to respond with faith. Hebrews 11 makes clear that this dynamic of promise and trust is the nature of the relationship between God and his people throughout the Old Testament. The most obvious example is Abraham. When God announces his intention to Abraham, an intention which in the light of the circumstances seemed improbable to say the least, we are told 'Abraham believed the Lord, and he credited it to him as righteousness' (Genesis 15:6). Abraham was not perfect, as the succeeding chapters of Genesis show quite clearly. He could not and he did not earn God's favour. But God was worth trusting. What he promised to do he would do. Abraham knew that and he responded by trusting God. God declares that response to be righteousness.

Throughout the Old Testament the promise of salvation points to the future. The search for the seed of the woman, which began back in Genesis 3, generates a restlessness which drives us from the Old Testament into the New. None of the great figures of faith in the Old Testament actually received what had been promised (Hebrews 11:39). They died in faith, trusting that the fulfilment was still to come. God had promised and they believed him. They, like Abraham, were right with God.

Jesus appears against this background, as the fulfilment of God's promises and the object of faith. He stands in stark contrast to the performance-oriented Judaism of the time, a grotesque mutation from the covenantal faith of the Old Testament. He exercises an 'authority to forgive sin on the earth' in unexpected directions (Mark 2:10). He is happy to be described as 'a friend of tax collectors and sinners' (Luke 7:34). His controversial parable about a Pharisee and a tax collector exposes the bankruptcy of all attempts to relate to God on the basis of performance. The tax collector who had nothing to plead before God, not the Pharisee with all his boasts, 'went home justified before God' (Luke 18:14). At Jesus' death, those who trumpet their own righteousness mock him, while those who recognize that their only hope lies in him hear the words of forgiveness and assurance (Luke 23:40-43).

Paul's teaching on justification is perfectly consistent with its embodiment in the ministry of Jesus. God is the one who 'justifies the ungodly' (Romans 4:5). A right standing with God comes not through personal or corporate religious performance but 'through the faithfulness of Jesus Christ' (Romans 3:22). Those who put their trust in Jesus are right with God and need no longer fear the prospect of condemnation (Romans 8:1-4). Our new standing with God is not our own invention; it is his declaration in the face of the effective atonement made by Jesus on the cross and our faith in him (Romans 3:22-26).

'Justification by faith alone' is a slogan which reflects the New Testament teaching of 'justification apart from works of the law' (Romans 3:28). It safeguards the Christian insistence that our boast lies in

God alone (1 Corinthians 1:30-31). However, nowhere in the New Testament or the Old is it suggested that this is the end of the matter. Genuine faith changes lives. In the matter of salvation, faith stands alone as our appropriate response to what God has done. Nevertheless, genuine faith is never alone. Living faith is bound to reveal itself in repentance and embracing a new life as God's children. The biblical insistence on faith alone does not compromise the biblical concern for godliness in the life of the believer, rather it places that concern in its proper context (Romans 6; James 2).

Throughout Christian history, gospel-minded men and women have remarked on the importance of 'justification by faith alone'. This doctrine plays a pivotal role in Christian theology, safeguarding the initiative of God in salvation and undermining all human boasting. It focuses our attention on Christ and his cross rather than our performance.

In recent years, some very sophisticated attempts have been made to modify this doctrine, and to displace it from the centre of evangelical theology. Scholars associated with the 'New Perspective' on Paul have argued variously that 'justification by faith' is a peculiarly Pauline doctrine, that it is restricted to his concern for Jew-Gentile relations and that it is more about corporate covenant membership than individual standing with God.

However, evangelicals are bound to point out that, whatever the covenantal background or context, Paul remains deeply concerned over the fate of the individual before God. His teaching about the way God 'justifies the ungodly' reflects, as we have seen, the teaching of the whole Bible, and is embodied in the ministry of Jesus himself.

5. The Necessity of the New Birth: A Distinctive View of Grace and the Spirit
Jesus' death and resurrection remains the one and only basis for our acceptance with God. We are called to respond to that marvellous provision by repentance and faith. However, such a response does not come naturally to human beings who are trapped in the slavery and death of sin, both guilty and corrupt. God must work a miracle within us, creating the very things which cannot be produced from the depths of a depraved heart.

John's Gospel emphasises this human inability to believe without the miraculous intervention of God. Christians are not children of God by virtue of a human decision (John 1:12-13); rather, through the work of God's Spirit, they must be 'born again' (John 3:3,5). The use of imagery from Ezekiel 36 in Jesus' conversation with Nicodemus reminds us that this 'new birth' has always been God's intention. This teaching of Jesus is highly significant. Both the objective and subjective dimensions of salvation are the work of God: God has provided the atonement in Christ, and God has brought us to new birth by his Spirit in order that we might enjoy the benefits of Christ's atonement. Christians stand as grateful recipients of a full and final salvation, not as its initiators or contributors.

Here is the most basic evangelical understanding of the work of the Spirit. In recent years some have suggested that evangelicalism has ignored the Holy Spirit. This is simply not true. The person and work of the Holy Spirit have never been neglected by evangelical writers. Evangelicals have always maintained the significance of the Spirit in creation, redemption and the life of the church. They have always spoken of the Spirit's vital role in the greatest miracle of all: bringing a person from death to life. What is distinctive is their steadfast refusal to trivialise the work of the Spirit or to ignore the fact that the sword of the Spirit is the Word of God (Ephesians 6:17). The Christian response to God's mercy in Christ is impossible without the work of the Spirit: the new birth. The Christian life is life in the Spirit. 'If anyone does not have the Spirit of Christ, he does not belong to Christ' (Romans 8:9). Personal conversion is the outward manifestation of this inward reality.

This is precisely why evangelical theology cannot be described as abstract or merely intellectual. It is profoundly experiential, for it recognises that the beginning of the Christian life is the experience of new birth brought about by the Spirit of God. So while evangelicalism can only be defined theologically, its theology is intensely practical, proclaiming the direct personal address of the living God to one made alive by the Holy Spirit.

6. The Imminent Personal Return of Jesus to Judge: A Distinctive View of Universal History
The urgency of the gospel call to repentance and faith is anchored in a future reality guaranteed by the resurrection of Jesus from the dead. God has 'set a day when he will judge the world with justice by the man he has appointed. He has given proof of this to all men by raising

him from the dead' (Acts 17:31). The culmination of human and universal history will be the creation of a new heavens and a new earth (Revelation 21:1), but this will be preceded by the judgement of all men and women (Revelation 20:11-15). In the light of these realities Christians can be described as those who have 'turned to God from idols to serve the living and true God, and to wait for his Son from heaven, whom he raised from the dead — Jesus, who rescues us from the coming wrath' (1 Thessalonians 1:9-10).

There are a variety of views, even within evangelicalism, on the chronology and precise nature of the events leading up to the final judgement. In part these arise from our difficulties in understanding the apocalyptic language of the Book of Revelation. Nevertheless, the personal return of the glorified Lord Jesus and the reality of universal judgement are beyond dispute. What is also clear is that the only hope of rescue lies in Jesus Christ himself. It is this sure and certain rescue which takes the fear out of the future for the Christian and makes the promise of Jesus' return a message of comfort (1 Thessalonians 4:13-18).

Such a view of the future carries with it a distinctive view of the present. The New Testament is full of warnings about the unexpectedness of Jesus' return and the Book of Revelation concludes with Jesus' promise to come soon (Revelation 22:7). It also presents us with the reason for an interval between Jesus' ascension and return: 'The Lord is not slow in keeping his promise, as some understand slowness. He is patient with you, not wanting anyone to perish, but everyone to come to repentance' (2 Peter 3:9). The present time is an opportunity for repentance and faith. The end of all things is delayed so that others might be included in the great Rescue. That is the great concern of God for the present age. That is the great concern of those already rescued for the present age.

It is no surprise then that evangelism is at the forefront of evangelical practice. This commitment springs not only from our view of the future and the present, but also from our understanding of the Bible, the human predicament, the work of Christ and the necessity of faith and new birth by the Spirit. God's kindness in rescuing us through Christ creates in us a desire to see others rescued too. The reality of judgement and the magnitude of God's mercy in Jesus combine as a most powerful motivation for evangelistic ministry (2 Corinthians 5:11-21).

The Critical Coherence of Evangelical Theology

Clearly these six fundamental perspectives do not exhaust evangelical theology. Evangelicals have much to say about the Trinity, creation, and the church, amongst many other things. This article has not been intended as an exercise in determining the minimum one must believe to be considered an evangelical. However, it is these six biblical truths which give evangelical theology its basic shape. They cohere in their relation to the gospel of Jesus and their foundation in the text of Scripture. Therefore, it is the modification of theology at these critical points that characterizes a shift from evangelicalism.

In today's climate the modifications rarely take the form of negation. Though there are some who would deny one or other of these perspectives and still claim the label 'evangelical', the more dangerous — and sadly more frequent — modification comes through addition. This has always been the case. Reformation theology is often summarised by the slogans 'Scripture alone', 'Christ alone', 'Grace alone' and 'Faith alone', all of which guarded against modification by addition. Jim Packer has echoed the concerns of the Reformers when he wrote:

> 'You cannot add to evangelical theology without subtracting from it. By augmenting it, you cannot enrich it; you can only impoverish it. Thus, for example, if you add to it a doctrine of human priestly mediation you take away the truth of the perfect adequacy of our Lord's priestly mediation. If you add to it a doctrine of human merit, in whatever form, you take away the truth of the merits of Christ ... The principle applies at point after point. What is more than evangelical is less than evangelical. Evangelical theology, by its very nature, cannot be supplemented; it can only be denied.'[5]

Put another way, the crucial questions are ones of sufficiency. Is the Bible sufficient as the saving revelation of God? Evangelicals have answered 'yes' to this question; those outside the evangelical tradition have supplemented the Bible with human reason, church pronouncements, or private visions, dreams and prophetic statements. Is Jesus' death sufficient to deal with our sins and secure our relationship with God? Again evangelicals have answered 'yes', while non-evangelicals have argued that the ministrations of the church play a role in this as well. Is faith sufficient as the appropriate response to the offer of for-

---

5. James.I. Packer, *The Evangelical Anglican Identity Problem: An Analysis,* Latimer Studies 1 (Oxford: Latimer, 1978), pp. 17-18.

giveness? The evangelical affirmative to this question stands in stark contrast with the imposition of works, or ceremonies, or second experiences.

Room to Move

Evangelicalism, even when defined in terms of its theological distinctives, is not entirely monochrome. Outside of these distinctives there is room for difference and even disagreement without resorting to disenfranchising one another. However, the fundamental perspectives of evangelical theology ought to inform the way we handle such points of difference.

Some points of difference arise on matters about which the Bible is largely, and in some cases completely, silent. The decisions about when and how to baptize seem to fall into this category. While good cases can be mounted for both infant and adult baptism, the fact is that the Bible says little about baptism in relation to the children of believers. The appropriate evangelical response to such differences is to recognize the issues as matters of Christian freedom. We have no right to bind the consciences of other believers in ways that the Scriptures do not. We might hold firmly to our own view as a legitimate expression of biblical principles. Nevertheless, it is a mistake to invest those views with the same authority as the teaching of Scripture.

Differences of another kind also emerge within an evangelicalism which remains true to the theological foundations outlined earlier in this article. These are differences over what precisely the Bible is saying on a given issue it addresses. A commitment to the truth of Scripture and its authority for faith and practice demands a quite different response in these cases. Because understanding what God has to say on the issue is of paramount importance, and because we acknowledge the pervasive influence of sin on our hearts and minds, evangelicals are committed to dialogue and the repeated re-examination of the passages in question. This is not always easy because it involves admitting that we may have misunderstood what a particular passage is saying. Nevertheless, the truth is more important than maintaining a position or winning an argument. Sometimes, the questions of a critic are an important step along the way to a clearer understanding of just what the Bible is saying.

Love and Truth

Evangelicalism can only be defined theologically and in relation to the gospel of Jesus Christ because 'evangelical' is simply another way of saying 'biblical Christian'. Yet this is a dangerous business. It alienates those who, for whatever reason, wish to retain the label while 'growing out of' its basic beliefs. It raises the question of theological truth and implies that other Christian traditions (Catholic, charismatic, liberal) involve some kind of error. Surely, some have argued, it would be more loving to define evangelicalism in another way, one which would allow us to soften those distinctions and embrace the ecumenical spirit.

In the last few years attempts to do this have been made; attempts to go beyond a theological definition of evangelicalism. Using a much broader brush than I have in this article, it is possible to paint a rosy picture of the onward march of evangelicals and a new golden age for the church. What was once seen as theological difference is now being cherished as diversity (one book I've read actually listed the 'twelve tribes of evangelicalism'!). We are told that mature evangelicalism rejoices in its new-found diversity, discovering brotherhood in the most unlikely of places. A new positive outlook has replaced the negativity which characterised evangelicalism for so long.

Yet the sad truth is that such redefinition results in an evangelicalism with no heart. The evangelicalism it describes has surrendered to a caricature of itself as narrow-minded and negative, and obligingly transformed itself into an amorphous entity which stands for nothing and smiles benignly at the compromise of its most cherished beliefs. It has forgotten that genuine Christian unity is unity in the truth. It has in effect pursued a *balance* of love and truth rather than both love and truth. This 'new evangelicalism' needs to be reminded that love built on a lie is not love at all and stands opposed to the purposes of God in both the Old and New Testaments.

The heart of genuine evangelicalism is the gospel of the Lord Jesus Christ. This gospel is the only hope for a world heading towards judgement. Evangelicals cannot afford to be distracted from its proclamation. Our distinctive theological framework urges us to this task. In the final analysis, the vindication of evangelicalism does not lie in gaining the attention of the world at the end of the twentieth century, but in the salvation of men and women who have heard the truth and believed.

3

Currents of change
Trends in Anglican Evangelical Theology Today

Melvin Tinker

Introduction

There is a spirit of triumph if not of triumphalism amongst many Anglican evangelicals today. There are more archdeacons and bishops with evangelical pedigrees than at any other time this century. Evangelical scholarship is now being treated with studied seriousness instead of being dismissed as amusingly obscurantist. In this regard the words of Browning capture the mood of many:

> 'The lark's on the wing;
> The snail's on the thorn:
> God's in his heaven –
> All's right with the world!'

Or at least with the Anglican evangelical world.

But is it?

While not wishing to minimise many of the advances evangelicalism has made during the latter half of this century, it is important that if such gains are not to be lost a careful check needs to be made upon evangelical *theology*. On closer inspection there are certain cracks appearing which indicate weaknesses at the level of basic foundations.

It is the purpose of this chapter to offer a critique of some present trends in Anglican evangelical theology, together with some constructive correctives. The hope is that this will stimulate a more consistent evangelical approach to matters of doctrine. What is offered are some select examples which illustrate such trends, with accompanying comments rather than in-depth analysis. There are two basic reasons for selecting the following examples for our study: first, they touch upon issues of fundamental importance for evangelical belief and practice, and second, the writers involved are quite influential amongst Anglican evangelicals and therefore their views require serious consideration.

The misuse of the biblical concept of the Kingdom of God

Certain biblical concepts are presently in danger of having their biblical sense obscured and other meanings gradually attached to them; concepts such as 'Kingdom' and 'Justice'. Some of these terms function as 'buzz words', creating an approving resonance in the minds of the hearers and so act as means in forwarding certain theological agendas. If the words are used often enough in this way, then it is only a matter of time before the new meaning takes over from the Scripturally intended meaning.

One example of this is the way the term 'The Kingdom of God' is being employed by some evangelicals.

Think of the way the term 'Kingdom' is now frequently used as an adjective. Books are appearing thick and fast with titles such as 'Kingdom Living', Kingdom Ministry', Kingdom Praying'. Indeed, it appears that one sure way of gaining a ready market for a book is to have the term 'Kingdom' appearing somewhere in the title. This, however, is not the way the New Testament uses the term. It is the Kingdom of God (*he basileia tou Theou*), the focus being God who exercises his kingship. But even this has to be qualified given the New Testament's emphasis upon God's saving kingly rule exercised through Jesus Christ. Hence, George Beasley-Murray's helpful rendering 'the *saving* sovereignty of God'.[1] In other words, a conceptual distinction has to be made between the 'universal reign of God' which carries the sense that God is sovereign ruler over all (Psalm 145:13, and God now ruling through Christ, Ephesians 1:20-23), and the 'kingdom of God' understood with specific reference to Jesus Christ and salvation. The latter is a kingdom which must be sought and entered into. It requires poverty of spirit, submission to the will of God and an entering through the 'narrow gate' (Matthew 5:3; 7:21; 7:13). Indeed, one has to be born from above even to see this kingdom (John 3:3). This is a spiritual kingdom, one which is 'not of this world' and therefore it is not appropriate to use worldly means to achieve its ends (John 18:36). To come into this aspect of the reign of God is to enter into eternal life – the sphere of salvation. As Don Carson rightly argues, the Kingdom of God understood in terms of salvation is a subset of the universal reign of God which is now mediated through the risen and ascended Christ.[2]

1. G.R. Beasley-Murray, *Jesus and the Kingdom of God* (Paternoster Press, 1986).
2. D.A. Carson, *The Sermon on the Mount*: An Evangelical Exposition of Matthew 5-7 (Baker Book House, 1982), pp.11-15.

Why is it important that attention be drawn to this? For the simple reason that such a distinction is being overlooked by some evangelicals with far-reaching implications for the way we understand both the nature of the gospel and the way in which God extends his saving rule in the world.

Amongst those who would wish to own the term 'radical evangelical', the New Testament sense of the term 'Kingdom of God' is seriously being misused and reduced to the idea that 'God rules'. Those who adopt this position maintain that wherever social justice and peace are promoted, there we are to see the Kingdom of God, even if Christ is not acknowledged or salvation experienced.[3] One leading advocate of the 'Kingdom' approach to social ethics writes: 'Jesus' rule and action are cosmic. He has disarmed the principalities which create division in society. Where we see barriers broken down, can we divorce this from God's will seen in Christ's victory over the powers on the cross? (eg between Jew and Gentile, slave and free ... in Galatians 3:28)' and 'this understanding gives us a basis for seeing God at work in society beyond the church applying the effects of Christ's victory on the cross through social change'.[4] Another leading exponent of this position states: 'The Kingdom comes wherever Jesus overcomes the power of evil ... Jesus' death was also a decisive victory over the disordered, rebellious structures of our socio-historical existence'.[5]

Such statements are very reminiscent of the 'Social Gospel' movement which developed in the USA at the beginning of this century under the theologian Walter Rauschenbusch. Rauschenbusch was a thoroughgoing theological liberal, adopting a theology of the Kingdom of God espoused by Albrecht Ritschl. However, as White and Hopkins insist 'The theology of Walter Rauschenbusch was rooted in evangelical piety'.[6] He condemned the toleration of sin in society and sought through social change to assist in the practical realization of the

---

3. So George Carey writes: 'The Kingdom comes when lives begin to open to the claims of Christ and surrender to him; *it comes also when God's peace, love, joy and righteousness are reflected in human society; it comes as the bonds of alienation are cut from the lives of men.*' *'I Believe in Man'*, (Hodder 1977) p.125.
4. Sugden in *Kingdom and Creation in Social Ethics* (Grove Ethical Studies, No 79, Sugden and Barclay, 1990).
5. R. Rider, *Evangelism, Salvation and Social Justice* (Bramcote, Notts: Grove Books, 1977).
6. R.C. White Jr and C.H. Hopkins, *The Social gospel; Religion and Reform in Changing America* (Philadelphia, 1976) p.17; also p.249.

kingdom of God in the world. He also saw the 'unChristianized' nature of American capitalism as being a stumbling block preventing non-Christian nations responding to missionary work. The cross, however, did not largely figure in his theological framework whereas it is central to the understanding of the new radicals (e.g. 'Wherever evil is over-come in society it is due to the work of the cross'[7]).

Nonetheless, there are similarities between the old social gospellers and the new radical evangelicals. Both have the Kingdom of God as their theological centre-piece for mission. Both see social action as being integral to mission and forwarding the Kingdom in the world. Both see non-Christians as in some way experiencing the redemptive scope of the kingdom.[8] As Brian Stanley observes: 'This is extremely difficult to distinguish from the claim of Rauschenbusch that wherever corporations abandon monopoly capitalism for the "law of service" or undemocratic nations submit to real democracy "therewith they step out of the Kingdom of Evil into the Kingdom of God".' [9]

But in extending the term the Kingdom of God to embrace people and actions which are not Christian, a most serious misuse of a fundamental biblical concept is taking place. What Scriptural warrant is there for claiming that 'Where evil is overcome in society this is due to Christ's work on the cross'? Much is made of reference in Colossians and Galatians to the defeat of the 'elements of the universe' (*stoicheia tou kosmou*), as if it is crystal clear both what these 'powers' are and that whatever influence they have in the socio-political sphere can be altered by political change which can be traced back to the cross.[10] However, it is highly questionable that this is a correct reading of the term as employed by Paul.[11] Certainly in Colossians it would seem that the main thrust of Paul's argument is that it is as people become *Christians*, now living under the Lordship of Christ, that such spiritual powers are

7. C. Sugden, *Op cit*, p.13.
8. C. Sugden, '*The Kingdom of God in Social Ethics*', unpublished paper 1984, p.10.
9. B. Stanley, '*Evangelical Social and Political Ethics: An Historical Perspective*', unpublished paper 1986, p.11.
10. So R. Sider writes: 'Colossians teaches that Jesus death did more than accomplish atonement for believers. Jesus death was also a decisive victory over the disordered rebellious structures of our socio-historical existence.' *Salvation and Social Justice*, p.9.
11. For a thorough discussion of the meaning of the 'Elements of the Universe', see Peter O'Brien in his *Colossians, Philemon*, commentary (Word, Waco, Texas, 1987), pp. 129-132.

denuded of their influences over them. Similarly it is questionable whether the 'principalities and powers' of Ephesians 6 can be identified with political structures as some like Ron Sider and John Howard Yoder have proposed.[12]

It is also implied that the miracles and healing ministry of Jesus can be understood not simply as signs of the inbreaking of the Kingdom into the present age, but as equivalent to present day efforts to bring about justice in society. Indeed, some go further and claim that *any movement*, Christian or not, which takes place to establish social justice and righteousness are to be interpreted as having the same character as Jesus' Kingdom acts of power and healing.[13] But one must ask whether the Bible is being handled properly to justify such thinking. Thus, when it is said that wherever just relationships are established we are to take these as signs of God's Kingdom, and Galatians 3:28 is cited in support, it must be pointed out that Paul is referring to what happens in the *church* as a result of people hearing the gospel, and not 'just relationships' in society at large.

The great commission, the example of the early church in Acts and Paul's teachings to Christians, all show that the way the saving Kingdom of God relates now to God's wider rule is through people being converted, then adopting new priorities and values. Such people will seek to improve the lot of their fellow men out of obedience to Christ and his call to fulfil the law of love.[14] It is *in making disciples* and the working out of that discipleship in society that cultures are transformed.[15] The church itself, which although not to be identified with the

---

12. See J.R.W Stott, *Ephesians,* The Bible Speaks Today Series, (IVP, 1979), pp.267-275.
13. See Vinay Samuel and Chris Sugden, 'God's Intention for the World'; tensions Between Eschatology and History, in Tom Sine (ed), *The Church in response to Human Need* (Montrovia 1983), pp.225-6.
14. For a discussion on how Christian ethics be commended to society at large see, M. Tinker, 'The Priority of Jesus: a look at the place of Jesus' teaching and example in Christian Ethics' in *Themelios*, Vol 13, No 1 1987.
15. Russell Shedd's comment is worthy of consideration within this context when he writes: 'Replacing unjust structures with more equitable ones will finally be crowned with failure unless a far more profound transformation is wrought in the men who establish them and wield their power. For this reason evangelicals must ever contend that the first responsibility of the church is the proclamation of the gospel and depend upon the consequential spiritual change wrought by the Holy Spirit to create a community in which the unconverted may see a model of the Kingdom of God.' 'Social Justice, Underlying Hermeneutical Issues', D.A. Carson, *Biblical Interpretation and the Church – Text and Context* (Paternoster: Exeter, 1984), p.201.

Kingdom of God, is the locus in which Christ's rule should be most visibly and clearly expressed.[16] As such, Christians individually and collectively should both put society to shame and indicate the way forward to more wholesome God-approved patterns for living.

If the New Testament understanding of the Kingdom of God is not adhered to, what will result will be 'another Gospel', one in which redemption from sin is absorbed in policies for socio-political change. Salvation is then conceived as rescue from structural sin rather than from the wrath to come.

False relation between doctrine and experience

The relationship between Christian doctrine and Christian experience is much more intertwined than we often suppose. There is a sense in which doctrine enables us to interpret experience. For example, in talking with a non-Christian who may be experiencing some sense of meaninglessness, the doctrines of creation, the nature of man and the consequences of the Fall could be brought to bear so that the experience may be properly understood as a prelude to presenting the gospel. However, it is vital to stress that it is in and through Christian truth that one comes to experience God. Doctrine 'informs' experience, it structures and interprets it.

But not all view doctrine and experience in this way. One writer describes the relationship between doctrine and experience as follows: 'Underlying the Christian faith is first and foremost an experience, rather than the acceptance of a set of doctrines. The New Testament bears powerful witness to the experiences of the first Christians – an experience of the presence and power of the risen Christ in their lives, charging them with meaning and dignity.... The essential purpose of Christian doctrine is to provide a framework within which the experience of the first Christians may become ours'.[17] Elsewhere he writes 'Experience of God provides the stimulus to develop doctrines about God. Thus the Christian belief in the divinity of Christ did not arise as an intellectual theory, but through the impact of experiencing Jesus Christ as God.'[18] But is this actually the case?

In countering what can be called incipient gnosticism, John in his

16. See I.H. Marshall, 'The Hope of the New Age, the Kingdom of God in the New Testament', *Themelios*, Vol 11, No. 1 1985.
17. A.E. McGrath, *Justification by Faith*, (Marshall Pickering, 1988), p.129.
18. A.E. McGrath, *Understanding Doctrine*, (Hodder and Stoughton, 1990), p.40.

first letter writes: 'That which was from the beginning, which we have heard, which we have seen with our eyes, which we have looked at and touched with our hands – this we proclaim to you concerning the Word of life.' Howard Marshall in commenting on these verses writes: 'Our writer here wants to emphasize that the Christian message is identical with Jesus; it took personal form in a person who could be heard, seen and touched'.[19] In other words, the apostles' experience of Jesus was not simply some existential 'I-Thou' encounter which led them to search around for appropriate concepts to express that experience. Rather, the experience itself involved hearing propositional truths – teachings – received from Jesus about his person and work, explained within the framework of the Old Testament Scriptures.

What is more, the apostles' Spirit-enabled task was to 'witness' to Jesus, bringing other people to faith through their message (John 16: 13: 17: 20). It is by embracing this message (with definite doctrinal content) that fellowship is had with God and other believers (1 John 1:5). Certainly this is more than intellectual assent (*assensus*), it is whole-hearted trust (*fiducia*). But doctrine does not follow some experience of God, it is the means by which we come to recognise him and so experience him. Furthermore, it is as revealed truth is embraced, animated by the Holy Spirit, that a whole host of other Christian experiences are to be had such as conviction of sin, repentance, forgiveness, joy unspeakable (1 Peter 1:3-12 is most instructive here). It is not the case that 'Experience and meaning are two sides of the same coin'[20], but rather that in order to experience the gospel one must respond to its meaning.

The relationship between doctrine and experience is such that belief in erroneous doctrine can generate erroneous experiences which if not anti-Christian may well be sub-Christian. To help us understand how this is so, let us think of the way language in general functions. Language is used to talk about things (informative) and to think about things (cognitive). It is also used to get things done and bring about a change of affairs; promises and commands do this (performative). Language is also used to express and elicit feelings (expressive and evocative) as well as bind people together in a common solidarity

19. I.H. Marshall, *The Epistles of John, in New International Commentary on the New Testament* (Eerdmans, Grand Rapids, 1978), p.102. See footnote for discussion on the interpretation of verse 1.
20. A.E. McGrath, *The Genesis of Doctrine*, (Blackwell, Oxford 1990) p.70.

(cohesive). Doctrines function in much the same way. They relate truths about who God is and what he has done (informative). They provide categories by which we might think about God and ourselves aright (cognitive). They can bring about a state of affairs, so for example, in hearing and responding to the doctrine of justification we are declared to be in a right relation to God (performative). Through doctrines about the holiness of God, his saving righteousness and so on, our feelings may be stirred to adoration (evocative) and by using the appropriate language of praise and penitence we may express such feelings (expressive). Furthermore, through adherence to common biblical doctrines, we enjoy a common evangelical solidarity (cohesive).

Now we can see that far from Christian doctrine merely being some sort of mould by which formless experience is given shape, it actually gives Christian experience its character. Thus to change doctrines which function in the ways just outlined is very serious indeed, for if such changes are substantial what results is something *other* than *Christian* experience. What *counts* as Christian experience will, in part, be determined by the doctrinal grid through which it comes. If that grid is not biblical, the experience won't be Christian.

Let me give a personal example of what I mean. When I was a student we had a speaker at the Christian Union who, with impressive rhetoric, told us that he had received a 'word from the Lord' loosely based on John 15 that there were two types of Christian; those who were servants of God and those who were friends of God. The servants of God had a dutiful service, but the friends of God were those who having being baptised in the Spirit knew a joy and intimacy which the others could only envy. 'Which are you?' he challenged. 'Which do you want to be?' he enquired. The answer, of course was a foregone conclusion. Practically everyone in the meeting, including myself, felt impressed, convicted, and cast down. But was such an experience 'Christian'? The answer must be 'no', for no such division of Christians is to be found in Scripture and no alleged 'filling' of the Spirit is proffered as a solution. The truly Christian experience came for me when, in reflecting upon what was said in the light of Scripture, I saw the teaching to be bogus and realised afresh the wonderful liberty of being a child of God.

Now we can see why a Bible-centred ministry is so vital to the spiritual well-being of the church and why evangelicals of all people should not give way to other things which would displace it. It is through such ministry, by the agency of the Holy Spirit, that people's minds are

shaped and hearts are moved to know, obey and so experience God as
he has revealed himself through his Word.

Subversive Hermeneutics
In an article entitled 'It seemed good to the Holy Spirit and to Us?',[21] one
Anglican scholar has argued that those who have changed their mind on
the issue of ordaining women to the presbyterate have done so in the
light of certain recent changes. It is acknowledged that society has
changed and is 'impatient' with the few remaining bastions of male
privilege. The church, and therefore the gospel, is 'for many tarred with
the brush of chauvinism and of injustice'. The church too has changed,
'moving away from the one man band form of ministry causing many
to appreciate the ministry of women.' But thirdly, and perhaps most
significantly, hermeneutics has changed, that is, the principles and
methods applied in biblical interpretation and application, particularly,
under the influence of what is sometimes called the 'new hermeneutic'.
So now, says the writer 'we have come to realise that it is possible on
some issues to argue in quite opposite directions from Scripture depending on what texts you take as your starting point, and what relative
weight you give to different aspects of the whole scriptural revelation'.

Having acknowledged the traditional approach to this matter, namely
considering those texts which seem to apply specifically to the issue –
1 Corinthians 11, 1 Corinthians 14, 1 Timothy 2 and so on, he suggests
a different approach. This is to look at the broader sweep of Scripture,
one which sees women in the Old Testament from time to time taking
a leading role, the way Jesus related to women and challenged conservative Jewish attitudes, and the alleged 'impressive way' Paul viewed
women as we glean from the way he greets and speaks of certain leading
women in Romans 16. So he writes:

> 'The effect of this chapter is so striking that one wonders how it could
> derive from the same Paul who is responsible for 1 Timothy 2:12. If it does,
> as I believe, then the question must surely be raised whether Paul meant in
> that passage quite what he is generally understood to have meant, or
> whether there was something specific to the situation in Ephesus at the time
> which caused him to make a more restrictive ruling apply'.

So we have a choice: 'Whether, we take our stand on 1 Timothy 2 and
related passages, and somehow make the prominent role of women in

21. R.T. France, 'It seemed good to the Holy Spirit and to Us?' *Churchman*, 1994, Vol. 3.

first century Christianity fit in with them or we start with the more general picture as it is summed up in Galatians 3:28 and ask how the more restrictive passages can be explained in that context'. In addition, he says, we have to face the more demanding hermeneutical question that even if we follow the traditional reading of Paul, how do we apply that teaching to the very different circumstances in which we find ourselves today?'

There are several issues here.

First, should we not detect signals when it is admitted that one of the main stimuli for a re-examination (and re-interpretation) of biblical texts is changing attitudes in society? Thus, Paul accommodated his teaching to the culture of his time (and from one point of view was inconsistent going against the principle of Galatians 3:28) and we are to do the same. Does this mean that if our society developed in a more male dominant direction then we had better re-read Paul again and go back to a more traditional interpretation?

Secondly, the writer inverts a very important principle of Biblical interpretation. Instead of reading passages which clearly and specifically deal with an issue – e.g. eldership/teaching ministry within the church – and reading the less clear passages in their light, it is suggested that the more obscure passages, such as the listing of women in Romans 16, be taken as key and the more specific passages such as 1 Timothy 2 be viewed against this backdrop, thus not only explaining them but explaining them away as culturally specific.

The fact is, Paul in the one passage dealing with the issue refers back to the creation order for his ruling and not to the specific context of the church situation. Therefore, we need a hermeneutic which will enable us transpose this principle of headship, that is Christ-like male leadership and teaching, to the situation in the church today, and not a hermeneutic which violates it.

The main concern with a hermeneutic which emphasises the difference between our world and the world of the New Testament over and against the sameness, is that too much weight and influence is given to the prevailing beliefs of the present day. One cannot help but see a parallel between the arguments used for the ordination of women – relativising those texts which address the issue – and the arguments for legitimising practising homosexual relationships. Supposing the prevailing attitudes in society were to change to such an extent that, to modify the words of our writer, 'it became impatient with the few remaining bastions of heterosexual privilege and began tarring the church, and therefore the gospel, with the brush of homophobia and injustice', does this mean that we should go back to the Scriptures and reinterpret those texts which appear to rule out such practice? If we are to be consistent, then the answer must be 'yes', and conveniently a hermeneutic is ready at hand to enable us to do so.

In fact this has already started to happen. Here is part of an article which appeared in a recent Anglican evangelical journal. [22] Notice the formal similarity in the argument used to legitimise homosexual relationships and the arguments we commonly hear to justify the ordination of women to the presbyterate. Referring to Romans 1:26-27 this writer states,

> 'Paul's argument is Greek in form. He draws on the notion of the natural
> (*phusis*) which was very important in a wide range of Greek philosophies
> (but relatively unusual in the biblical tradition). It is a word which means
> more than 'normal' or 'conventional', but it does not mean natural in the
> sense of a fixed law in physical nature of a purely factual kind. The natural
> is not that which is simply observed in nature, but rather it is a human moral
> reflection on the natural world. It includes a sense of human judgement
> which can be enshrined in cultures and laws. Thus, when Paul speaks of it
> being natural for women to wear their hair long (1 Corinthians 11:14), he
> is using the word in a typically Greek sense .... I suggest that Paul's
> argument in verses 26f is similar to that in 1 Corinthians 11:14, based on his
> own moral reflection of the natural order he comes to the conclusion that
> male/male and female/female sexual relationships are idolatrous ... my
> argument is that based on the openness to reflection of the concept phusis,
> we need not necessarily share his conclusion today. It is significant that Paul
> and his world had no word for homosexuality, they did not know that some
> human beings have sexual orientation that seems deeply fixed in a homo-
> sexual mode. As a consequence they lumped together pederasty, homo-
> sexual prostitution and sexual debauchery. It seems to me that we could
> claim today that living and committed homosexual relations are natural
> within the Greek sense of the word *phusis* ...'

He then goes on to say:

> 'Because it uses a moral argument based on the Greek *phusis*, Paul's
> reasoning in verses 26f means that in our different empirical and moral
> setting we can come to a different conclusion in the specific case of

22. M. Williams, 'Romans 1: Entropy, Sexuality and Politics', *Anvil* Vol 10/No 2/1993, p105-10.

committed homosexual relationships. We can thus remain faithful to the deep argument of Paul's text ...'

and the conclusion?

'We ought to accept homosexual relationships that are not idolatrous as being part of the variety of creation. Those who are convinced under God that this is the form of life that they are called to ought to be respected whether they are lay or ordained.'

Is there not something perverse in a hermeneutic which can lead us to say the exact opposite of what Paul is saying and at the same time claim that we are being faithful to him?

The development of a hermeneutic which has the effect of imprisoning Paul's teaching within the confines of his own culture and ideological preunderstanding, so relativising and silencing him, reached a new stage in a subsequent article dealing with the same issue.[23] Here it is argued that Paul's world-view need not be ours, indeed, the recent insights of psychology and sociology make it almost impossible for us to adopt Paul's 'weltenschaung' with integrity:

'Current thinking generally considers homosexual orientation to be 'natural', physiologically present in a person. Sexual relations should be between equals and with consent of both persons .... Our world view is very different from Paul's. Paul condemned same-sex acts in the light of his differentiated and structured view of creation, in which the male and female roles should be distinct and heirachical. Is such a world-view normative for Christians today? There are many aspects of Paul's thinking that we no longer accept uncritically; we condemn slavery more forthrightly than he did; we do allow women to teach, and in few churches are women silent and hatted, and in those churches seldom do men lift up holy hands as part of their praying.'

The writer concludes by presenting us with a stark choice of alternatives either to use the Bible 'pre-critically', in which case, he argues, we have to go the whole way to be consistent, strict adherence to the Torah, speaking to one another in psalms, etc, or we adopt a 'post-critical' position, allowing our interpretation of Scripture to be the result of a

---

23. P. Reiss, 'Sexuality, Symbol, Theology and Culture: A reply to Francis Bridger', *Anvil*, Vol 11, No. 1, 1994.

'dialogue' with 'the best of psychological and sociological insights'.

But surely this is a false antitheses. In the first place it is quite evident that this proposed 'dialogue' is a very unequal one, effectively rendering the authority of Scripture in any meaningful sense void. The presentation of the 'traditional' evangelical approach is a gross caricature which is most reprehensible. It has been demonstrated by eminently able evangelical scholars that it is possible to adopt an approach to interpreting Scripture, based upon the grammitico-historial-theological method, which enables us to make some distinction between those elements of Scripture which are solely or largely the cultural expressions of theological principles (wearing veils, lifting holy hands, etc) and those which have absolute, universal application (e.g. the prohibition of same-sex genital relations).[24] To place Paul's treatment of homsexuality in the same category as wearing veils is naive and mischievous. In a variety of places and in a variety of ways, Paul propounds a theology of male-female relations, grounded in the doctrine of creation-fall-and redemption. It is this framework which makes same-sex genital relations 'unnatural'. To jettison such an understanding, as this professing 'Anglican evangelical' writer does, is to engage in a serious departure from a view of biblical inspiration and authority which has been one of the defining elements of evangelicalism. While one is wary of the 'slippery slope' argument, one wonders what, if anything, will be left of Paul's teaching which we can consider as having any validity today.

Several years ago Carl Henry commented:

> In recent years a type of theft has emerged as some fellow evangelicals wrest from the Bible segments that they derogate as no longer the Word of God, some now even introduce authorial intention or cultural context of language as specious rationalizations for their crime against the Bible, much as some rapist might assure me that he is assaulting my wife for my or her own good ... they misuse Scripture in order to champion as biblically true what in fact does violence to Scripture.[25]

This is a most pertinent comment on some trends presently taking place in Anglican evangelicalism.

---

24. *Hermeneutics, Authority and Canon.* Ed. D.A. Carson and J.D. Woodbridge, IVP, 1986.
25. C.F. Henry, 'The Bible and the Conscience of Our Age' in *Hermeneutics, Inerrancy and the Bible'* ed. Radmacher and Preus.

A new commitment

Of all the weaknesses reviewed, the last is perhaps the most worrying. It has been a hallmark of evangelicalism that Scripture is supremely authoritative and sufficient for matters of faith and conduct. While the question of the authority of Scripture is the subject of another chapter in this book, it might be helpful to raise one or two points in conclusion.

What does it mean to hold to the authority of Scripture? One helpful way of considering this question might be to think of the way any form of communication functions. In this regard valuable assistance can be afforded by the insights provided by brain science at the level of communication engineering, as propounded, for example, by the late Professor Donald MacKay.[26/27] Put simply, any form of communication (whether true or false) is designed to shape the way we relate to things, what is called our 'conditional states of readiness'. How this works can be illustrated by way of analogy: In a railway shunting-yard there will be a signal box of levers. When the levers are set up in a certain pattern the yard is 'conditionally ready' to deal with traffic in a corresponding way. Change the pattern of the switches and you change the conditional readiness to cope with the traffic. Words can be thought of as specially designed tools for adjusting the switch settings of our brains – having a shaping function, so that we can become ready to act. So it is with God's communication with us in the Bible. It is designed to shape the way we relate to reality – the reality of God, the world, each other and so on. Hence, Jesus' often misquoted statement in John 8:31: 'If you *hold* to my teaching, you are really my disciples. *Then* you shall know the truth and the truth will set you free'. Understanding and obeying the truth of God co-inhere. It is impossible to have obedience without understanding.

The implications of this are quite far-reaching.

First, it is an incentive to put teaching where it ought to be, namely, at the centre of Christian ministry. For it is through proclamation, teaching and admonishing (Colossians 1:28), that people's states of readiness are shaped so that they will think and behave in God-approved ways. We must not underestimate what happens Sunday by Sunday or on any other occasion when God's Word is opened.

Secondly, it means that in addition to attempting to be as accurate as

---

26. D.M. MacKay, *Human Science and Human Dignity*, (Hodder and Stoughton, 1979), pp.80-102.
27. D.M. MacKay, *Behind the Eye*, (Blackwells, Oxford, 1991), pp.112-116.

possible in conveying Christian doctrine, we must pay close attention to the non-verbal aspects of our communication which can be just as effective in their shaping effect on people's minds as the actual words used. By this one does not simply mean the manner, intonation and demeanour adopted in preaching (although these things are included), but, for instance, the 'style of worship', the form as well as the content of the services. Are these subject to God's authority? Are they designed to have the shaping effect in people's lives that God intends? Or is something else being conveyed such as: 'This is being done because it is 16th-century language' or 'Worship is having a happy self-indulgent time with good vibes all around'? To acknowledge the authority of Scripture in *practice* means acknowledging and submitting to God's right to shape our conditional states of readiness.

This brings us to our third point, namely, the extent to which we are submitting to that authority can in part be gauged by our responses to situations as they arise. In other words, our behaviour often serves as a fair indicator of what our true beliefs are and what is *really* exercising its authority over us. For example, in spite of what Article Six of the Thirty Nine Articles says about the authority of Scripture, in practise many Anglicans evangelicals are more or less being required to adopt as an article of faith that only 'priests' can officiate at Holy Communion. This is not required by Scripture and one may argue that a good Scriptural case can be made that it should not be so. (A similar position has now arisen with the measure permitting the ordination of women to the presbyterate.) What are Anglican evangelicals' conditional states of readiness with regards to such matters? Are we being ruled by God's Word or by denominational regulations? What are we willing to do about it?

There must be a new and deliberate undertaking by Anglican evangelicals to promote the belief and practice of the authority and sufficiency of Scripture. This will involve exposing and resisting some of the trends that have already been noted. It will involve encouraging ministers in particular to develop and maintain the priority of the teaching ministry and to call for those who are so gifted to engage in doing the necessary theological graft to promote a coherent and contemporary evangelical theology for our generation. This will not be a matter of doing the theological equivalent of re-inventing the wheel, but it will be part of contending afresh for the faith delivered once for all the saints. And it is to this task that all evangelicals must commit themselves with renewed vigour.

4

Whatever happened to the authority of Scripture?
Gerald Bray

Classical Protestant Hermeneutics

Everyone knows that the authority of the Bible was one of the chief points of debate at the time of the Reformation, when Luther's cry of *sola Scriptura* ('Scripture alone') became one of the distinguishing marks of the Protestant movement. Luther believed that the doctrine of the church must be determined only by appeal to the Bible, so that anything which was not contained or taught in it could have no final authority for Christians. His opponents agreed that Scripture was the primary authority for doctrine, but they also believed that it must be interpreted with the help of tradition. This allowed them to accept doctrines, like the existence of purgatory, which were not clearly taught by the Apostles, but which had grown up over the centuries of pious devotion.

Luther was not putting forward a new doctrine, but reaffirming an ancient teaching of the church which he believed had been obscured by the misuse of tradition. In both patristic and medieval times, it had been a theologian's proudest boast that he was 'learned in the sacred page' (*in sacra pagina doctus*), i.e. that he was a master of the art of Biblical interpretation. It is true that nobody explicitly stated that Scripture was the *only* authority for doctrine until John Wyclif (d.1384), who was condemned for it, but the great classical doctors of the church treated the Bible with such reverence that no other authority could rival it. Luther believed that he was following them, and that Wyclif's position was basically correct.

But Luther was not content merely to affirm *sola Scriptura*. Along with that came his conviction that justification by faith alone was Scripture's basic message and that everything in the Bible must be read in the light of that principle. This was not a new doctrine, but Luther's defence of his position by systematic Biblical exegesis was unprecedented. A third factor was that Luther took his convictions and started to preach them. What might have remained an academic argument between learned monks spilled over into the church at large, where it provoked an upheaval.

Luther's work was carried on and developed by John Calvin, who accepted Luther's teaching and systematized it. His writings fall easily into three main categories. First there are his *Commentaries*, which were intended to cover the entire Bible and provide a clear guide to its interpretation. Then there are his *Institutes*, which created a systematic framework in which the teaching of Scripture could be understood. Finally, there are his *Sermons*, in which the fruits of his Biblical exegesis ('study of the meaning of the Scriptural texts') and the content of his systematic theology (the logical synthesis of his exegesis) were fused into a powerful weapon for transforming the church.

Calvin did not live to complete *Commentaries* and *Sermons* on every part of the Bible, but his followers built on his foundations and continued his work. By the middle of the seventeenth century, there had appeared a Reformed tradition which took the Covenant theme as the fundamental principle uniting its exegesis, its doctrine and its preaching. Covenant theology became the classical Protestant hermeneutic, enshrined in documents like the Westminster Confession of Faith (1647) and repeated, with varying degrees of consistency, by one generation of theologians after another.

In this system of thought, pride of place belongs to thorough and responsible exegesis, which is the *source* of all true doctrine. The Reformers insisted that *only* a careful and scientific investigation of the Biblical text, taken in its intended (or so-called 'literal') sense, could provide a secure basis for the Church's teaching. They believed that the Bible was basically self-interpreting, because its main message was clear to anyone who had the ability to read it. On the other hand, they did not deny that it contained many hard and confusing passages, and they had no time for fanatics who took a few verses out of context and built an entire doctrine on them. They believed that exegesis was a scientific discipline which required careful study and great patience if it was to achieve the correct results. The methods they used could be defended in academic terms, and were available to anyone with the appropriate training. It was not necessary to be the possessor of some esoteric knowledge (such as that afforded by mystical contemplation) in order to understand the plain meaning of the Bible.

The second principle is that Scripture is a unity, and that its teaching can therefore be systematized in a coherent structure of belief. This offers a guide to the correct interpretation of difficult passages and provides the foundation for the Church's teaching ministry. Theology is neither a luxury which can be dispensed with, nor an imposition on the pristine purity of a self-evident text, but a necessary tool, revealing the *system* which undergirds the witness of Scripture. Without that, Biblical interpretation becomes disjointed and loses its meaning, since the reading of a particular verse or passage is not connected to what the Reformers liked to call 'the whole counsel of God'.

Particularly important is the distinction which systematic theology makes between what Scripture teaches and what it merely records, or tolerates. For example, many Biblical passages *record* instances of polygamy and slavery in a way which indicates a certain tolerance of these social customs. Hard though it may be for us to understand why neither of them is openly condemned by Scripture. Yet the Bible *teaches* that male and female were meant to live together as equals, just as it teaches that all human beings are created in the image and likeness of God. The fact that Abraham, the father of our faith, was polygamous and may have owned slaves without incurring God's condemnation, does not mean that this is God's will for us. Our practice must be determined by what Scripture teaches, not by what it merely records.

The third principle is that a theology is valid only if it can be preached. It is only as the message is proclaimed and applied to the life of the believer and the church that its true *sense* is revealed. Biblical interpretation and systematic theology are necessarily the work of specialists, but they are not meant to become esoteric pursuits for the chosen few. Unless and until the findings of scholars can be unpacked for the edification of the believing community, they remain fruitless. If it is discovered that scholarly conclusions have no echo in the life of the church, then the classical Protestant position is that it is up to the scholars and theologians to recognize that somewhere along the line they have gone wrong, and that their efforts are no longer serving the community which has called for them in the first place.

The Breakdown of the Classical Framework

The classical Protestant hermeneutical framework did not enjoy unchallenged pre-eminence for long. Even in the seventeenth century there were those who could not accept the Covenant theology which the Westminster divines and others of similar views were hammering out. One group, the so-called 'High Church' party, disagreed with the way in which the Puritans were applying the principles of *sola Scriptura*. They maintained that while Scripture was clearly the supreme authority in matters of faith, other authorities, notably the tradition of the universal church, should also play a part. Only when it could be shown that this tradition had departed from the plain teaching of the Bible should it be rejected. The practical consequence of this was that the High Church group saw no reason to abandon traditional structures of church government and worship which were not obviously incompatible with the teaching of the New Testament, whereas the Puritans believed that a new system should be created, based on the practice of the New Testament church. Their failure to agree on what this should be was a powerful argument in favour of the High Church position, which had the added advantage of maintaining the stability of the traditional order. The High Church party tried to emphasize the continuity of the Church of England with the primitive church, an exercise which led it away from the systematic, towards a more historical approach to theology. In their preaching, they were more inclined to follow the mystical, allegorical tradition of the Church Fathers rather than the scientific exegesis of the Reformers, as can be seen from a glance at the sermons of Lancelot Andrews, for example.

Beginning in the 1630's, a few anti-Calvinists, who had been influenced by Dutch Arminians like Hugo Grotius, began to advocate a kind of non-doctrinal Christianity. They did not believe that it was possible to build an entire society on exclusively Biblical principles, and accused the Puritans of manipulating Scripture to suit themselves. For them, the Bible was a useful guide for morality, but not an all-encompassing authority, and it was among them that the idea of using science to disprove the supposed claims of Scripture first gained an audience.

The majority of eighteenth-century intellectuals dismissed large portions of the Biblical text as myth, or as a record of events which were unworthy of a rational Deity. Only a small minority tried to defend traditional orthodoxy, by claiming that there was nothing irrational or morally unacceptable in Scripture, but their apologetic efforts were not very successful. Too much smacked of special pleading, and the rationalists had little difficulty in demonstrating that their opponents were motivated by dogmatic considerations which were inimical to the pursuit of true science.

The final blow to the traditional order was struck, somewhat paradoxically, by the Evangelical revival of the mid-eighteenth century. In many ways, this was a conservative movement, a popular protest of piety against the ungodly rationalism of the intellectuals. Unfortunately, the Evangelical revival was quickly divided by its own doctrinal differences over the relationship between divine sovereignty and human freedom. John Wesley and his followers became 'Arminians' who denied that predestination could stand in the way of making a decision for Christ, whilst George Whitefield and the majority of those Evangelicals who remained within the Church of England were 'Calvinists' who put their emphasis on divine sovereignty in the work of conversion.

For Wesley and Whitefield, doctrinal issues were sufficiently serious to cause lasting division. But in a movement of spiritual revival, where most ordinary folk had little understanding of the theological issues at stake, such a division was hard to maintain. Any conflict between theological principles (like predestination) and practical experience would inevitably be resolved in favour of the latter, and it was usually possible to discover a Scriptural text to support this. Wesley himself gradually came to accept a doctrine of human perfection, based on the experience of a second blessing, which he defended from such verses as 'Be ye perfect, even as your Father in heaven is perfect' (Matthew 5:18). How could a quotation from the Sermon on the Mount, of all things, be regarded as teaching an unscriptural doctrine? The result was a method of interpretation which may be described as 'find a text to back up your inspiration/experience', and this was to become characteristic of much of the Evangelical movement.

In many circles, there was a strong sense that the Calvinist-Arminian divide was an unnecessary distraction, harmful to the task of preaching the gospel, and plenty of revivalists were ready to blame 'dead doctrine' for the lethargic and divided state in which they found the church. If only Christians could forget theology and restrict themselves to the Bible, there would be no problem! *Sola Scriptura* was thus dusted off and reinterpreted to mean something which Luther would never have contemplated!

By the middle of the nineteenth century, Scripture no longer exercised any real authority in academic circles, which were dominated by the rationalism of the Enlightenment. Systematic theology, though it still existed, became increasingly less biblical in its orientation. For if the Bible could be shown to be a collection of discrete, and mutually contradictory documents, how could a theological system be constructed out of it? Theology could only be rescued from rationalist attacks on the Bible by giving it a new theoretical basis. In the hands of Friedrich Schleiermacher and his disciples, it became a kind of religious philosophy whose business it was to discourse on spiritual realities which were note susceptible to the methods of scientific reason. And so it remains. Writing in the *Church Times* of 11 June 1993, Peter Baelz criticized the conservative doctrinal series, *Contours of Christian Theology,* in the following terms:

> 'A fundamental difficulty for some readers of this series will be its presupposition that Christian doctrine is an articulation of biblical doctrine. Certainly no theologian belonging to the mainstream of Christian reflection would want to see a sharp division between Bible and doctrine. However, many will take the view that the Bible is a varied and complex collection of books, reflecting different stages in a people's history and self-understanding. They will doubt, therefore, whether there is any such thing as a single coherent Biblical theology ... Scripture can provide the basis for more than one theological system.'

This is a statement by a leading theologian of the Church of England, who is far from being a radical liberal. Yet he cannot imagine how anyone can hold to a theological principle of *sola Scriptura*. For him, the Bible is an important resource, but it cannot be regarded as definitive for theology.

Evangelicals reject what they see as the 'liberalism' of Baelz's position, but it is not clear what they would put in its place. They continue to affirm the Reformation principle of *sola Scriptura*, but without the Reformation framework of systematic Biblical doctrine. Many would agree, implicitly, that doctrine merely gets in the way of understanding the Bible, and that experience is the ultimate criterion of truth. The result is a situation in which the authority of Scripture is affirmed in theory but often denied in practice, because of a faulty method of interpreting it.

Sola Exegesis

What has happened is that modern Evangelicalism has been shaped by what can best be called a policy of *sola exegesis*, not *sola Scriptura* as the Reformers understood it. For a generation now, Evangelical exegetes have laboured to bring their perspective to bear on the interpretation of the Bible. They have accepted the rules of the academic game and done their utmost to demonstrate that there is no incompatibility between their academic research and their faith commitment. This claim has not always been received by non-Evangelical scholars, as the work of

James Barr has shown.[1] Many Evangelicals have replied to Barr, but none had done so as thoroughly or as graciously as Dr. R. T. France, who has written quite extensively about his views.[2] Perhaps inadvertently, Dr. France has in the process also demonstrated very clearly what the effects of a *sola exegesis* position can be.

In his analysis of contemporary Evangelicalism, theology is mentioned only in connection with the doctrine of Biblical infallibility and/or inerrancy, which touch directly on the exegetical enterprise and are generally thought to give Evangelical scholarship its 'fundamentalist' tinge. One of Dr. France's main concerns is to demonstrate that Evangelical scholars are not fundamentalists, and to do this he uses the authorship of different New Testament books as a case study. At one time, he says, Evangelical 'orthodoxy' (note the word) would have insisted even on the Pauline authorship of Hebrews, but that era is now long gone. Modern Evangelical scholars are prepared to question, and many of them actually reject, the traditional ascriptions of many New Testament books, including Matthew, John and Revelation. Particularly serious is the rejection of the Pauline authorship of the Pastoral Epistles and the Petrine authorship of 2 Peter, because the texts themselves (unlike Matthew and John) claim these authors. Here as Dr. France readily admits, a theological issue is at stake – are these books telling the truth or not?

But it is precisely at this point that Dr. France cannot give a satisfactory answer to his own question. Instead, he defends modern Evangelical scholars on the ground that they have found a new way of reconciling their theological commitment to Biblical authority with the latest critical findings. It is all a matter of *interpretation*! Dr. France does not spell out what this might mean, but others have.[3] It seems that the *doctrine* of a pseudonymous book is authoritative in so far as it accords with apostolic teaching, but the *incidental details* of the book may be dispensed with. In the case of 2 Timothy, for example, this would mean that 3:16 ('All Scripture is inspired by God') is authorita-

1. J. Barr *Fundamentalism*, SCM Press, London, 1977 and 1981; 'The Problem of Fundamentalism Today' in *Explorations in Theology 7*, SCM Press, London, 1980, pp. 65-90; *Escaping from Fundamentalism*, SCM Press, London, 1984.
2. See *Anvil* 8, 1991, pp.51-64, with Professor Barr's reply, *ibid.*, pp.141-52. Also, 'Evangelicalism and Biblical Scholarship:2. The New Testament' in R.T. France and A.E. McGrath edd., *Evangelical Anglicans*, SPCK, London, 1993, pp.47-546.
3. See David G. Meade, *Psudonymity and Canon: An Investigation into the Relationship of Authorship and Authority in Jewish and Earliest Christian Tradition*, Eerdmans, Grand Rapids, 1986, pp.203-215.

tive for the church, but that 4:12-18 ('Tychicus I have sent to Ephesus. When you come, bring the cloak that I left with Carpus at Troas' etc.) are fictitious embellishments which the original readers of the book would have recognized and accepted as such!

Dr. France welcomes this new development, though he admits that many people in the church find it hard to understand. As he puts it: 'what was an unsettling new perspective for many ordinary church members has proved a liberating one for the evangelical scholarly enterprise'.[4] Dr. France does not quite say that those who do not go along with this are not on the same intellectual level as those who do, but the implication is certainly there. In the modern world, it is not a compliment to suggest to someone that he/she has not been liberated!

The traditional, or less 'open' Evangelical would want to reply that it is bad scholarship to doubt the authenticity of a text without good reason to do so. In the case of the New Testament documents, the doubts of modern scholars were heard at least as early as the third century, and were fully debated. It may be true that pseudonymity was more widely accepted in antiquity than it would be today, but there is no indication that Christians were prepared to accept pseudonymous works in the canon of Scripture. Had the majority in the church been persuaded that these books were not of apostolic origin, they would not have been included in the canon.

When these points are taken into account, it becomes clear that the real issues are somewhat different from what Dr. France presents us with. On the purely scholarly level, there have long been disputes about certain books of the New Testament, and these will probably continue until our Lord's return. A conservative answer to the question is not the preserve of Evangelicals, and it will doubtless be advocated by some as long as scholarship exists. Whether Evangelicals ought to be committed to a conservative standpoint is another matter, which must be decided on different criteria. [5]

---

4. Op. cit., *Evangelical Anglicans*, p.53.
5. David Meade has attempted to answer this question. He recognizes that Paul was worried about a false letter (2 Thessalonians 2:2), but claims that this was mainly because it contained heresy, not because it was inauthentic. His basic argument is that apostolic doctrine, not apostolic authorship (or commendation) determined canonicity. But quite apart from the difficulties which such a definition entails, there is no evidence to support it. Even Meade has to confess that the Early Church soon discouraged anonymity and pseudonymity (p.206). Need we ask why?

If it can be shown that the Pastoral Epistles and 2 Peter are not apostolic, then on historical grounds they ought to be excluded from the canon. Are Evangelicals who take this position prepared to see these books relegated to the level of the *Didache* or the *Shepherd of Hermas*? If not, why not? They could hardly accept that the books ought to remain canonical for traditional reasons, because the tradition which made them canonical did so in the belief that they were apostolic. But the canon, as Brevard Childs keeps reminding us, is essentially a theological concept. For a book to be in the canon means that it is theologically authoritative for the church. Why should this be so, if the book is not apostolic in origin? Here we have gone beyond the limits of a *sola exegesis* approach and entered the realm of systematic theology, which modern Evangelical scholars run away from, but which is essential if their exegetical efforts are going to have any relevance to the life of the church.

This brings us to the heart of the matter. Anyone who tries to preach the results of exegesis (as distilled, for example, in the average modern commentary) will soon discover one of two things. Either he will end up lecturing on the meaning of a particular verse or passage – an activity which may appeal to an intellectual minority but is unlikely to make a lasting impression on anyone's life – or he will abandon any serious attempt to apply the text and retreat to the old stand-by of experience, using the text as an introduction to what he really wants to say.

This state of affairs is now so common that many Evangelicals are incapable of recognising or appreciating serious exposition of the Bible. The idea that we ought to *submit* our thoughts to the Word, as opposed to reading them into it, is foreign to a large part of the Evangelical constituency. Moved as many of them are by emotional currents of spiritual 'renewal', they may well turn up to church half an hour before the service begins, in order to participate in a 'time of worship', and they may also be prepared to stay on afterwards for what they call 'ministry'. These have become the highlights of their churchgoing – what happens during the official service is almost boringly irrelevant by comparison. Certainly, the sermon counts for very little, and may often be replaced by an audio-visual 'teaching' slot geared more to amusing children than to teaching adults. Even then, the emphasis is almost certain to be on informing the audience about the contents of the Bible, rather than on applying it to the spiritual needs of those who have come to the service. It is little wonder that additional forms of 'ministry' have become so popular!

The inapplicability of *sola exegesis* becomes very clear when we start to consider ethical issues. Here more than anywhere, Biblical practice appears to many to be out of date. Whether we are discussing nuclear weapons or personal sexuality, it is often hard to see how the Bible can be applied directly. Either it says nothing about the issues raised, or what it does say is liable to be understood too simplistically.

A hermeneutic which relies on *sola exegesis* will soon discover that there are whole realms of human experience which cannot be brought under the authority of Scripture, because there is no verse which speaks clearly about them. As a result, Christians either retreat into an unthinking conservatism ('it must be wrong') or make their decisions without reference to the Bible, because they can find no guidance in its pages. Either way, the authority of Scripture is effectively denied.

The absence of fundamental principles makes itself felt even in cases where the Bible does appear to speak clearly on a particular issue. The recent debates over women's ordination provide a good example of just how inadequate the *sola exegesis* approach can be in determining the way forward for the church. In the course of this debate, enormous effect was expended on the interpretation of one or two verses of the New Testament, as if these can be read in isolation from the whole. At times single words have become the focus of attention, as with the true meaning of the Greek word *kephale* (head) in 1 Corinthians 11:3. Absurd attempts have been made to demonstrate that this verse does not mean what it clearly says, entirely in the interests of demonstrating that the female does not have to submit to the authority of the male in the life of the church. Even if it could be demonstrated that *kephale* might mean 'source', instead of 'head', it clearly does not do so in this passage. But even if it did, it would not make any difference to the meaning, since for the male to be the source of the female would also imply that he had authority over her!

The real problem here is not the precise interpretation of the text in question, but rather that a debate of this kind could happen at all. How can we have reached the point where a highly dubious interpretation of a single word can influence the church's life to such a momentous degree? Some would say that that is the price we must pay if we are to take the authority of Scripture seriously, but the object of that particular exercise was to neutralize a text of Scripture which says something which the supporters of women's ordination do not want to hear. The intention is not to exalt the teaching of Scripture, but to get around it – the authority of the Bible is recognized, but as the enemy!

From there it is but a short step to rewriting the sacred text whenever its words do not accord with popular sentiment. Many translations of the Scriptures are currently being redone in order to take out what is perceived to be 'sexist' language, which means language in which the masculine is used to include the feminine as well. Given that that is standard Biblical practice, extending even to the point where a male represents the entire human race on the Cross, the changes required are numerous, and have far-reaching consequences. In the forthcoming revision of the NIV, for example, the Greek word *adelphoi* ('brothers') will apparently be replaced, not by 'brothers and sisters', which is felt to be too unwieldy, but by 'believers' – a totally different word! What has happened to the authority of Scripture when the plain reading of the text can be altered like this, purely in response to a current social fad?

Protests against this sort of thing abound, but they are largely ineffectual. Faced with the overwhelming desire to satisfy the demands of modern feminism, who would dare to worry that the inner integrity of an ancient text is being sacrificed to this new idol of our time? The fact that many Biblical scholars have acquiesced in this kind of thing – some are very enthusiastic supporters of it – demonstrates only too clearly what the limitation of a *sola exegesis* approach are. The biblical passages which deal with the place of women in the church may be hard to relate directly to the question of ordination, but the overall pattern of male headship, in the church as well as in the home, is clear enough. By concentrating on parts – sometimes on very minute parts – they have sacrificed the perspective of the whole, and allowed unbiblical conclusions to be drawn from what purports to be the interpretation of Scripture!

Can the authority of Scripture be recovered?

Recent events have clearly demonstrated that the modern church, including its Evangelical wing, is unwilling to submit to the authority of Scripture. If what the Bible teaches is uncongenial, then scholarship is put to work to demonstrate that the text either means something other than what it plainly says, or else that it cannot be applied to the issue at hand. Groups pressing for change have few problems with this, though some non-Evangelicals, who fail to see why anybody should bother to consult the Bible at all, might think that this procedure is an unnecessary waste of time. But the fact is that some Evangelical leaders, who ought to be among the leading opponents of this new non-hermeneutic, are actually some of its more enthusiastic supporters!

For those committed to the Reformation in principle of *sola Scriptura* this is a depressing situation. *Sola Scriptura* can only work effectively if there is an agreed understanding of what it means, and that implies a systematic theology. But the history of divisions on this score is such as to have created a deep-seated suspicion of theology among many Biblical scholars, including those of a conservative stripe. To be fair to them, there is also the problem that in an age of specialization, it is difficult to be equally adept in exegesis and in systematics, especially when the skills needed for the one are not always appropriate to the other. A good exegete needs to be analytical in his approach, whereas a good systematician needs to be capable of synthesizing his material into a coherent whole. How many of us are able to handle both of these with comparable ease?

These are real difficulties, and it would be foolish to underestimate them. But if scripture authority is ever to mean anything, it must be supported and defended by a coherent theology. Failure to do this will lead either to an arbitrary use of the Bible, subject to the whims of prejudice or expediency, or (as in many parts of the church today) to the abandonment of Scripture as a serious guide to current thinking and practice.

The reconstruction of a serviceable theology, in which *sola Scriptura* can find a meaningful place, will not be a simple matter. Quite apart from the various prejudices which have to be overcome before the task can even begin, there are a number of practical problems to face. Would such a theology be basically denominational or basically Evangelical in character? In a mixed denomination like the Church of England, it is hard to see how any agreement along denominational lines could ever be reached. Mixed churches are coalitions of interest groups which combine (or split) in different ways from time to time, but which seldom present a common front. A pan-Evangelical approach, on the other hand, runs the risk of resurrecting old quarrels (like the debate over infant baptism), without being able to influence the practice of any particular church. Perhaps the best solution, at least in the short term, is that like-minded fellowships should be formed within particular denominations, which could maintain friendly relations with each other but fight for their principles inside the currently existing structures.

In the Church of England, it seems obvious that such a fellowship would be formed from among the Evangelical wing, but it would be idle to pretend that the two would be identical. Some Evangelicals, particularly those who believe that they are fully represented within the *status quo*, would resist the whole idea, and trying to include them would scuttle the whole project from the start. A restructuring of the current Evangelical scene along doctrinal lines would be a painful exercise for those who have grown used to thinking in terms of club membership, but if being an Evangelical is more a matter of who you know (and get along with) than of what you believe, the principle of *sola Scriptura* will never be more than an empty phrase, trotted out on ritual club occasions but completely ignored in practice.

Of course, it would be extremely important to agree on acceptable boundaries for a workable theological system. Proponents of the Reformation principle would no doubt want to begin by saying that what Scripture affirms must be affirmed, that what it denies must be denied and that what it is unclear about must be left as a matter of indifference. That is fine in theory, but we must not be blind to the practical problems which such a formula creates. Systematic theology is basically about God, not about the Bible, and that focus must not be forgotten. It is what Scripture affirms *about God* which must be emphasized, not what it says (or is thought to say) about politics, biology or whatever. Hard though it may be to avoid, we must not get caught up in arguments about social or evolutionary theories about which Christians may and do legitimately differ.

To the objection that an overemphasis on systematic theology will lead back to the 'dead orthodoxy' which so afflicted later Puritanism, we must reply that the recovery of doctrine only makes sense if it goes hand-in-hand with current exegetical efforts, and leads to the revival of an effective preaching ministry. A truly Reformed perspective keeps all three of these in balance, and the only justification for paying special attention to doctrine is that it is the weakest link in the chain at the present time. But we must also recognize that a theology which cannot be preached is a disaster which, if it were allowed to develop, would kill all efforts at recovering *sola Scriptura*.

Good preaching is the way in which good theology and good exegesis are communicated to people and change their lives. It is the way in which faith is born and nourished, and thus it constitutes the vital link between principle and practice. The test of preachability is essential for any theology, and those who advocate Reformation principles must be the first to insist on this.

On a somewhat different front, we must recognise that there are some issues about which Scripture is unclear, like forms of church government. Here diversity of practice may be legitimate in principle, but if an organization is to hold together, there has to be an agreed policy. It ought to be understood and accepted that in these matters the church acts in ways which common sense and existing structures determine. Some people will always find themselves living within constraints which they would rather do without, and most of us will be in that opposition at some time or other.

But here we must be prepared to compromise, by recognizing that the Bible does not define church government in details, that there is no fundamental doctrinal principle at stake, and that perfection is unattainable in this life. For example, nobody is ever going to have the perfect baptismal policy – the important thing is to have one which is theologically defensive and pastorally consistent. A certain amount of reform will be necessary to achieve the former, and the situation would presumably have to be kept under review, but once the doctrinal and liturgical principles are settled, pastoral practice ought to be recognisably similar in every parish. This would require compromise on the part of idealists and perfectionists who find it hard to put up with what they see as inadequacies, but it is a compromise which is needed if the credibility of the church as a whole is to be maintained.

Lastly, proper discipline would be vital for the maintenance of Scriptural authority. The difficulties surrounding this are so formidable that discipline of any kind has now been almost totally lost in the church. Heresy trials have long since been discredited and are now unthinkable, though there is plenty of scope for covert discrimination against people who disagree with the prevailing consensus – over the ordination of women, for example. Evangelicals are not immune to this – indeed, they are among the worst offenders. The deplorable tendency for doctrinal disputes to degenerate into personality clashes is one of the worst failings of the modern church. Realistically speaking, there is no prospect of exercising serious discipline in the church as a whole; the most that a doctrinally-sensitive fellowship could hope to do would be to establish proper criteria for its own members and institutions.

It cannot be stressed too strongly that whatever system of discipline is adopted must at all costs be as objective and as fair as possible. This means, among other things, that discipline cannot be exercised in a private or confidential manner. However embarrassing it may be to some people, the issues at stake must be public, so that everyone has a clear understanding of what is going on. This goes right against the grain of the 'club' atmosphere which dominates so much of present-day Evangelicalism. But even in cases where privacy might be desirable, the scope for injustice is so great that it is a luxury which the church cannot afford. One of the major points in favour of a *sola Scriptura* doctrine is its openness – the Bible is there for all to read. If a person is to be accused of corrupting or dishonouring its teaching, then the facts ought to be made public so that everyone knows why discipline must be exercised. This procedure might well cause divisions, and it would probably mean that disciplinary action was rarer than might be ideal. But better that than the opposite, where a small clique, or even a single individual, could attack others under the cloak of confidentiality and get away with it!

Openness in disciplinary matters is also necessary to preserve variety and balance within a doctrinally-committed movement. It is all too easy for one personality-type to dominate the proceedings, and discriminate against others on that basis. A conservative leadership will not appreciate the prophetic voice calling it to continuing reformation, but if such voices are stifled the church will not hear the healing and redeeming Word. Whoever sits in judgement on people like that needs the wisdom of Gamaliel!

In conclusion, we may say that there is no simple solution to the problem of Scriptural authority in the church today. Agreement in principle means nothing if it cannot be applied in practice – but there's the rub! Unless we can come to a common understanding of what Biblical authority entails and until we can agree on a way to make it effective, we shall never recover it for the church. On the contrary, if the past is any guide, we shall almost certainly continue to fall farther and farther away from it, leaving the next generation in an even greater disarray than that in which we now find ourselves.

5

Men, Women and God

Douglas Spanner

Women's ordination is now an established fact in the Church of England, so it may seem superfluous to publish any further comments about it. However, it has raised questions so fundamental to the relationship of men and women that the debate is not going to be laid to rest merely by a vote in the General Synod of the Church of England. I want therefore in this chapter to put forward some considerations that have not received a very wide airing in the public debate. They concern not just the question of ordination but also the wider issue of the harmony between the sexes in today's society.

Why not?

I may say at once that my own opposition to the 'priesting' of women does not turn on any special notion of 'priesthood', nor of the inability of women, for gender reasons, to 'represent Christ at the altar'. The New Testament teaches the priesthood of all believers; and the finality of the Cross means no human priest (male or female) can ever again minister at a visible altar. Any objection on these grounds therefore, in the light of the New Testament, is ill-conceived. What then has been wrong with the pressure for women's ordination?

Let me start with an examination of the well-known passage in Paul's first letter to Timothy.[1] One thing which has been disputed here is the

---

1. The interpretation placed here on 1 Timothy 2:11-15 and Ephesians 5:21ff. is rather different from that of many recent writers. It presupposes that sufficient clues to understanding the first citation are 'on the spot'; they lie in the Old Testament passage itself to which reference is made, the narrative of Genesis 3. They are thus accessible to every generation of readers, and do not rely on a detailed understanding of the educational position of women in first century Ephesus society, something which requires considerable research to establish and which would certainly not be available to many early (and not-so-early) Christians. Since the issue is a matter of evergreen and agelong importance – the relationship of husband and wife – the former presupposition would seem to be a *priori* more in keeping with the genius of inspiration. That is one reason why I prefer it.

meaning of the Greek verb *authentein* which occurs only this once in the New Testament. It is sometimes translated 'to have authority' or 'dominion',[2] but is often given a rather harsher tone: 'to usurp authority',[3] 'to dictate',[4] 'to domineer',[5] 'to tell [a Man] what to do'.[6] This harsher sense has been strongly argued for by some evangelical supporters of women's ordination, such as that able expositor Steve Motyer:[7] 'domineering bossiness' is his understanding.[8] This raises at once the question of why Paul forbids this to women but makes no mention of men; are women the only ones liable to be bossy and domineering? I do not think this suggestion would commend itself to many! Steve Motyer is very hesitant himself to offer a reason, but one is surely not far to seek.

Paul's train of thought here seems to be fairly clear. For he goes on at once to speak of the creation order in Genesis 2, and then of the temptation in Eden. It is entirely in keeping with this[9] to understand him as implying first, the ordained leadership of the man (*'first formed'*);[10] and second, that this was ignored by Eve when the serpent approached her. The scenario for the temptation I take to be this: Adam and Eve were at least within earshot in the garden.[11] The serpent, eminent for subtlety and carefully choosing its words, approached Eve rather than Adam – no doubt judging her (rightly or wrongly) to be the more readily taken in ('deceived'). In circumstances such as these it would have been both possible and right for either human partner to have first consulted the other; but this would have been especially so for Eve since she had presumably learnt of the divine command only through her companion. Fatally, Eve did not. She acted independently

---

It supports this interpretation to recall that just as the term 'God' is used both of the Godhead and of the Father, so the term Adam ('man') is used both of humankind and of the first husband (Genesis 1:26; 5:1-3).

2. New International Version, Revised Standard Version, New King James Version, Revised Version.

3. Authorised Version.

4. Revised English Bible.

5. New English Bible.

6. Jerusalem Bible.

7. Lecturer, London Bible College.

8. *The Church of England Newspaper.*

9. Note the 'For', introducing v.13.

10. *Cf.* Matthew 10:2.

11. Note the 'with her' in v.6 (R.V., N.I.V., J.B.); the contrary, had it been the case, would surely have been more worthy of remark.

on her own initiative and 'took and ate' the forbidden fruit. Still in the lead, she gave it to her husband, and he ate. Is this where the *authentein*, the 'dictating', 'domineering' 'telling [a man] what to do', comes in? It would seem that the unbroken flow of Paul's thought indicates that *authentein* belongs somewhere in the Eden narrative; and where else than here? It makes good sense of his linking it only with woman, and also to his proceeding at once (puzzlingly to many exegetes) to stress a *genuinely* God-ordained function for womanhood, namely childbearing. If leadership is for man, Paul seems to be saying, here is an immense honour for woman – bringing a new human soul into the world. In *this*, Paul says, she shall indeed find divine approval.[12,13]

But to return to the Genesis narrative: of course the Lord God knew already exactly what had happened when he walked 'in the garden in the cool of the day'.[14] Why then the call 'where are you?' directed specifically to Adam, not to Eve? (Note that the two were apparently together.) Surely because it was upon *him* that the responsibility for strict obedience had been imposed. Instead of facing up to that responsibility he had 'listened to the voice of his wife' (a more than possible suggestion that she had exercised some sort of pressure); and it is for this precise reason that his labour henceforth is to be burdensome. Divine judgement has often a very subtle character: with profound irony, God engineers (for instance) that exact opposite of what sinful man has attempted to seize. The one who exalts himself finds abasement; professing himself wise he becomes a fool; promising liberty he turns into a slave of corruption; and so on. The ironical element is frequent in Scripture: think of Jacob's life of deceiving – and being deceived! Is it any wonder that in this seminal passage woman, attempting to dominate, is reduced to having her husband 'rule over her'? Or that man, taking with fatal ease what is forbidden, is to find henceforth that what is freely given can only be won with sweat and toil? And is it not right to interpret these very judgements as falling intentionally upon the roles for which, first and foremost, each sex is divinely fitted: man to be breadwinner, woman to be mother of children? I find it hard not to think so.

If this exegesis is accepted Steve Motyer's understanding of

---

12. Note the allusion to Genesis 3:16 in John 16:21.
13. Paul's 'saved' does not necessarily imply physical safety; Luke 21:14-19; Romans 8:28 and 2 Timothy 4:18 R.V. offer a possible understanding here.
14. Psalm 139:1ff.

authentein seems to make his case (for uniform equality) worse, not better. In public function, the man is *primus inter pares*; man and woman are not on a dead level. Leadership as a principle has been imposed on the man, and where he is weak, unworthy or otherwise not fit for it and woman has to take his place the situation is to be regarded as sub-standard and non-ideal.[15] A very emphatic endorsement of this under-standing is in Revelation 12:1ff., where the woman, Israel, brings forth 'a man child' (lit. 'a son, a male', with a distinct stress on the male-ness) 'who is to rule all nations with a rod of iron', the fulfilment of man's primal responsibility.

Feminine figures of speech for God

It is often argued that feminine metaphors or similes as well as male ones are used for God and that this permits us to use unsexed or even feminine language for him. Examples often quoted are Isaiah 66:13 ('as one whom his mother comforts so will I comfort you'); Luke 13:34 ('as a hen gathers her brood under her wings'); Isaiah 42:14 (' I [the Lord] will cry out like a woman in travail; I will gasp and pant').

But there is an immediate explanation for this. Feminine meta-phors are used simply because they are the most vivid available, and no gender significance whatever is in mind. We use language in this way frequently ourselves: Bismarck, we say, *conceived* the idea of a united Germany, and Einstein that of General Relativity; an inventor has a very *fertile* brain; we refer to a *miscarriage* of justice, or of a scheme which *aborted*. The Bible itself speaks quite often in terms like this: the wicked man 'conceives evil and is pregnant with mischief and brings forth lies' (Isaiah 59:4, Psalm 7:14). What about Galatians 4:19 where (contrast 1 Corinthians 4:15) Paul uses a powerful feminine metaphor (*Odino*) of himself? What about 1 Thessalonians 2:7, 11? No one can possibly read a gender reference in any of these, and the appeal of Christian feminists to such metaphors used of God really does their case more harm than good.

What is much more significant in the Bible is not only that Deity is represented *passim* exclusively by masculine pronouns or titles, but also that we are actually instructed to do so (as in the Lord's Prayer), and that in cases where a feminine term might seem a logical desirabil-ity it seems to be studiously avoided. There is a rather striking example

---

15. Isaiah 3:12; perhaps Judges 4:9; 1 Kings 19:1ff., 21:25ff.; Revelation 2:20; Nehe-miah 13:26d.

of this in James 1:18 where the verb for 'brought forth' (*apokueo*) is 'the medical word for birth at the close of pregnancy', yet it is associated with two masculines (*bouletheis, autou*). In a rather similar way, Isaiah 66:13 runs into masculines ('his' twice) in the very next verse; and the female metaphor of 'pinion' and 'wings' (*cf.* Luke 13:34) is joined with masculines in Psalm 91:4. Similar comments apply to Isaiah 42:14 (*cf.* verse 13c). Why is there never a 'she' or 'her' in these passages? The Greek for Spirit is *pneuma*, a neuter word, and so a neuter pronoun is grammatically quite proper. But in numerous places in John's Gospel where the Spirit's personhood is being stressed an emphatic (and ungrammatical!) masculine pronoun is used (*ekeinos*: John 14:26, 15:26, 16:8, 13, 14). The argument from feminine metaphors for justifying unsexed language for God thus rather recoils upon itself; resorting to it is time misspent.

A statistical digression

Suppose we assemble a fair number of men, chosen at random, and measure the height of each to the nearest inch. The results can be represented visually by drawing a horizontal line marked to show height and on this erecting at the appropriate points vertical lines whose length is proportional to the number of individuals scoring the corresponding feet and inches. The result will be something like this:

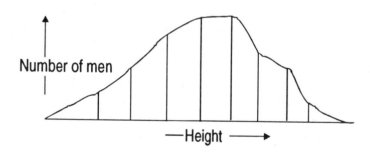

Joining the tops of the verticals gives a bendy bell-shaped line. Making the measurements more accurate (say to the nearest one hundredth of an inch) and including also more men (or the verticals would become progressively shorter), this line becomes more like a smooth curve, and eventually when the intervals are vanishingly small it become a real one:

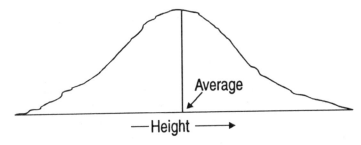

The resulting curve is called the 'frequency curve' for height. It tells us that we can expect to find men with any height between the upper limit A and lower one B but with increasing rarity as we approach the lower slopes on the 'hill'. The average height will of course be at the centre. If we repeat the whole exercise but this time with women, and then place their frequency curve on the same diagram, it will look like this:

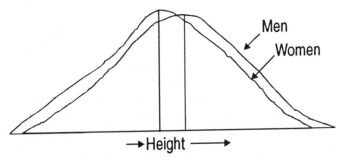

It is the displacement of the women's curve to the left of the men's that justifies us in saying that men are taller than women; however it is important to recognise that it does not mean that in a mixed group any man will be taller than any woman, or even that the tallest individual will be a man. Of course not! There is quite a good chance that it will be the other way round, though not so high as a 50/50 chance. To say that men are taller than women is a *statistical* statement, one about averages, not one about selected individuals.

Men and Women
The purpose of this digression has been to introduce what is a more contentious issue. How do men and women compare when it comes to intellectual and other gifts?

Are men and women equally gifted? Remember we require a *sta-*

tistical conclusion, not a comparison of one selected individual with another.

Take the incidence of genius. History records far more geniuses among men than among women. Genius in fact seems to inhere relatively rarely in womanhood. Where are the female artists, composers, sculptors, architects, dramatists, philosophers, mathematicians, scientists, surgeons and so on who can match the brilliant array of names on the male list? One has to search very hard to find them. There are obvious ripostes in as this already noted: women have had to bear and rear children; men are physically stronger and have made one-sided demands on the time and energies of their womenfolk; and so on. But this cannot be the whole story or anywhere near it. For one thing, there are a few spheres in which women have been the equal or nearly equal to men – as novelists, for instance. Emily Bronte's *Wuthering Heights* is one of the greatest novels ever written, and women novelists have many other claims to fame. So why have they not excelled everywhere? Again, many male geniuses have been without family obligations – Beethoven, Kant, Newton, Kierkegaard, Michaelangelo and so on. One might have thought there would have been supremely gifted women similarly unencumbered. The great Danish philosopher-theologian Kierkegaard once had a dispute with the fairy-story genius Hans Christian Andersen. The latter maintained that genius 'needs favourable circumstances for its development'. Kierkegaard's reply was otherwise – 'Genius is like a thunderstorm which comes up against the wind'. Genius will out, in other words, whatever impediments it faces. This also must surely be conceded, for many men of genius have faced tremendous difficulties, and triumphed.

All things considered, it seems difficult to deny that supreme ability is much more common among men than among women. Of course in more everyday and commonplace cases this must be interpreted with a due regard to local conditions; the best cook in a given company may well be a woman, and the one cleverest with a needle a woman too, if only for the reason that there are more women than men in these occupations.

Are women inferior?

In view of the relative rarity of genius among women is it to be concluded that women are, in the widest sense, somewhat inferior to men? Certainly not!

Consider the life of Jesus of Nazareth. When the Word of God became flesh, he did not choose to come as a genius. To call him such is nearly as derisive as to call him a superstar. At best, it is to seek for him worldly praise. He had none of the characteristics of genius. He bequeathed to culture no great works of art; he made no outstanding contribution to abstract thought; he advanced the practice of his trade by no striking new techniques or inventions; he enriched political theory with no brilliantly novel ideas. He left no great literature; his recorded sermons are not rhetorical masterpieces. No doubt all he produced as a working man was competent and of good quality; but so far as we know it never raised him to recognition as any sort of prodigy. He chose to come among us as a common man; 'He had no beauty, no majesty to catch our eyes, no grace to attract us to him. He was despised ...'[16] Yet Jesus of Nazareth, all Christians agree, excelled all other men. In what respect did he do so? Viewing his life with purely human eyes there is probably no better way of expressing it than by using J.A.T. Robinson's phrase: he was 'the man for others'.[17] He came to *serve* and to *give* (Luke 22:27; Mark 10:45). More colloquially (and speaking strictly on a non-theological level), his purpose was to make life easier, richer and happier for others – men and women and children alike (John 10:10).

And it is just in this direction that I believe women surpass men. Their specific gift is to excel, in many ways, in 'making life easier for others'. Men are not quite so quick or adept at doing it! This endowment is the centre-point in God's design in given woman as a 'helper suitable for' men. If this is true, it is an immensely significant recognition; woman's character is a little closer than man's to that of the human Jesus of Nazareth. She is one jump ahead, one step neared to that perfection to which we are called as his followers. 'Christ Jesus made himself of no reputation, took upon him the form of a servant,[18] and became obedient'. This is the ideal to which God is working for fallen humanity; and womanhood, true to itself, is nearer naturally to it than manhood is. Of course, we are speaking again statistically, of averages. In any given company the most Christlike individual may be a man. But it is more likely to be a woman. Genius in the end will pass away and be forgotten; but love (and it is an aspect of love that we have been talking about) will abide, and for ever. No; women are not second-

16. Isaiah 53:2,3 (R.E.B.).
17. J.A.T. Robinson, *Honest to God.*
18. Note, not the form of a genius.

class, inferior to men, and all that has been said above about genius does not imply this. The trouble is, much secular feminism has erred here and taken misguided aim. In so doing it results have been to demean womanhood, not to exalt it. And some of its misguidedness has damagingly infected religious thinking. One of the best comments ever made on woman is that of the old Puritan, Matthew Henry, in his famous biblical commentary:

> If man is the head she is the crown; a crown to her husband ... the crown of the visible creation. The man was dust refined but the woman was dust double-refined, one remove further from the earth ... She was not made out of his head to top him, not out of his feet to be trampled upon by him, but out of his side to be equal with him, under his arm to be protected, and near his heart to be beloved.[19]

This is not the progressivist emphasis of today; but I believe it is true to the ideals of the biblical picture, and gives far more honour to womanhood than anything for which secular feminism is striving.

Why is God 'He' in the Bible?

God is spoken of in the masculine gender in the Bible (and exclusively so). The use of feminine metaphors, as I have argued, constitutes no exception to the generalisation. This exclusiveness is such an obvious fact that it is liable to pass almost unnoticed for very familiarity, and its significance is thus often missed. That Emmanuel, God with us, was a man and not a woman expresses the same great archetypal principle: that in a universe of rational creatures with any degree of individual freedom, harmony can prevail only if all recognise one supreme authority; and authority can be permanent and stable only if it has the ultimate sanction of force. This is a position the Bible surely abundantly endorses.[20]

Even within the Trinitarian Godhead the fact of one *locus* of supreme authority can be argued from biblical premises. 'Thus *sendest forth* thy Spirit' (Psalm 104:30); the address of Wisdom in Proverbs 8:22-36 in the light of John 1:1-5, 14, 18; and the reference to the *Servant* and the Spirit together in Isaiah 48:16cd are Old Testament instances which support this assertion. The New Testament ones hardly

---

19. Matthew Henry, *Commentary on the Bible* (1708-1710).
20. *E.g.* Psalm 93, Isaiah 45:23; Matthew 25:34, 41; Revelation 19:6,15.

need listing: the Father is the found of *Deity in eternity* (John 5:26 and 1:4); the Son is *begotten*; the Spirit *proceeds*. Of course, within the limitless perfection of the divine love the sanction of force would be an absolute irrelevance; but in connection with the finite created order it is otherwise. *The necessity for the ultimate sanction is surely the reason for God referring to himself as 'he' and not as 'she'.* It is not that God is male; Isaiah 45:9, 10 and Deuteronomy 32:18 with their parallel 'father' and 'mother' allusions are two references among many which serve to deny this. Job 38:28f. is another interesting one. It is rather that man possesses to an extent greater than woman what is implied by necessary authority. He has superior physical strength, a more masterful voice, and, it can be argued, a greater ability to assess accurately and to control effectively a dangerous situation. Again I must stress that I am speaking statistically, about averages. There are women who are superlative at controlling dangerous situations; but they are rarer than men, and most would agree that the popular image of the female (which is inevitably based on averages) does not suggest to potential trouble makers the no-nonsense authority required.

It would seem to be the case that it is in connection with the matter of authority that God has chosen in the Bible to be thought of as 'he' rather than 'she'; for he has sovereignly given to the one sex, in comparison with the other, a general superiority in whatever qualities help to establish and confirm the impression of authority – physical strength and stature, capacity to make rational and objective judgements, creative ability in the world of thought and action. This is not to say that woman is far behind in these qualities; but she *is* behind, and that is what counts here. Her own superiority lies in another direction altogether, a direction that is characterised by the biblical conception of love which gives and serves. And as Paul has so eloquently told us, the things in which man excels will one day cease; those in which woman excels will abide. Fortunately, man need not be far behind in these things either; but he *is* behind.

Western Society today

One does not have to look far to see how prevalent violence is in our society, nor how pervasive it is in all levels. Murder, rape, child abuse, public act of terrorism are, it can be argued, almost expected as natural accompaniments of twentieth century life. Teachers are attacked in schools and doctors and nurses in hospitals; unwanted babies are battered to death. There is no fear of God as once there was (at least to some degree, and within living memory). Churches are robbed, despoiled or otherwise violated as much as anywhere else.

My purpose in writing about this is to draw attention to an often unremarked feature of this phenomenon: who are the chief offenders? It can hardly be denied that men, especially young men, are nearly always in the lead. It would seem right to say that they are far more often the culprits than their opposite numbers, the young women. Who are in the gangs bent on destructiveness, looting, football hooliganism, vandalising of young trees, or reckless driving in stolen cars? 'Young men' is nearly always the answer. Young women have their own faults; they can bring out the worst in young men, and often do so provocatively. But it is still the young men who in the great majority of cases take the decisive step in law-breaking. They are the leaders; when young women are involved they usually stand behind, inciting them in one way or another to express their contempt for authority.

This highlights two things. First, in such wanton incidents it is both natural for men to take the lead and for women to expect them so to do. Second, that somewhere there has been a serious breakdown in the process of instilling into young men (and young women too) respect for authority – a respect which is by no means arbitrary and superfluous. Every one who thinks seriously at all must especially in a world like ours. There may be room to disagree about how authority should be constituted, but there rarely is about the need for it to be constituted somehow, and respected. For anarchy as a principle sooner or later (and usually sooner) shames itself into undeniable disrepute.

How then are young men to learn respect for authority? Primarily it must be from their fathers. Mothers can exert an enormous and irreplaceable influence for good. But obviously they are not usually so tough in the ultimate sanction of force may be unavoidable. God himself uses it with rebel societies; Isaiah 1 expresses a biblical commonplace. In family matters too it has his authority: Deuteronomy 21:18ff. (which Jesus himself – Mark 7:9ff. – confirmed as God-given) express this. 'For him who has power to cast into hell' he also warned us. It may not be a doctrine popular today in religious circles, but that God threatens and then uses the ultimate sanction of force is *passim* in the Bible. No doubt love is the dynamic impelling of all God's action towards his creatures (Psalm 145:8,9), but that does not invalidate what has just been said, unless the biblical writers are hopelessly inconsistent.[21] The Bible leaves us with the impression that in this balanced respect too we are to be 'imitators of God as dear children'.[22] All this would seem to point to a very definite role for the father as the centre of authority in the home, strict when necessary; and this in turn would seem to point back to the appropriateness of masculine terminology for God.

The place of men and women in society

It is often remarked by feminists – Christian as well as secular – that women today have entered with distinction many professions previously regarded as exclusively male. Women are doctors, barristers, scientists, Members of Parliament, even Prime Ministers. This is true, and there is no reason why it should not be so – with certain provisos. The ultimate rule for the life pleasing to God and for that very reason fulfilling for man is this: 'Not my will, but thine'. Self-pleasing, one of the supreme motivations of disordered humanity, is fatal in the long run for happiness. In the desire for a career therefore Christian women (and men) have to ask themselves 'Are there any indications that this is not the will of God for me?' Such indications may be particular, that is to relate to myself in my particular individual circumstances; or they may be general, and relate to the general class in which in his wise providence God has placed me. Obviously in connection with the present debate on women's ordination it is indications of the latter type which are the relevant ones. Has God given any general indications that it is not his will that women should be ordained? I shall not spend much time in listing those which spring most readily to mind (our Lord's choice of men exclusively for the apostolic band for instance), but concentrate upon some less often cited.

Let me say at once that where deep-seated differences between men and women exist we have to make up our minds beforehand whether we are to regard these as *accidental* or *providential*; that is, whether they are the result of blind, purposeless forces of nature acting by 'Chance and Necessity' as Darwin postulated; or whether they are the result of the Creator's wisdom and will. If the former, we are free to seek to set them aside by legislation, education or any other available means, provided we do so with due care and thoughtfulness. If the

21. These two aspect of the Divine character often appear in close juxtaposition: see, for example, Jeremiah 33 and Ephesians 5:1f.,6.
22. Ephesians 6:4; Hebrews 12:5-11.

latter, our right course is clearly to bow to them and to work within their constraints. Some Christian thinking today fails to face this issue; it never isolates and examines its presuppositions. Here then are some considerations that spring from the biblical conviction that the differences are *providential*.

One outstanding difference between the sexes is that women alone can bear children. They are therefore essential for the continuance of the human race. With the availability of artificial insemination (as in stock breeding) it becomes apparent that the race could continue with the male cloning, the male could actually become entirely obsolete. This leads us to ask why the Creator made us male and female with a built-in chromosome mechanism for ensuring roughly equal numbers of each? One answer clearly indicated by the Bible is God's design that man and woman should unite in exclusive faithful lifelong partnerships within which godly children could be raised and trained.[23] But this has serious requirements. In such little communities where shall ultimate authority reside? It is quite unrealistic to suppose that it could safely be shared equally by the two partners, even if their love were perfect. Differences of opinion are built-into the very notions of creaturely freedom and responsibility; and if the family is to stay together there must be a prior understanding of who has the last word, and a willingness in the other to accept it. What ship is ever sent to sea with two captains? It makes sense therefore to believe that a wise Creator has given to one partner in an unambiguous way gifts of leadership, creativity and physical strength superior to those he has given to the other; and there is no doubt that this is a position the Bible endorses.[24] It is this quality of manhood that balances-out the superior importance of womanhood mentioned above (the basic principle operating here is stated in 1 Corinthians 12:22-26).

Such a conclusion of course needs to be well substantiated, for it is being very strongly challenged today. I have argued that it conforms to natural observation; but for the Christian it is even more important that it be fully authenticated from the Bible. I have quoted Ephesians 5:22f. in support and I will defend this further below; but it is upheld by other quite different lines of testimony. The formation of Adam was prior to that of Eve; could they not have been formed simultaneously? Presumably; so there must be some significance in the particular order God

---

23. Malachi 2:15.
24. *E.g.* in Ephesians 5:22f.

chose in which to describe his work. It is really no satisfactory riposte for the feminist to claim that the highest kinds of animals were formed last! Eve was not just dust as they were. I have argued earlier that in one way woman is inferior to man, in another superior, and the points just made (formed *last*, but not out of *dust*) are consistent with this.

Again, one notes that in Scripture God names himself *in a particular way*: 'I am the God of Abraham, of Isaac and of Jacob' he says. Never does the formula become 'I am the God of Sarah, of Rebekah and of Rachel', however true that would be. To reply that it was only because society was patriarchal that this is so is to betray the presupposition that God has to take history as he finds it; that is, that it is accidental and not providential. But this is a position quite unbiblical, however tempting and fashionable it may be in many theological circles today.

The Bible of course does record women on several occasions as holding positions of eminence in Israel. Deborah, for instance, was a prophetess who judged Israel during a time of bitter oppression by neighbouring enemies.[25] She summoned Barak to raise ten thousand men to engage the enemy. She dominated the scene enough by her faith and strength of character for him to beg her to accompany his troops to battle. She was a married woman, but her husband seems to have had little significance. Huldah was also a prophetess, and again a married woman, in the critical days of Josiah (2 Kings 22). She had to deliver him a momentous message about the nation. And there are others. So there cannot be an absolute biblical injunction against women in places of leadership in public life. There is even a possibility in New Testament times that a woman was thought of as an 'apostle'.[26]

But these instances were rare and they all concern what might be called the more 'unstructured' type of ministry, composed of special individuals raised up for the occasion like Amos.[27] Such ministry was not constituted formally by God as a feature of Israel's established religious life, which was served rather by the priesthood; and from this women were excluded. Of course, this does not constitute a conclusive argument against the ordination of women; *men* from tribes other than Levi were excluded too (perhaps after the incident of the Golden Calf), whereas the New Testament makes priesthood the privilege of all be-

---

25. Judges 4.
26. Junia, Romans 16:7.
27. Amos 7:14f.

lievers.[28] But as a contribution to the debate it is not without force.

Further, the incident in which Miriam figures in Numbers 12 has another contributory lesson. Pressure for personal recognition as a spiritual leader is a very perilous business, and God found Miriam here seriously at fault. No doubt she felt 'pain' at not being officially acknowledged, but she would have been wiser surely to have left the matter to God, and if necessary, gone without. Many features of the propaganda battle over women's ordination (on both sides) convey the impression that God is conceived as a passive spectator, hoping things will turn out to his satisfaction, instead of as the One who calls sovereignly and irresistibly to spiritual prominence those he will, and none can refuse or stand in his way.[29]

The legacy of Secular Feminism

Feminist pressure is having many strange effects on present-day society. In saying this I am not arguing for a return to previous relations between the sexes. None has ever been perfect or even nearly so, and many have been very imperfect. But the 'swing of the pendulum' is a familiar phenomenon, and in many respects this particular pendulum has swung too far. What are some of the adverse results noticeable today?

For one thing, the secular feminist claim for all-round equality with men has, I believe, made a very significant contribution to snuffing-out what used to be called 'gentlemanly behaviour'. Men no longer offer their seats in a crowded train or bus to a woman as woman, open the door for her, or treat her with any special consideration. The effect on family life has been destructive too. The headship of the father being no longer accepted as a fact of nature, children lose the sense of a firm *locus* of authority in the home, and become unruly. Married women claiming a high career profile for themselves have eroded their husband's sense of responsibility as breadwinner; this tends to be shared now as a matter of equality. Parents look at each other with a degree of ambivalence, and their mutual loyalty is subject to new latter-day strain. An ancient element in their felt necessity of and for each other has withered, and cohabitation becomes preferable to marriage. Lacking a clearly defined function in the family men hive-off, and single-parent families proliferate. Children find themselves living with the new temporary boyfriend, and the stage is set for child abuse. If women are the

28. 1 Peter 2:5,7.
29. Exodus 3:10f.; Jeremiah 1:4f.; Luke 1:26f.; Acts 9:15f.

equals of men in the way many now claim, they can fend for themselves! Men cease to feel they have protective roles, in fact the reverse may prevail; gratuitous humiliation is contemptuously added to violence. Respect between the sexes falls to a low ebb, and with it the well-being of society of which it is a major ingredient. Men and women lose their sense of being necessary to each other; they become cynics and rivals, and homosexuality flourishes as an acceptable alternative to the providential order.

Of course, thankfully, things in our society have not become universally bad; there are fine stable families even where both parents have careers, and where the father possesses an acceptable and considerate authority. But increasingly they have an old-fashioned air about them. Of course, secular feminism is far from being the sole or even post potent cause of all this; the matter is intricately complex. The general decay of religion (especially in its classical form of 'the fear of God'); the destructive effect of theological liberalism on belief in biblical standards; the spread of the youth culture and the popularisation of psychedelic drugs may be even more powerful; but secular feminism does contribute its share to the general malaise. One symptom of the demoralisation of, especially, thoughtful men is the frequency with which one finds them giving in to its pressure. Steven Weinberg, a leading theoretical physicist and Nobel prizewinner, is an example. Writing about how highly abstract theories become generally accepted by the scientific community, he says:

> In the case of a true prediction, like Einstein's ... it is true that the theorist does not know the experimental result when she [sic] develops the theory ...[30]

So far as I am aware, there was at that time no outstanding female theoretical physicist anywhere in sight! The well-intentioned bouquet to womanhood will strike many as both patronising and faintly ridiculous; I feel sure I would resent it were I a woman. It suggests a pretence; a transparent effort to disown a male superiority in which furtively the writer probably really believes. But women, I have argued earlier, have no need of being ashamed of themselves and patronised like this. Today's theologians are addicted to the same sort of window-dressing too. In a recent book[31] Keith Ward has five 'shes' and hers' in

---

30. S. Weinberg, *Dreams of a Final Theory* (1993).
31. K. Ward, *A Vision to Pursue* (1991).

a paragraph about theists and Buddhists, and similarly in another on 'the fully human person'. Males seem to have disappeared without trace! Perhaps it is men who are ashamed of themselves; perhaps women think they ought to be.

There are other signs too. The suicide rate of young men is rising and well in the lead; what ultimate need, after all, has society for them? Reviews in the Arts section of *The Times* of well-known male authors discuss men's growing feeling of being increasingly unaware of their place in the scheme of things; and so on. Unemployment bears heavily on men; they go to pieces more readily under its influence than women do. Naturally, the more current secular feminism persuades women of the superior status and rewards of work outside the home the more married women will seek it, and this is bound to have *some* impact on men's opportunities.

Of course none of this is anywhere near being a knock-down argument against women working outside the home! They have an assured place in that sphere. It has been expressed rather to counter the prevalent aggressive disparagement of the work women have traditionally done *within* the home. Home building – no work is potentially more important. The hand that rocks the cradle still rules the world, and the break-up of home life is one of the great sicknesses of our society. Please God it may not be unto death.

Hierarchy in the home?

One factor which Christian feminism tends to have in common with its secular namesake is the denial of any degree of hierarchical order in the home, that is, that the husband is (in the traditional sense) the 'head' of the home. Without claiming that the Bible's teaching on this has been correctly understood in the past (or even nearly so), I would nevertheless argue that the pendulum today is swinging too far in the other direction. Take for instance Mary Evans' otherwise excellent little book *Woman in the Bible*,[32] a work of careful scholarship and loyalty to Scripture. She allows, almost inevitably, that the meaning of *kephale*, 'head', is hierarchical in content in Ephesians 1:21, 22, as it is also in the Septuagint (where it translates the Hebrew *rosh*); there, this use is quite common.[33] But when she comes to Ephesians 5:23 she argues for a meaning drawn from *secular Greek* ('source', which she says is 'some-

32. M. Evans, *Woman in the Bible*.
33. *E.g.*, Exodus 6:14; Joshua 11:10; 2 Kings 2:3; Hosea 1:11.

times used' there) as against that derived from the Old Testament. This is a rather questionable procedure! Paul is constantly referring his hearers, many of the Gentiles, *back to the Old Testament*; he does so later in this very chapter.[34] It is worth quoting C.E.B. Cranfield in his *Commentary on Romans*. Of the nineteen occurrences of *dikaioun*, 'to justify', in Paul's epistle 'none' he says, 'can be at all tolerably explained on the basis of the word's use in secular Greek'.[35] In spite of the fact that *kephale* of verse 23 is sandwiched semantically between the two uses of *hupotasso* ('submit') of verses 22, 24 (which must surely slant its meaning), Mary Evans defends her exegesis by explaining that in Ephesians 5:24 'it is the self-giving' [not the hierarchical] 'aspect of Christ's relation with his church that is paralleled in the relation of man and wife'; [this]] 'is confirmed in verse 25'.[36]

However true this is (and it looks a little like begging the question), the most vivid and poignant expression of the self-giving of our Lord was surely the washing of the disciples' feet; but on this very occasion he chose to assert quite pointedly that he was 'Lord and Teacher';[37] the relation between him and them was emphatically hierarchical, and this must never be forgotten. If one gives this incident (of which Paul apparently knew)[38] due exegetical recognition, the introductory *But* of verse 24 (to which Mary Evans draws attention) assumes importance. Paul is implying that even if the husband is truly self-giving to the same profound degree as the Lord was, the wife must not presume to think herself above 'submitting to him in everything'. The remarkably strong language of Ephesians 5:33b supports this understanding. No, the human relationship between them is not one of exactly symmetry, and Ephesians 5:21 (on which I comment further below), hardly allows us to think otherwise. The relationship follows, at an almost infinite distance, that of Christ to the church.[39] Even if 'source' is part of the meaning of *kephale* it cannot be all; the word is linked too intimately with hierarchy in another Pauline passage (Colossians 1:15-18) for this principle to be so easily eliminated here.

Mary Evans seems rather inadequate too in her examination[40] of

34. verses 28, 29, 30, 31.
35. C.E.B. Cranfield, *Commentary on Romans*, p 95.
36. *Op. cit.*
37. John 13:13,14.
38. 1 Timothy 5:10.
39. Ephesians 5:25; *cf.* John 13:14.
40. *Op. cit.,* p. 67.

hupotasso ('submit', 'be subject to'), a common enough word in the New Testament (nearly forty times). She appears to have mistaken it for *tasso* in quoting its 'root meaning' as 'to order, arrange, put in place'. The prefix *hupo* ('under') changes the meaning significantly. In the middle voice (which is the relevant one) the sense is: 'to subject oneself, obey';[41] 'to take rank under'. This puts a different complexion on things; the idea of hierarchy is inescapable with this military term. Nor can it be replied that the injunction of verse 21 ('submit yourselves *one to another*') enjoins something equal and reciprocal between husband and wife; compare the very similar use of *allelois* ('to be another') in 1 Peter 5:5 where the idea of simple reciprocity would be absurd. Yet a good deal of the author's understanding of the husband-wife relationship seems to turn on these points. She is no doubt right in suggesting[42] that in Colossians 3:18 Paul uses *hupotasso* in connection with wives in 'carefully-chosen contrast' to the distinct *hupakouo* ('obey') of verses 20, 22 for children and slaves. Behind this may lie a thought recalling our Lord's contrast in John 15:15; husband and wife are uniquely *friends*. If so, it certainly does not negate the idea of obedience (see verse 14 of John).

But this suggestion of Mary Evans invites another. By the same token, Paul no doubt uses *hupotasso* for the wife in Ephesians 5:22 and later *agapao, heauton paradidomi* for the husband in 'carefully-chosen contrast' too.[43] For the wife, total submission; for the husband, total self-sacrifice. If this be accepted, it establishes a matter of importance for our discussion. For wifely submission means *conceding* the leadership; husbandly self-sacrifice means *taking* it. Good it was for us our Lord did take it![44] If Paul means anything, he means that the husband has this positive obligation too. So here again there *is* a gentle hierarchy in the marriage relationship; but it is of leadership of a quite costly and unworldly kind, rare even among Christian men. It is a position of which they should be only subliminally aware; not something for them to demand, but for their wives rather to bestow. This is the divine ordering.

---

41. G. Abbott-Smith, *Manual Greek Lexicon of the New Testament.*
42. *Op. cit.,* p. 77.
43. See also Colossians 3:18,19 where something very similar occurs.
44. Romans 5:6.

Conclusion

It is time to conclude this study. It has not been comprehensive; it did not set out to be. Its main premise has been that it is to man that the Creator has given the responsibilities of leadership and of providing for his own, and to woman those of helping and, within the family, of bearing and rearing children. Neither of these tasks is to be considered inherently greater than the other; the Lord does them both.[45] To both sexes has been given a balance of gifts suited to their responsibilities; to man, more of those needed for bold leadership and the exercise of authority, and to woman, more of those needed for caring and sustaining. These characteristics are patent to common observation. But no gift (except the purely biological) is exclusively the property of either sex; it is only the balance that is different. So there may be great woman leaders, and very gentle and caring men. But this balance of characteristics must be regarded as providential, not accidental; that is, as something to be attributed to the gracious design of the Creator's will, and men and women should regard themselves accordingly. Of course, marriage and parenthood do not come to all, though they can be taken as the Creator's general design ('Be fruitful and multiply' was his first directive to Man in Genesis 1); but the same principles nevertheless apply, even to those who have not children of their own. Poignant human needs of all sorts cry out constantly and everywhere for help!

Within the Holy Trinity all Persons are equal in Deity. But the Bible gives us reason to say that *functionally* (if we may reverently use that term) the Father is *primus inter pares*.[46] (It was after all in eternity, not

---

45. Psalm 23; Deuteronomy 32:15.
46. In the New Testament the Godhead is revealed as a Trinity of Persons: Father, Son and Holy Spirit. The unqualified term 'God' is customarily reserved for the Father, (as in 'the God and Father of our Lord Jesus Christ'). He is thereby represented as *primus inter pares,* the 'first among equals'. The Father and the Son are declared to love each other (John 1:18, 3:35, 3:20, 14:31), but corresponding language is never used of either in connection with the Spirit. Why is it? Perhaps because the Holy Spirit is the great *Communicator* off the divine love; he is the *vinculum caritatis* (as Augustine termed him), the active bond of love between the Father and the Son. (It is consistent with this that the 'gift of the Spirit' brings the believer intimately into the very circle of the divine love: John 14:16, 17 with 21, 23; Romans 5:5.)

Now as 'made in the image of God', something of this Trinitarian character might be expected to be dimly realised in the constitution of humankind, and it is hardly far-fetched to see it in this: man, woman, and the strong and particular bond of love established by the Creator between them (Genesis 2:18, 21f.). The latter becomes a sort of miniature replica of the divine *vinculum caritatis,* and one which is at least *associated*

in time, that the Father gave the Son to have life-in-himself).[47] If the man had a similar *primus* within the constitution of mankind 'made in the image of God' this will not be surprising; nor will it be in any sense a denial that woman, equally with man, is made in that image. With this understanding it would be inappropriate for the Bible to speak of God in the feminine gender; in his self-revelation to the created order his authority, no less than his wisdom, love and power, must be emphasised beyond misunderstanding. The church thus has no licence to speak of God as 'she'.

Has all this anything to do with women's ordination? Without going into the evils of what we might call 'masculinism' (they have historically been, and continue to be, many and very great) I have tried to suggest some of those of even Christian feminism, which more immediately concern this essay. On the practical level it must be remembered that women considerably outnumber men in our congregations; is this imbalance likely to be reduced if women flood into the ministry? Or is man's masculine conceit going to make it worse? I fear the latter. That the only structured order in the religious life of Israel was exclusively of men, and that our Lord's personal ordinations were similarly exclusively so, are also considerations which are bound to influence the view we take. But whether the case incidentally made here against the ordination of women is a good one or not I must leave my readers to decide. It certainly is for a fundamental reappraisal of the all-important relationship between men and women. At the moment this is a shambles, with far-reaching and devastating effects on society: on men, on women, and on children. Men and women have lost faith in each other in every sector and level of society. No wonder cohabitation (or in a different way homosexuality) has become a better gamble than 'till death us do part'. The beauty of the whole thing has

with personhood (through procreation) and which transcends the ordinary societal bonding of our race.

If this analogy is valid it throws a revelatory light on human family relationships: the Father gives his name to the husband (Ephesians 3:15 R.V. marg.; 1 Corinthians 11:7); and the Son, within the Trinity, is the Beloved (John 1:18; Mark 1:11, 9:7; Ephesians 1:6). The analogy is not, and cannot be, exact; but it is clear enough for the language of Philippians 2:6 (N.I.V., R.E.B.) to suggest God's will for the Christian wife in her relation to her husband. There is a lesson too in the outcome of the Son's submission to the Father, Philippians 2:9. Perhaps this is something for the husband to ponder; compare also the teaching of Matthew 19:30.

47. John 5:26 with 1:4; *cf.* also 1 Corinthians 15:24ff. and the Trinitarian reference to John 14:6.

faded; its romance has gone. Over it is written ICHABOD, the glory is departed. This may be an exaggeration, but it is not an outrageous one. One of the most urgent tasks of Christian feminism (and Christian masculinism too) is to try to restore it in accordance with its Maker's instructions and in the fear of God to its true wonder and God-intended loveliness.

6

Towards an Evangelical view of the Church

Melvin Tinker

Evangelicals and ecclesiology

In his address at N.E.A.C 3 in 1988, the then Archbishop of Canterbury, Robert Runcie, extended a challenge to Anglican evangelicals to do some serious thinking about ecclesiology and said:

> If the current evangelical renewal in the Church of England is to have a lasting impact then there must be more explicit attention given to the doctrine of the church.

Twenty years earlier in 1968, Professor Klaas Runia commented that

> There is an erroneous doctrine of the church, which is so often found among evangelicals. Many of them tend to regard the visible organised church as relatively unimportant, primarily because in it one finds many who have little faith, if any at all.

He then goes on to urge evangelicals to

> give special attention to the biblical doctrine of the church ... If ever we want to solve the present problems of the church, we must first know what the church really is according to Scripture.[1]

In all honesty we have to admit that generally speaking there is some substance in what is implied by these two statements, namely, that there is a certain weakness in the way many evangelicals think about the church. If an evangelical were to be asked to say what he believed about the death of Christ or the inspiration of Holy Scripture, then in most cases he would be able to do so with relative ease. But if that same evangelical were to be asked to relate the essentials of his beliefs about the church, that might prove to be a little more difficult.

---

1. Klass Runia, *Reformation Today*, (Banner of Truth, 1968) pp. 44f.

94

As a result of this lack of clarity in thinking about the church, evangelicals become all the more prone to accept views about the church which are far from Scriptural, and certainly in the Church of England that means quasi-Catholic views of the church, this happening almost by default.

However, from another standpoint, evangelicals have been giving a great deal of time to thinking about the church in the last twenty years from a more practical point of view. Much of the discussion concerning the work of the Holy Spirit in the sixties and seventies was often ecclesiological, concerning every-member-ministry for instance. Who is more concerned with evangelism and church growth than the evangelical? That is why it is not that wide of the mark to say that an evangelical's view of the Church of England is captured by the saying that it is 'the best boat to fish from' – this encapsulates, perhaps in a crude form admittedly, a deep scriptural truth. When evangelicals are patronizingly dismissed by some as having no ecclesiology, what critics often mean is that they do not like the ecclesiology that evangelicals have. As we shall see, evangelicals do have the richest, most authentic ecclesiology there is, because it is rooted in, and arises from, Scripture.[2]

The Nature of the Church

According to Paul Minear[3], the Bible uses over eighty figures and symbols to depict the church's nature, but we shall focus only upon one, namely, the church as the people of God.[4]

The apostle Peter takes the Old Testament term 'People of God' and applies it to the New Testament church (1 Peter 2:9) and so, as with many ideas and themes in the Old Testament, this finds its fulfilment in Christ and the age of the New Covenant. The actual word for church *ekklesia*, which is the Greek rendering of the Hebrew *qahal*, basically means 'assembly' or 'gathering'. It is a term which describes the covenant-making assembly at Sinai (Deuteronomy 9:10) as well as Israel gathered before God for covenant renewal (Deuteronomy 29:1). In the New Testament this term is taken and almost exclusively applied to young Christian communities after Pentecost, in contrast with the term

---

2. For a detailed response to the Archbishop's call see Tim Bradshaw's, *The Olive Branch. An evangelical Anglican doctrine of the church,* (Paternoster, 1992).

3. Paul Minear, *Images of the Church in the New Testament*, (Philadelphia, 1960).

4. See E. Clowney's article 'Church', in *New Dictionary of Theology*, (Edd. Ferguson and Wright, Inter-Varsity Press, 1988) p.140.

'synagogue' used to refer to the Jews – the two exceptions being Acts 7:38, where Luke uses the term *ekklesia* to describe Israel in the wilderness, and James 2:2 where he uses the term 'synagogue' to refer to the Christian congregation. So in what sense was the term *ekklesia* used in the New Testament to depict the people of the New Covenant?

It is interesting to note that in the New Testament epistles the plural is used when more than one church is in view: 'the churches of God' (2 Thessalonians 1:4) and the 'churches of God in Judea' (2 Thessalonians 2:14, cf. 1 Corinthians 7:17; Romans 16:4; Galatians 1:2). It therefore appears that the term was only applied to an *actual gathering of people*.

Theologically we therefore need to ask: What is the relationship – between 'the Church' and 'the churches'? This is a question that has been explored to great effect by Peter O'Brien[5], who points out that the 'assembly'/'congregation' is theologically construed in the sort of thinking expressed in Hebrews 12:22-24:

> But you have come to Mount Zion, to the heavenly Jerusalem, the city of the living God. You have come to thousands upon thousands of angels in joyful assembly, to the church (singular) of the first born, whose names are written in heaven. You have come to God, the judge of all men, to the spirits of righteous men made perfect, to Jesus the mediator of a new covenant, and to the sprinkled blood that speaks a better word than the blood of Abel.

Christians thus participate in the heavenly, eschatological church of Jesus Christ. This is what Paul primarily has in mind when he speaks of Jesus as being the 'head of the church' (Colossians 1:18). Therefore, each local church is not to be seen as one member parallel to lots of other members which together make up Christ's body – the church. Nor is each church 'the body of Christ' as if Christ has many bodies. Rather each congregation is the full visible expression in that place of the one true heavenly church – an outcrop or colony of heaven – reflecting the eschatological gathering of God's people around God's throne. In the words of O'Brien:

> 'Paul consistently refers to the church which meets in a particular place. Even when there are several gatherings in a single city (e.g. at Corinth) the

---

5. P.T. O'Brien, 'The church as the Heavenly and Eschatological Entity' in *The Church in the Bible and the World*, (Paternoster 1987) Ed D.A.Carson.

individual assemblies are not understood as part of the church in that place, but as one of the churches that meet there. This suggests that each of the various local churches are manifestations of that heavenly church, tangible expressions in time and space of what is heavenly and eternal'.[6]

In parenthesis we might want to ask: Where does this leave us viz a viz our denominations? Does it mean that we become independents or congregationalists? The answer is no, such a conclusion does not follow from the premise. There are plenty of reasons, theological and practical, why congregations should be associated with each other. But it does mean that a denomination is not a church, it is an association or federation of churches, which in fact is the classic Anglican position. So long as the denomination sees that, with its role as serving the local churches and the diocesan structures functioning more like a 'parachurch', all will be well. But, as is increasingly happening, when the denomination or diocese is seen as the main unit, with the local churches there to serve them, then we are not only being unbiblical, but we are in danger of having the gospel life blood sapped away. For example, is it in accord with what has been said so far, that for the sake of 'fair distribution' evangelical curates are not being allowed to be placed in evangelical parishes? Should the local churches have increasing financial burdens placed upon them to finance non-gospel activities or personnel in the diocese? What the local churches should be saying is, 'No we don't want this, this is not why we belong to this federation which is meant to serve our interests – gospel interests – and we do not want men or money being detracted from this.'

What many Anglican evangelicals have done is to adopt an ecclesiology which is not biblical. The unbiblical ecclesiology is the one which sees the denomination as primary and its structures the place to be, so that occupying a diocesan post, being an archdeacon, bishop, or archbishop – is seen as 'promotion' or to use that awful term 'preferment'. It may not always be voiced in that way, but sadly that is the unspoken feeling of many. This does not mean, of course, that we should not seek to have evangelicals in these positions if we can afford the manpower, but let us see these positions for what they are, namely posts in a servicing industry – ideally servicing the local congregation which is Christ's church. We have deliberately given a fair amount of space to discussing this idea of the church as the assembled people of God because it is

6. P.T. O'Brien, *Colossians and Philemon*, The Word Commentary Series (Word,1982) p 61.

fundamental to the New Testament and in practice far removed from the present outlook predominant in the Church of England.

Aspects of the Church

On the basis of the biblical emphasis upon the *spiritual* nature of the church, the Reformers saw quite clearly that the church had two aspects – what we can call the invisible church and the visible church, or the church eternal and the church temporal. In saying this the Reformers were not claiming that there are two churches, one real, the other apparent, but rather that there are two aspects of the one reality which is the church. Thus the members of the invisible church (invisible to us – that is why we say we *believe* in one holy, catholic and apostolic church) are also members of the visible church, but exactly who they are is only known to God. Ultimately it is only the elect which constitute the church of Christ; and one day, when Christ returns, the invisible will become visible. In other words it is made up of those whose names are written in the Lamb's book of life (Revelation 21:27). But let us not think that the Reformers in reaction to Rome, who equated the visible mediaeval church with the true church, took flight in the invisible church, because they did not. Calvin in particular placed great store in the visible aspect of the church. He saw the church as being an earthly community where God's Word was preached and the sacraments administered:

> Wherever we see the Word of God purely preached and heard, and the sacraments administered according to Christ's institution, there, it is not to be doubted, a church of God exists.[7]

The same thought is expressed in Article 19 of the Thirty Nine Articles. The visible churches are only provisional; they will always be in error. So to state as the Archbishop of Canterbury did at N.E.A.C.3 that 'If it is the Body of Christ, the church too demands our belief, trust and faith', betrays an abuse of the metaphor between the visible and invisible church. What is more he was extolling an essentially Roman Catholic view of the church as found in the Pope's *Mystici Corporis Christi.*

---

7. *Institutes*, IV.1.9.

Attributes of the Church

The Nicene Creed confesses 'One holy, catholic and apostolic church' – the four essential attributes of the church.

First, the church of Christ is *one*. This as we have already seen is essentially a spiritual unity, as indicated in the oft misquoted prayer of our Lord in John 17:21 – a favourite of the ecumenists, 'May they all be one; as thou, Father, art in me and I in thee, so also may they be in us, that the world may believe that thou didst send me' (New English Bible). This does not describe an external organization – a church as some multinational ecclesiastical company – but a church of a deeply personal and spiritual nature, as is the mystery of the Trinity itself. The fact is, all true believers *are* one (we are back to the invisible or heavenly church again) and so are to express that oneness in action.

Secondly, we believe the church to be *holy*, set apart from the world for God, something increasingly being brought into question by the flagrant disregard of plain biblical teaching on morality. How can the holiness of the church be taken seriously when we have bishops and reports extolling homosexuality as a perfectly valid lifestyle?[8] We are to be in the world, but not of it; and this is something we desperately need to recapture if we are going to make an impact in our society today – holiness without which no man shall see God.

Thirdly, the church is *catholic*, which means universal and non-sectarian. If ever there has been a term which has been abused, it is this. For all the Church of England's claims to be catholic, it is really sectarian in practice, for example, in not recognizing the orders of a non-episcopally ordained man whose rule is the Word of God. We must recapture its true meaning, namely the universality of the church; indeed the first time the term was used in Christian literature by Ignatius of Antioch, it referred to the heavenly church (*Smyrna 8*). What is the true test of catholicity? It is that which the early church had – submission to the Word of God, the teaching of Christ and the apostles.

And so we come to the fourth attribute of the church, that it is apostolic. Again we must stress the negative that this has nothing to do with so-called apostolic succession by the laying on of hands. This is an idea that was largely introduced into the Church of England in the last century by the Tractarians, and has nothing to do with historic Anglicanism. Rather it is that the church is founded upon the teaching

---

8. E.g. *Homosexual Relationships – a contribution to discussion,* (Church Information Office, London, 1979).

of the apostles, it is in the succession of the apostles' teaching that the church is truly apostolic (2 Timothy 2:2). Such a view was common to both the English and Continental Reformers as is summarized by Paul Avis in his excellent treatment of the subject:

> By making the gospel alone the power at work in the church through the Holy Spirit, the Reformers did away with the necessity of a doctrine of apostolic succession, replacing it with the notion of a succession of truth. Correspondingly, the gospel of truth was held to be sufficient to serve the catholicity of the church.[9]

It is possible, as history sadly testifies, to have an unbroken line in bishops but for that 'church' not to be apostolic but apostate in perverting the apostles' teaching.

The Marks of the Church

We have already touched upon this when we looked at the question of the visible church. The church has certain distinguishing features, just as a living body has certain features which indicate that it is alive – like respiration, movement, etc. We refer to Article 19:

> The visible church of Christ is a congregation of faithful men, in which the pure Word of God is preached, and the sacraments be duly ministered according to Christ's ordinance in all those things that of necessity are requisite to the same.

Three marks are to be found there: The preaching of the Word of God in pure form, that is unadulterated by human speculation, whether by tradition or, as is more the case today, by liberal theology. Then there is the due administration of sacraments ('due' – 'proper') in which the ministry of the visible Word is to be linked to the audible word. This would seem to rule out any *ex opere operato* view of the sacraments which works regardless of belief on the part of the recipient.

Also it has been suggested by some that contained within this is discipline as a mark of the church, for here we have a congregation of *faithful* men. Here there is no question of judging who is and who is not finally saved – only God can do that – but there is the call to discern whether a person professes faith, a faith which is credible, one which shows itself in day-to-day living. This, sadly, is not exactly the

---

9. Paul Avis, *The Church in the Theology of the Reformers*, (M.M.S., 1970) p.28.

mark of the church which is to the fore today. We now find ourselves in the extraordinary situation where a Bishop can deny the virginal conception and bodily resurrection of our Lord with impunity, but let an ordinand take a stand on not wearing a stole for ordination and he will soon have to give an account to someone in authority.

Even if we were to agree with the later Calvin (his definitive *Institutes* of 1559) that discipline does not constitute one of the marks of the church, it is surely nonetheless vital for the church's spiritual health and well-being.

The Purpose of the Church – Distinguishing AD from BC

If we were to get the emphasis right on the *local* church, there is yet another attendant danger which in practice leads to a faulty ecclesiology and that is a failure to distinguish AD from BC., that is failing to take seriously how Old Testament promise is met by New Testament fulfilment and is therefore abrogated. Instead, what tends to happen is that practises and models are lifted straight from the Old Testament and applied with one or two adjustments to the church today. So we have the localisation of God either in the reserved sacrament or in the 'hallowed' building. With this there is a ministry of priestcraft with robes to match. What is more, we are often being told that the most important activity for Christians to engage in when they meet is 'worship' with the primary movement from man to God which may either be in the form of a eucharistic celebration or a celebration of praise and prayer. But what we have to think through and translate into practice, is the difference Christ's person and death makes to the people of God. If in Jesus we have God's final work and God's final word (Hebrews 1:1-4), then this has an earth shattering significance not only for our view of the nature of the church, but what the church's primary purposes are; what the church is meant to be doing.

What then is to happen when God's people gather together? As we have seen from Hebrews 12 that gathering is an expression on earth of the heavenly gathering around the throne of Christ. Following this imagery through (which is taken by the writer from Deuteronomy 10 and transformed through the filter of Christ), first and foremost we must submit to the one who rules through his Word. In other words, the primary movement is one of grace from God to man. Architecturally, let the building reflect this – let the pulpit occupy a central position. More importantly, let it be expressed ministerially with the minister

functioning and looking not like a sacrificing priest but a teaching pres-
byter. Let everything communicate not barriers but access which has
been achieved by Christ's sacrificial death.

This leads us to the next element of what is meant to happen when
God's people assemble; they are to edify and encourage each other:

> 'Let us consider how we may spur one another on towards love and good
> deeds. Let us not give up meeting together, as some are in the habit of
> doing, but let us exhort one another – and all the more as you see the Day
> approaching' (Hebrews 10: 24-25).

The reason why God has given apostles, prophets, evangelists, pastor-teachers is so that God's people might be prepared for works of
service for the building up (*eis oikodomen*) of the body of Christ (Ephesians 4:11ff). Note again the downward movement from God – his
gift of ministries to the church – then the outward movement amongst
his people – works of service – so that they might grow upwards in
Christ. When we use the term 'edify' (*oikodomeo*) we tend to think of
it individualistically and pietistically. That is not the way it is used in
Ephesians 4. On this subject David Peterson[10] writes:

> 'Perfection is not an ideal to be attained but a reality to be met in Christ.
> Put another way we may say that the purpose of Christian ministry is to
> prepare the saints to meet their Lord. All ministry should have an eschato-
> logical focus and perspective.'

He later adds:

> 'Edification occurs when Christians minister to one another in word and deed,
> seeking to express and encourage a Christ-centred faith, hope and love.'

What should we be doing when we meet? 'Edifying' – and that of
course is the test Paul applies in 1 Corinthians 14 as to whether certain
things should be done and how they should be done.

From what has been said so far, we must not make the mistake of
thinking that church-'gathering' is synonymous with introversion and
exclusivism. Certainly in a very profound sense the church is exclusive, but theologically it is necessary to coordinate the notion of 'gathering' with 'dispersion' – 'calling' with 'sending' so that we may, to

---

10. David Petersen, 'The Biblical Context of Edification', in *'Church, Worship and the
Local Congregation'*. Explorations 2, Ed. B.G. Webb. Lancer Books 1987.

use the language of 1 Peter 2:9, 'declare the wonderful excellencies of him who called you out of darkness into his marvellous light'. One of the criticisms of the idea of the church we have been exploring is that it 'may lead in practice to a lack of a Christian face towards the world, and with it social introversion'.[11] Although this may be the case it is not necessarily so.

How, then, are the ideas of being 'called together' and being 'sent out' with a view to evangelism and acting as salt and light in the world to be understood? Maybe in the following way: It is the church, which by definition, is called together. While it is assembled the gospel may be presented and some unbelievers present might be converted. But, by and large, the notion of 'sending out' with a view to proclaiming the gospel is not the task of the church qua the church (i.e. as a gathering or 'institution'), but the task of individuals or groups of individuals. Apostles are sent. Evangelists are sent. In one sense all Christians are sent (John 20:21), but the church-assembly is not sent. The purpose of the sending is to gather in people by the proclamation of the gospel. The goal is the church, its upbuilding and completion.

Let us follow through the implications of this biblical ecclesiology as it impinges upon two major areas of present concern for Anglicans, the question of episcopacy and church unity.

Episcopacy
There is little doubt that evangelicals in particular within the Church of England are giving a fair amount of time and attention to the question of episcopacy. The Anglican Evangelical Assembly of 1990 devoted a whole conference to the subject, and this is all part of a wider concern to grapple with the issue of ecclesiology. But why focus on episcopacy? For two main reasons. The first is a very practical and immediate one. There are now a number of evangelical bishops in the Church of England and they are asking for help to think through their role and their position within the church structures. Secondly, as the failed Methodist-Anglican reunion scheme has shown, the question of episcopacy is one which is central (as far as many Anglicans are concerned) to ecumenical relations: to what extent is it legitimate to view episcopacy as being essential to the being of the church?

Of course in putting the question in this form one has in mind a

---

11. Graham Cole, The Doctrine of the Church: '*Towards Conceptual Clarification*'. Ibid.

certain view of episcopacy – the view which came to the fore in Anglican circles with Newman's first *Tract for the Times*, which saw the threefold institution of bishops, presbyters and deacons as being divinely ordained, stemming from the apostles and secured by an unbroken line of ordinations. In 1946, the book *The Apostolic Ministry*[12] was published which made a distinction between those ministries which were essential (that is, having an unbroken link with the apostles) and those which were dependent. So the question revolves not so much around episcopacy per se – after all Free Churches have oversight and eldership – but rather apostolicity understood in terms of succession being maintained by the laying on of episcopal hands, which is a different concept altogether.

It really is quite astounding that within such a relatively short space of time, such a view should become so widely accepted as if it were main-line, historic Anglican teaching – let alone Biblical teaching! More recently Carey and Hind have spoken of apostolic succession as precisely the 'recognition that the special ministry is a gift of God to, in and through the church and the continuity in office and responsibility is one of the signs of the continuity of the whole church in the faith and witness of the apostles ... one of the symbols [i.e. both signs and instruments] of the univerisality of the church ... [The] historic and distinctive ministry is one of the constitutive elements of the church of Jesus Christ: one of the means by which he himself exercises his own headship of his body and by which the Holy Spirit reminds Christians now of what Jesus taught his disciples and leads them into all truth'.[13]

But how can such a statement be taken at all seriously when we have had popes making declarations about infallibility, the immaculate conception and the like? Are we seriously to believe that here the 'Holy Spirit is reminding Christians now of what Jesus taught his disciples and leads them into all truth'? What of duly ordained bishops who deny the fundamentals of the faith? Is it really through such as these that 'Christ is exercising his headship'? One only has to ask such questions to reveal how vacuous and dangerously romantic such thinking is.

12. *The Apostolic Ministry,* (Ed. K. Kirk, London: Hodder & Stoughton).
13. Carey and Hind, 'Ministry, Ministries and Ministry' in *Stepping Stones,* (Ed. C. Baxter, London: Hodder & Stoughton, 1987) p.59. The same outlook is expressed in *Episcopal Ministry* (Church House Publishing, 1990). For a helpful critique of this see C. Green's *An Oversight? What Bishop's think about Bishops and how evangelicals reply* (REFORM booklet, 1993).

What are we say to such claims?

First of all from a biblical standpoint, such a view of apostolic succession cannot be demonstrated. There is no indication that a congregation had to wait for an apostle to come along to authorize it. There certainly were ministries in Rome and Antioch long before an apostle visited these places. Why, if such succession is essential to the church, is no mention of it to be found, especially in the pastorals? The silence is deafening. As we have seen there is an apostolic succession but it is the concern to ensure the continuity of apostolic doctrine (2 Timothy 2:2).

Secondly, from an historical standpoint this view leaves much to be desired. The one who placed great emphasis upon bishops as a means of ensuring unity in the church was Ignatius of Antioch in the second century, but even here we find no mention of manual transmission of apostolic authority. In a concern to fend off heresy, Ignatius urged Christians to conform to the mind of Christ, which, he argued, meant conforming to the mind of the bishop, even to the extent that the congregation was not to do anything without the express permission of the bishop (understood in terms of area oversight). For some this would be enough to provide some support for the present view of bishops prevalent in the Anglican communion – but is it? Professor Geoffrey Bromiley has this astute comment to make:

> Ignatius' programme could not work out historically because it rested upon a naive and unsupported assumption, *viz*, a supposedly self-evident equation of the mind of the bishop with the mind of God ... God did indeed choose apostles, and through them pastors and teachers ... but he also laid upon them a responsibility of faithfulness to the spoken and written tradition. Far from enjoying a direct identity with the mind of God and a consequent infallibility, they had thus to be subject to God's own word in the apostolic testimony.[14]

In other words, if we were to take the *principle* that Ignatius is promoting, 'unity by conformity to the mind of Christ', and translate that into contemporary thought, it would be that a ministry which is truly apostolic is one which renounces self-opinion and humbly tunes itself to the mind of God as expressed in the apostolic, Biblical teaching.

Thirdly, from the standpoint of Anglican teaching is it acceptable? Again the answer must be 'No'. According to Article 6, we are re-

---

14. G. Bromiley, *Historial Theology*, (Edinburgh: T. & T. Clark, 1978), pp. 53-54.

quired only to believe those things demonstrable from Scripture. As we saw in Article 19, succession is not offered as one of the marks of the church. Richard Hooker, who although he prized episcopacy, did not consider it necessary and said that 'The church hath power by universal consent to take it away.' But not only in accordance with traditional Anglican teaching is episcopacy not of the *esse* (essence-being) of the church, neither is it absolutely vital for its *bene esse* (well being) – we are merely told that it is something which has been received from ancient times and is continuing; it is something which is not contrary to Scripture. So as far as traditional historic Anglicanism is concerned, episcopacy is a matter of indifference.

We should, therefore, not be enticed into accepting a view of episcopacy which is scripturally and theologically deficient. We are not to allow this innovative doctrine to hinder fellowship and work with fellow believers who have a different ministerial structure, so that they cannot enter our pulpits or celebrate around the Lord's table – that is a scandal and must be overcome.

Even one such as Professor Geoffrey Lampe has written that we should be 'increasingly reluctant to be committed as Anglicans to a position in which our church too often seems to the rest of the world to be concerned with a gospel which is no gospel, a gospel of the grace of God in bishops'[15] – how true!

Turning to the present situation, many Anglican evangelicals are tending to approach the question of episcopacy from the standpoint of accepted historical-sociological convention [the Anglican episcopate as we have it] and then try and read into it the roles and functions of episcopacy as we find it in the New Testament (teaching, pastoral care, mission etc.), with the resulting call for more bishops with more power and smaller dioceses to enable such roles to be fulfilled in today's society.

However, such a procedure needs to be stood on its head for it to be truly evangelical (*sola Scriptura*). We need to apply the principle of the 'dynamic equivalent' in our Biblical interpretation and application, and ask: who are the 'dynamic equivalents' to the presbyters/overseers in the New Testament? The answer, of course, is the pastor-teachers of the congregations, the Vicars and Curates.

Therefore, in order for New Testament oversight to be translated into a living reality today, we do not need to multiply the number of

---

15. G. Lampe, 'Episcopacy and Reunion', in *Churchman*. Vol. 75, (1961), p.16.

existing Anglican Bishops, but to increase and facilitate the number of pastor-teachers in our congregations, seeking people whose rule is God's Word, and whose 'focus of unity' is the gospel.

If the present Anglican episcopate structure is to be retained (although it may help if a term other than 'bishop' could be adopted), it could be reformed in a direction away from the monarchical model towards a truly servant role, whereby as area spiritual advisers and enablers, they commit themselves to encouraging, training and resourcing the true bishops of congregations to fulfil their calling – to teach the faithful and reach out to the unevangelized. Instead of the diocese being seen as the primary reality of which the congregation is but a small part, the situation would be reversed so that the concern of such 'area enablers' would be to make every resource available to foster the work of Christ where he is present, in the midst of his people, the congregation.

This would not only have the advantage of removing the delusory 'career ladder' which exists, but bring us back into line with the Scriptural emphasis upon the local congregations as the primary loci of God's activity and objects of his concern. It may also be a great step forward for such 'area advisers/bishops' to be elected by the diocese itself and for a shorter fixed period of time so that he may return, at a future period, back to a congregation (if he were to leave one at all). In any event, more radical thinking in the light of Scripture is surely required.

Ecumenism

As we saw earlier, the unity of the church is one of the essential aspects of the doctrine of the church. The very term *ekklesia* means 'gathering' – the people of God gathered around the Messiah. This too is linked to the 'catholic' dimension, so that there is one shepherd and one flock (John 10:16) – (a favourite text of the Reformers) and there are others who are to be gathered in by the teaching of the apostles as we read in John 17:20-21. There is no doubt that this prayer of Jesus, 'that they may be as one even as the Father and the Son are one', was fulfilled at Pentecost: the spiritual unity was brought about by the Holy Spirit, a unity which was made manifest in terms of fellowship and submission to apostolic teaching. So it is not surprising to find that in the New Testament the proclamation of the fact of Christian unity is followed by a call to be 'eager to maintain the unity of the Spirit in the bond of peace' (Ephesians 4:3).

The unity that the New Testament speaks of and urges is never uniformity, nor is it seen as some multinational conglomerate. It is a unity 'in Christ', emphasizing its spiritual and personal nature; and a unity in truth, emphasizing its doctrinal nature: after all it is possible to be united in error, a point once graphically brought home by Jewel: 'There was the greatest consent that might be amongst them that worshipped the golden calf and among them who with one voice jointly cried "Crucify Him!"'[16] Also Latimer was to remark, 'We ought never to regard unity so much that we would or should forsake God's Word for her sake'.[17] The New Testament never sees 'unity' as an end in itself: it is something which arises out of God's gracious movement towards us in Jesus Christ and which we are to work out in dependence upon him.

This means that there will be limits to unity. Where the apostolic truth is rejected, no unity exists. Paul pronounces upon those who promote error a curse (Galatians 1:8). John goes so far as to say that those who promote such heretical teaching never belonged in the first place (1 John 2:18ff; 4:1ff.). So not all so-called disunity is wrong. Indeed it would seem that in the New Testament there are two motifs for disunity, one which is unacceptable, the other necessary.[18] The first is what can be called the 'Apollos' motif as we find it in 1 Corinthians 1 and 2, where the local church is being split on purely personal grounds – for non-theological reasons – and that is condemned. The second is what can be termed the 'Anti-Christ' motif, as we find in John's letters, where one must separate oneself from those who are teaching serious error. So the first cause for disunity is lack of love, and this must be overcome; the second is lack of truth and the promotion of error, and this too, where possible, must be corrected, and if necessary, separation must occur.

Let us now work out some of the implications that this teaching has in two directions: what can we all 'external ecumenism' – the way churches of one denomination or none relate to others; and 'internal ecumenism' – how we might view churches within our own denominational structure.

The modern ecumenal movement as represented by the World Council of Churches and the new Inter-Church Process have as their focus external ecumenism, the bringing together of denominations and af-

---

16. Jewel, Parker Society, 3.69.
17. Latimer, Parker Society 1.487.
18. See Klaas Runia, *Reformation Today* (Edinburgh: Banner of Truth; 1968) p.61.

filiations of churches: and it is with visible unity that they are primarily concerned. But as we have seen, the unity which exists is spiritual and it is the invisible church which is truly one, although it is within the local church that that unity should be expressed visibly.

However, it would seem that one of the reasons why there is much confusion and frustration in modern ecumenism is because it is mistakenly thought that a denomination is a church. We believe in the church – yes – local and universal, but as we have seen, it is seriously wide of the mark to say that we believe in the church denominational. A denomination is more of a para-church organization, ideally organized to facilitate and encourage the work of the local church. As such it is not contrary to Scripture (as indeed other groups like the Church Pastoral Aid Society and Universities' and Colleges' Christian Fellowship are not). But to speak of a denomination as a 'church', as we do, is as misleading as to speak of a building as a 'church', which we also do. It is theoretically possible to have a 'unity' of denominations or only have one 'superstructure', and yet be far removed from the unity of which the New Testament speaks – unity in Christ and in truth. This is not to say that where possible one should not seek a greater understanding between such organizations, and where appropriate a sharing of resources – but is this really Biblical ecumenism? Would it not be more in line with the New Testament view of the church to seek closer fellowship, a recognition of ministries, a coming together between local churches which do confess and have that oneness in Christ and truth. That is what would commonly be called evangelical ecumenism? Should this not be the prayer of evangelical believers, as it was that of the great Richard Baxter? Is it right that for the sake of a para-church affiliation, that fellowship in the gospel should be hindered? Our survey so far would suggest not.

So what of 'internal ecumenism', which since the Keele congress of 1967 has seemed to be the main concern of Anglican evangelicals? Again we need to raise one or two questions. Is it perhaps the case that just as a confusion has arisen because of the mistake of identifying the church with denomination, so there is confusion because there has been the tendency uncritically to accept a congregation as being a 'church' simply because it belongs to a denomination? Supposing, without being harsh or judgmental, that there is a congregation called St. Swithin's. But as far as one can tell, the pure Word of God is not being preached, nor the sacraments duly administered, and discipline not exercised. If these marks of the church are absent, then can it be called a church? This does not mean to say, of course, that those amongst the number there do not belong to the universal church – the church invisible; but it does raise a serious question mark about the congregation's validity or at the very least its health. Now we obviously have to be very careful at this point. We are not saying that a congregation which contains error, or where immorality is to be found, is not a church – look at Corinth. But we surely do have to ask whether a gathering where the gospel is repudiated in both word and symbol can in all honesty – be conceived as a church, even though it belongs to a denomination. Such questions are not purely theoretical either: they have very practical and pastoral implications. For instance, one of your congregation is to move to a new town. Do you recommend that he finds the nearest church which belongs to your denomination or do you encourage him to find fellowship where the marks of the church are exhibited? As members of the Church of England, are we to put denominational loyalties above gospel loyalties in our working with other congregations? We have to face these questions honestly if we are going to understand our ecclesiology in practice.

Conclusion

It is time for Anglican evangelicals to get back to their biblical roots on the matter of ecclesiology. This will entail amongst other things:

(1). Affirming the priority of the local church;

(2). The implementation of biblical priorities and principles for the life of the local congregation;

(3). The promotion of evangelical cooperation for the spread of the gospel and

(4). Taking steps to prevent the undermining of gospel ministry presently being caused by the gradual slide of the denomination into a dead centralization of power upheld by bogus theology.

The challenge before us is formidable, but with the grace of God not impossible.

7

Never mind the quality, feel the width.
Comprehensiveness in the Church of England

J. I. Packer

One ingredient in today's Anglicanism is its claim to be comprehensive in a way that other traditions are not, and its confidence that this comprehensiveness is a fine thing. Many Roman Catholics, Eastern Orthodox, and non-Anglican Evangelicals have thought it irresponsible and scandalous, and made no bones of saying so. But there is, of course, at least in theory, more to comprehensiveness than this; though folk find it notoriously hard to get hold of just what.

Why is that? Because since the middle of the last century comprehensiveness has been paraded as an Anglican excellence from at least four distinct points of view, each observing it as a phenomenon and justifying it as a policy in a different way. While it was to be expected that Anglican comprehensiveness would comprehend different ideas of itself, the effect, here as in other areas of plural Anglican thinking, is to induce a degree of theological glossolalia which Eeyore would have labelled a Confused Noise, and which is as maddening and bewildering to observers as it is embarrassing and frustrating to those whose own utterances are part of it.

Inclusiveness

First, both historically and logically, comes the traditional understanding of comprehensiveness in terms of *calculated inclusion*. Here, comprehensiveness means a deliberate policy of so ordering the Church that it can be a spiritual home for all 'mere Christians' who do not insist on adding to the creed mediaeval and post-medieval novelties (papal claims, the Mass-sacrifice, etc.) or taking from it any of the Biblical fundamentals which it contains.

Comprehensiveness in this sense was the aim of the Elizabethan settlement, which sought a Church structure that might embrace the whole nation. The settlement took the form of a broad-based Protestant traditionalism circumscribed by the Articles and Prayer Book (two witnesses to a Biblical fulness of faith and worship), the royal supremacy (the sign that the Church was national and established), and the historic episcopate (marking continuity in space and time with the Church of earlier days).

Being Reformational as against Papal and Anabaptist and on the eucharistic presence Reformed as against Roman Catholic and Lutheran (Article 28), the settlement could claim to embody the essence of new Testament and mainstream patristic Christianity; thus it displayed true catholicity of substance. The doctrine of the Articles was put forward as a sufficient minimum, leaving a great deal undefined, and no terms of lay communion were imposed other than *de facto* acceptance of the established order; thus a truly catholic inclusiveness was achieved as well.

Archbishop Parker, the first Elizabethan bishop, spoke of the settlement in terms of 'golden mediocrity' ('*aurea mediocritas*', 'a golden mean' is what we should say). With this may be bracketed the familiar idea of Anglicanism as a 'middle way' (*via media*). What these phrases point to is Anglican unwillingness to shape the Church in a way that either needlessly cuts loose from the past or needlessly cuts out Christians who would be part of it in the present. The *via media* was never, as is sometimes suggested, a tightrope walk between Rome and the Reformation, nor between Romanism and Anabaptistry, but a pastorally-minded balancing of the claims of traditional faith and practice against the need to change for edification.

Its spirit comes out in the opening sentence of the Preface to the 1662 Prayer Book: 'It hath been the wisdom of the Church of England, ever since the first compiling of her Publick Liturgy; to keep the mean between two extremes, of too much stiffness in refusing, and of too much easiness in admitting any variation from it.' The Cranmerian Prayer Book in its 1559 and 1662 revisions was in fact for centuries the chief instrument of comprehensiveness. Following time-honoured forms within a Reformed-Augustinian doctrinal frame, it was phrased with such breadth and resonance that it could delight a wide range of theological and liturgical palates. Long before the age of fish and chips, the Book of Common Prayer was the Great British Invention, nurturing all sorts and conditions of Englishmen and holding the Church together with remarkable effectiveness.

The benefits sought through this policy of circumscribed

inclusiveness were two: catholicity for the Church and unity – religious, political, and social – for the nation. Until the nineteenth century the policy seemed on the whole to be succeeding, despite the lapses of leadership which squeezed out the Puritans and Wesley's people in the seventeenth and eighteenth centuries respectively. But when the Tractarians started to accuse the Church of defective catholicity because of what it jettisoned at the Reformation, and Newman to argue that for doctrine to remain the same it must constantly develop and change often, and liberals to deny that the Bible should be read as if God were its primary author, then not only Anglican unity but also the theological basis of the comprehensiveness policy itself were irrevocably undermined.

For the policy rested on agreed acceptance of what the Bible, Creeds, and Articles contain as normative revelation, or at least as catholic theologoumena that must not be spoken against. It expressed doctrinal modesty but not doctrinal indifferentism. Its demands and restrictions in matters of belief and behaviour were no less categorical for being minimal.

But once substantial bodies of Anglican theological opinion began to question these demands on grounds of catholicity and truth, some wanting to augment and others to reduce what was common ground before, agreement that the Anglican set-up secured genuine catholicity became a thing of the past, and the Church changed overnight from a community unitedly proclaiming an achieved catholicity as the basis of its fellowship into one unitedly seeking such a basis but divided as to what, if anything, needed to be done to secure it.

So for more than a century the Church has been a cockpit of debate between representatives of differently conceived catholicities trying to knock each other down and if possible out, or to elbow each other aside, or to find ways of taking into themselves the apparently opposed principles of the other views; and the debate continues.

Integration

Second comes F. D. Maurice's very influential reinterpretation of comprehensiveness as *Intergrative practice*: that is, the synthesizing in action of apparent theological opposites. Maurice (1805-72), an ex-Unitarian for whom the living Trinity was the key to everything, was a distinguished, original, and isolated figure in the Church of England whose influence, gone as it seemed long before his death, has remarkably revived during the past half-century.[1] He lived when Anglican party strife was at its height, and his highly individual plea for a non-party understanding of the Church of England fell on deaf ears. Today it chimes in with what many wish to hear, so Maurice is hailed as a prophet for our time.

Maurice held that the God who bestows national characteristics appoints distinct destinies for various national churches, and that part of the Church of England's special calling is to synthesize all the principles separately maintained as theoretical opposites by its three warring parties, Evangelical, Tractarian, and Broad Church. Each party contends for a positive principle, to which it adds antithetical, negative, restrictive, and sectarian notions in order to form an exclusive system of thought (Maurice detested systems). Thus Evangelicals contend for salvation in Christ and muddy it with Calvinism, Tractarians contend for the God-giveness of the Church and muddy their point with sacramentalist theory, and Broad Churchmen contend for freedom from bondage to intellectual systems of yesterday and link this with pleas to abolish the Articles and Prayer Book. But, all three positive principles were embodied already in the Church of England, with its creeds, sacraments, liturgy, and ordained ministry, and the rest of each position could be safely dismissed as mistaken.

Maurice contended that the union of the Triune God with mankind and the domination of Christ over his church, together with the institutional means by which this union and dominion are furthered, are more basic to Christianity than any theological formulations. In one sense, of course they are, for things talked about are always basic to talking about them; but Maurice meant that the church is primarily institutional and only secondarily confessional, and that is much more disputable. His approving comment on the English Reformation shows his attitude:

'Here the idea of the Church as a Spiritual Polity ruled over by Christ, and consisting of all baptized persons, did, owing to various providential circumstances, supersede the notion of the Church, as a sect, maintaining certain options; or to speak more correctly, the dogmatical side of Christianity was here felt to be its accessory and subordinate side, and the ordi-

---

1. On Maurice, see A. M. Ramsey, *F. D. Maurice and the Conflicts of Modern Theology*; Alec Vidler, *F. D. Maurice and Company*; W. Merlin Davies, *An Introduction to the Theology of F. D. Maurice*; Torben Christensen, *The Divine Order*.

nances, which were the manifestation of it as the law of our social and practical life, were considered its principle side'.[2]

Stephen Sykes judges that Maurice's view of Anglicanism has been 'theologically ... disastrous.' 'It must be said bluntly that it has served as an open invitation to intellectual laziness and self-deception ... the failure to be frank about the issues between the parties in the Church of England has led to an ultimately illusory self-projection as a Church without any specific doctrinal or confessional position.'[3] But this belief had in it less of prophetic insight than of theological oversight, for faith and theology cannot be thus separated. The Christ to whom each man's faith is a response is the Christ of the kerygma he believes, and to the extent that their understandings of the gospel vary, different Christians serve different Christs, or at least differently conceived Christs. If ever we wondered whence came the facile idea, often met, that the Church of England is a liturgical rather than a confessional church, now we know.

It is hard to dissent from Sykes' verdict, and no less hard to accept Maurice's view of the Church of England. For:

(1) in order to show how in Anglican practice the three party positions are complementary Maurice is forced high-handedly to redefine them in ways which neither Evangelicals nor Anglo-Catholics can own.

(2) Maurice's view implies that the crusading Anglicanism of a Simeon-or Ryle-type Evangelical, who wants to see the whole Church of England leavened with the gospel, is less authentically Anglican than that of a professedly anti-party institutionalist like himself.

(3) Since Maurice too was a theological crusader, advocating an account of universal redemption which neither Evangelicals nor Anglo-Catholics could accept, and basing his institutionalism largely on it, he should really be seen as a one-man party, unlike others in having private theological reasons for not wanting to change the Church's constitution, but possessing no better claim to be a mainstream Anglican than anyone else.

(4) To suggest that in the English Reformation as a whole (as distinct from the reign of Henry VIII, which only saw its beginning) the issue of theological truth ('the dogmatical side of Christianity') was not primary is to part company with all exponents of what happened

---

2. Maurice, *The Kingdom of Christ*, 1838, II, 338.
3. Stephen W. Sykes, *The Integrity of Anglicanism*.

for the first hundred years after the event, not to mention most since. Granted, the Reformers sought a reformed catholicism, not a new start; granted too, no fully interlocked Anglican system like that of the Tridentine decrees or the Westminster Confession was ever spelt out; nonetheless, what the Articles defined was set forth categorically and confessionally, to be the doctrinal standard for interpreting Anglican liturgy, and it is idle to say it was not. On this stubborn fact views of Anglicanism like Maurice's founder.

Tension

Third in order comes the semi-official twentieth-century understanding of comprehensiveness as a state of *inner tension,* indeed frank disunity on some matters, which the Anglican Communion is providentially called to sustain because, first, out of it will some day emerge a richer wholeness (catholicity) than the Christian world yet knows and second, it qualifies the Anglican communion to act as a 'bridge church' bringing into unity with itself bodies which cannot at present find unity with each other. Inner incoherence is the price Anglicanism pays for the privilege of fulfilling its unique vocation in reintegrating Christ's divided church.

Sometimes this view is presented as an extension of Maurice's, and historically it may have developed in that way, but theologically it is a different thing altogether. Maurice looked back to Christ's founding of the church as his kingdom, and sought a way of harmony between warring Anglican groups by appeal to historically given institutions of the kingdom: sacraments, creeds, worship, ministry. This third view looks forward, anticipates new developments and states of things, and finds the meaning of present conflict in future prospects. Let me illustrate. Here, first, is Almand de Medieta unveiling his vision for the church which he left the Roman communion to join.

> I am convinced that the historic mission or destiny of the Church of England, and, on a wider scale, the destiny of the world-wide Anglican Communion, is to make a theological and also a practical *synthesis* of Catholicism and Protestantism ... Our Church must bestir itself and *become* a genuine dialectial Church ... a dialectical Church is committed to the view that all these views or particular theologies (Anglo-Catholic, Evangelical, Liberal) must *all* be transcended in a higher *synthesis*.[4]

---

4. E., Amand de Mendieta, 'From anglican Symbiosis to anglican Synthesis' in *The Anglican Synthesis*, ed. W. R. F. Browning. The source of the 'dialectical church' idea

And here is the Church Unity Committee of the 1948 Lambeth Conference reflecting on the tensions set up in reunion discussion with non-episcopal churches by the coexistence of different Anglican views of episcopacy.

> We recognise the inconveniences caused by these tensions, but we acknowledge them to be part of the will of God for us, since we believe it is only through a comprehensiveness which makes it possible to hold together in the Anglican Communion understandings of truth which are held in separation in other Churches, that the Anglican Communion is able to reach out in different directions and so fulfil its special vocation as one of God's instruments for the restoration of the visible unity of His whole Church. If at the present time one view were to prevail to the exclusion of all others, we should be delivered from our tensions, but only at the price of missing our opportunity and our vocation.[5]

It would be hazardous to speak either for or against this noble and hopeful vision, and I shall limit my comments to a review of some relevant facts.

First, it is a fact, and a happy one, that within the past thirty years the previously felt convictional and kerygmatic gap between the more conservative Evangelicals and the more conservative Anglo-Catholics has shrunk.[6] On such matters as Biblical authority, justification, the efficacy of baptism towards salvation, and the balance of preaching and eucharist in worship, there appears a convergence, which the charismatic, liturgical, and evangelistic thrusts of our time continually help along. Today's Evangelicals see that tradition has value as an aid to understanding Scripture and a safeguard against bondage to present-day cultural prejudice. Today's Anglo-Catholics see that tradition, which purports to embody and express biblical faith, must be judged by those very Scriptures which it interprets and applies. Most Anglo-Catholics allow that those who took Evangelicals' *sola fide* to mean that justification is by feeling justified and sanctification is unreal or unimpor-

---

is acknowledged to be H. A. Hodges in *Anglicanism and Orthodoxy; a study in Dialectical Churchmanship*.

5. The Lambeth Conference 1948.

6. For evidence of this, compare C. Ol. Buchanan, E. L. Mascall, J. I. Packer, Bishop of Willesden (G. D. Leonard), *Growing into Union*, within *The Apostolic Ministry*, ed. K. E. Kirk, which argued the necessity of episcopacy to the church's very being, and the report Catholicity, which presented Protestantism as a total distortion of Christianity.

tant, misheard. Most Evangelicals perceive that the faith which Catholics inculcate looks to the Christ whose salvation the sacraments display, and not to the sacraments without the Saviour. Evangelicals nowadays carry conviction when they profess concern for the universal visible church even thought most of them still use the invisible-visible distinction to express their mind on the church's nature. Anglo-Catholics nowadays have largely ceased to speak as if the church's existence depends on the prior and independent reality of the ordained ministry, even though they still go beyond Evangelicals in their valuation of the historic episcopal succession. (The thought of the historic episcopate as a sign of the space-time continuity of Christ's ministry from heaven to his people has been found illuminating and unifying in some quarters.) Anglo-Catholics have helped Evangelicals to see Christianity as the baptismal life; Evangelicals have helped Anglo-Catholics to see it as a life of joyful assurance and expectant prayer. These are some of the more obvious points of convergence.

But it is also a fact that in recent years an enormous gap has opened up between Evangelicals and Anglo-Catholics on one side and, on the other, those liberals, heirs of the old Broad Churchmen, who since 1963, the year of *Honest to God*, have been called radicals – 'rads' against 'trads', or 'questers' against 'resters'. The Bultmannite hermeneutic, which treats New Testament narrative and theology as so much culture-determined mythology, celebrating and evoking the ineffable impact of God upon us while telling us nothing of a divine-human redeemer at all, has bred a worldwide crop of Christian reconstructions, all starting from a non-incarnational view of Jesus, all working with a unitarian idea of God seasoned with more or less of process-theology, all claiming that modern secular knowledge makes their type of view the only one possible, and all vigorously off-setting themselves from the categories and content of traditional belief. Many Anglicans, leading scholars among them, are in this camp. But the versions of Christian belief which the reconstructionists produce strike Evangelicals and Anglo-Catholics as forms of unbelief, or at least of intellectual besetting sin[7] and in relation to the fashion of thought that has produced them – which, please God, will pass, as fashions do – de Mendieta's 'higher synthesis' is out of sight.

Finally, it must be said that events since 1948 have not given any

---

7. This point is gently but firmly made by E. L. Mascall in *Theology and the Gospel of Christ*.

support to the notion of Anglicanism's providentially appointed 'bridge' role. In England the Anglican-Methodist unity scheme has failed, partly because of its problematical 'Service of Reconciliation' which maintained the rule, allegedly necessary to Anglican comprehensiveness, that non-episcopal clergy must receive the form of episcopal orders, and the subsequent multi-church discussions that produced the 'Ten Propositions' do not seem to have been notably enlivened by Anglican magic.

Overseas union schemes involving Anglicans have also collapsed or been put into store (New Zealand, USA, Canada, and several in Africa). In the world ecumenical movement Anglican leadership is a thing of the past. Pan-Anglican groups have talked to Lutheran, Roman Catholic, and Orthodox representatives, and come under suspicion of saying different and incompatible things to different churches. If the confidence of the 1948 Lambeth Conference about the Anglican calling rested in any measure on the Anglican track record of significant ecumenical initiatives during the preceding half-century, the past thirty years must be said to have left the idea less credible than it was before.

Relativism

The fourth and most recent way of understanding Anglican comprehensiveness is in terms of the belief, characteristic of the liberal tradition, that *theological relativism is inescapable,* and to make explicit provision for it is wise and healthy. No formulations of faith (it is urged) have finality; treat them as sacrosanct, and the Church stagnates; but let reason, informed by contemporary culture, revise and reshape them, and the Church will both appear relevant and be found enriched. Anglicanism, honouring reason in theology, has always instinctively made room for those who in the cause of truth and relevance have felt bound to challenge accepted formulations, and this comprehensiveness, whereby the Church in effect holds the ring for debate between advocates of the old and the new, is one main secret of Anglican resilience and vitality. So at least it is said.

To see what this viewpoint implies, we must be clear on some facts on which clarity is too often lacking.

First, the basis of all forms of this position is the hypothesis that no universally right way of thinking about God is given in Christianity. Evangelicals and Anglo-Catholics characteristically hold that there is a universally right way, given to us in the teaching and trains of thought found in the Bible. Catholics ordinarily make a point of adding that patristic tradition and conciliar definitions have authority as a guide to interpretation, setting limits within which all subsequent attempts to develop Biblical thinking should stay. But for a century and a half those known as liberals, modernists and radicals have found this incredible.

Unable to accept what might be called a Chalcedonian view of Scripture (i.e., that it is fully human as well as fully divine, and fully divine as well as fully human), they have doubted both the reality of the Chalcedonian Christ to whom the New Testament witnesses and the propriety of reading Scripture as more than a rag-bag of traditions, intuitions, fancies and mythology whereby good men celebrated and shared their sense of being in touch with God – a contact occasioned for New Testament writers by a uniquely godly man named Jesus. Scripture and the Christians' literary heritage are certainly stimulating, inspiring and effective in communicating God, but that does not make them true. So the constant endeavour of the liberal fraternity from the start has been to go behind and beyond biblical witness to reformulate the faith in terms which to them, as modern men, seem truer, clearer, and less inadequate.

Second, the liberal presence guarantees genuine contradiction of views. Sykes rightly says that it is a presence rather than a party; liberals have no united platform or policy, for they hold in common only the negations just noted, plus the sifting, re-shaping methodology which these negations entail. Sykes blames Maurice for leading Anglicans to think of liberals as a party in the Church parallel to the other two.

He notes that a 'liberal' theological proposal is always in the form of a challenge to an established authority, and thus necessarily implies a dispute about the appropriate norms or criteria for any theology whatsoever. He notes too that 'it is impossible to be merely a "liberal" in theology ... one's theology ... will be liberal is as much as it is a modification of an already existing type' – liberal catholic, liberal evangelical, or even liberal latitudinarian.[8] And he rightly stresses that any Church in which liberals do their thing, querying the traditional and jettisoning the conventional, will have to endure real divergences of belief as some negate what others affirm and affirm what others cannot but negate.

Third, the liberal method has gained acceptance in Anglicanism, as

---

8. Sykes, *op.cit.* (see last issue of *The Evangelical Catholic*, April 1987).

in most other large Protestant Churches. When in 1862 two of the authors of *Essays and Reviews* were tried for heresy, most of the novelties they affirmed were held not to be contrary to the doctrine of the Church of England.

When in 1921 Gore urged that modernists be disciplined for sitting loose to the creed, the response of the Archbishop of Canterbury, Randall Davidson, was to set up a commission to report on the state of doctrine in the Church of England, and its report, by acknowledging the liberals' contribution to the thought-life of the Church, was, says Sykes, an 'unambiguous victory' for them.[9]

The 1976 Doctrine Commission report, *Christian Believing*, distinguishes four attitudes of Anglicans to the creeds which they recite in worship. Some embrace them as norms, 'classical crystallizations of biblical faith'. Some recite them, despite reservations about their content, as a way of professing solidarity with the historic Church. Some 'can neither affirm nor deny the creeds, because they look to the present rather than to the past to express their faith, and attach more importance to fresh understandings of that continuing Christian enterprise which has its origin in Jesus'. Some feel the fallibility of creeds and cannot in principle regard them as expressing their loyalty to Jesus and the Creator, so feel uninvolved with them. The first attitude is characteristic of Evangelicals and Anglo-Catholics, the other three are liberals.

Fourth, all forms of liberalism are unstable. Being developed in each case by taking some secular fashion of thought as the fixed point (evolutionary optimism, historical scepticism, Marxist sociology, or whatever), and remodelling the Christian tradition to fit it, they are all doomed to die as soon as the fashion changes, according to Dean Inge's true saying that he who marries the spirit of the age today will be a widower tomorrow. The history of the past century and a half is littered with the wreckage of dead liberalism.

Some liberals cheerfully acknowledge this and never treat their current opinions as more than provisional, anticipating that they may think different next week. Others clearly cannot bear this prospect, and respond to factors which undermine their present opinions in the manner of King Canute forbidding the tide to come in; but the former group are more clear-headed. They measure the health of theology by its fer-

---

9. *op.cit.* The report was entitled *Doctrine in the Church of England*, The Report of the Commission on Christian Doctrine appointed by the archbishops of Canterbury and York in 1922.

tility in producing new options alternative to old ones, and value Anglican doctrinal tolerance (which they equate with comprehensiveness) because it removes all restraints on innovation.

Anglicans with a juster idea of what is given in Christianity see the matter rather differently. They judge of the health of theology by such criteria as fidelity to Scripture and in particular to the truths of incarnation and mediation, and the endless shifts of the liberal kaleidoscope remind them irresistibly of the folk whom the New Testament describes as always learning and never able to come to a knowledge of the truth (2 Tim. 3:7). Only by an agnostic judgment of charity can they treat exponents of non-incarnational Christianity as Christians, and they see all such doctrine as weakening the Church and threatening men's spiritual welfare.

From the foregoing survey we can now see precisely what Anglican comprehensiveness amounts to today. We perceive that, though all agree that catholicity requires as wide a comprehensiveness as the Christian revelation will allow, there is no common mind on how the current breadth of doctrinal toleration should be regarded.

Some still define Anglicanism in terms of the fundamentals set forth in the creeds and Articles, and challenge the propriety of clergy who sit loose to these ministering in the Church of England. Thus, for example, in 1977 the Church of England Evangelical Council declared:

> If, then, a time comes when a clergyman can no longer conscientiously teach something central to his Church's doctrine (such as the personal deity of Jesus) which he has solemnly undertaken to teach, we urge that the only honourable course open to him is to resign any post he occupies as an accredited teacher of his Church ... in the last resort (i) if a central Christian doctrine is at stake, (ii) if the clergyman concerned is not just questioning it but denying it, (iii) if he is not just passing through a temporary period of uncertainty but has reached settled conviction, and (iv) if he refuses to resign, then we believe the bishop (or other leader) should seriously consider withdrawing his license or permission to teach in the Church.[10]

Others continue to believe (though, it seems, myopically) that all Anglicans are 'really' united, whatever their views, by virtue of their common loyalty to the Anglican communion as a going concern, and

---

10. *Truth, Error and Discipline in the Church*; issued by the Church of England Evangelical Council (London; Vine Books, 1978, pp.12f).

that a transcendent synthesis of what now appear as contradictory theologies either exists already or will exist some day. So they decline to be troubled by any outbursts of apparent heterodoxy, or to be moved by others' distress at them, judging that the heretics' continuing loyalty to the institution suffices to excuse any unfortunate things they say. There is no official attitude to public heterodoxy among Anglicans, but this is the common attitude of officials in the Church's administrative hierarchy.

Finally, a strident minority, whose noise-to-numbers ratio in the Church of England reminds one of the 3,000-strong British Humanist Association in Britain's domestic affairs, insists that any ascription to Jesus and his church of any kind of ultimate significance should be accepted as a legitimate Christian option, since the focusing of this significance is what Christian theology with its inescapable conceptual relativism is really all about.

Advocates of the three positions understand Scripture and practise theology in such different ways that genuine communication between them is next to impossible. They are to each other very different animals, and from this standpoint comparing the Church of England which contains them to Noah's ark is not facetious but apt.

I do not suppose I am the only one for whom Anglicanism still means identifying with official doctrinal standards (creeds and Articles, historically understood) and appreciating the Anglican heritage: the 1662 Prayer Book, beside which modern alternatives seem so feeble and wet; the ethos of a biblically reformed and informed traditionalism; the concern for catholicity which makes Anglicans eager to embrace everything of value in other Churches' traditions; the hatred of sectarianism which makes them hostile to narrow one-sidedness; the practical, pastoral orientation of theological enquiry; the long-suffering tolerance which waits for things to be thoroughly discussed, lest consciences be wounded or truth squandered; and so forth. Nor do I suppose I am the only one whose active Anglicanism expresses, not complacency at what the Church is today, but hope of what it may be tomorrow, when (please God) it reapprehends its heritage and is renewed in so doing.

8

Preaching and Pastoral Ministry

Peter Adam

Whatever happened to Preaching?

It is one of the ironies of the currently celebrated Evangelical Renaissance in the Church of England that it seems to have lost its way in the area of Preaching. How has a tradition which looks back to Reformation Preachers including Bishop Latimer and Bishop Ridley, John Calvin and Martin Luther, whose commitment to Preaching is so perfectly expressed and reflected in the Book of Common Prayer, the Thiry Nine Articles and The Ordinal, and whose tradition of Preaching includes such masters as George Whitfield, Charles Simeon, John Stott and Dick Lucas, lost its way in Preaching in the 1990's? It is a double irony that while this Evangelical Renaissance is also celebrating the rise in Biblical scholarship over the last fifty years it should fail to ask the question why this outpouring of biblical scholarship is not producing great or even good Preachers.

This decline in Preaching among Evangelicals within the Church of England can be observed from the following evidence:[1]

Kenneth Hylson-Smith in his book *Evangelicals in the Church of England 1734-1984*[2] studies the growth and development of Evangelicals over 250 years. His section on the period 1945-1984 includes a number of themes of development within Evangelical thought such as social involvement, liturgy, hymnology, the ministry of women, the charismatic movement. It marks no comparable development in the theology or practice of Preaching. On the contrary, in his epilogue Hylson-Smith comments:

---

1. I am aware that I will need to convince some readers that all is not well with Preaching among Evangelicals in Anglican circles, so I have chosen evidence which cannot be easily dismissed as coming from an alarmist lunatic fringe.
2. Kenneth Hylson-Smith, *Evangelicals in the Church of England 1734-1984*, T & T Clark, Edinburgh, 1988

'as we have seen in scanning the past two and half centuries, no Christian tradition glories more than Evangelicalism in the supremacy of the Bible and the truth it contains. Nevertheless much contemporary Evangelicalism is "light weight, even flimsy compared with its antecendents". There is a wide-spread lack of seriousness, and a paucity of concern for searching the Scriptures and applying Biblical teaching to individual, church and community life.'[3]

Another commentator on modern Evangelicalism is Michael Sayward in his book *Evangelicals on the move.*[4] His comment on the modern generation of Evangelicals is 'excellent when it comes to providing religious music, drama and art. Not so good when asked to Preach and teach the faith or to express it in writing. As a publisher said to me 'where is the next Michael Green?'[5] Sayward quotes the Declarations of Intent from the Nottingham Conference of 1977. It is interesting to note that the Intentions do not include a commitment to Preaching and teaching the Bible.

Further evidence is the disquieting silence on the subject of Preaching in the recently published *Evangelical Anglicans: their role and influence in the Church today.*[6] The subject of the book is Evangelical contributions to Anglicanism, and it is intended to be a reflection and illustration of the kind of thinking that goes on within Evangelical Anglicanism today. With chapters on subjects like Evangelicalism and the sacraments, on social ethics and economic issues, and on the gender issue, one might have expected a chapter on Evangelicals and Preaching, a summary of the development of Preaching within Evangelicalism over the past fifty years and the good effect that this has had on the Church of England. No such chapter has been written, and the issue is too important to neglect. In fact the most extensive reference to Preaching is found in David Atkinson's chapter on pastoral ministry where 'the proclamation and teaching model' is one of five contemporary models of Evangelical pastoral care (the others are nurture, service, therapy and mission) and this model is described in one paragraph.[7] If David Atkinson reflects the state of Evangelical preaching accurately

3. Hylson-Smith, *op. cit.*, p.351-2
4. Michael Sayward, *Evangelicals on the move*, Mowbray, Oxford, 1987
5. Sayward, *op. cit.*, p.92
6. *Evangelical Anglicans: their role and influence in the Church today,* edited by R.T. France & A.E. McGrath, S.P.C.K., London, 1993
7. France & McGrath, *op. cit.*, p.154

then Evangelical Preaching is in a bad way.

It is no surprise then that John Stott who provided such an impressive model of Bible teaching and Preaching after the Second World War has written in his book *The Contemporary Christian*[8]:

'where are the Timothys of the next generation? Where are the young Evangelical men and women, who are determined by God's grace to stand firm in Scripture, refusing to be swept off their feet by the prevailing winds of fashion, who are resolved to continue in it and live by it, relating the Word to the world in order to obey it, and who are committed to passing it on, as they give themselves to the ministry of conscientious exposition?'[9]

Rather than Evangelicals succeeding in influencing the Church of England with a robust and forthright theology and practice of Preaching, the reverse seems to have happened, that is, Evangelicals seem to have been influenced by the prevailing mood of the Anglican Church and their society and submitted to the general decline in Preaching.

So Donald Coggan (who has been writing on Preaching for over fifty years) in a recent book *On Preaching*[10] writes of the dangers of contemporary Anglican practice.

'We shall rear a generation of Christians accustomed to the Eucharist but foreigners to many of the great truths of the Christian faith. They have never had the opportunity of listening, Sunday by Sunday, to a steady, intelligent, interesting exposition of the things most surely believed among us. They have been fed with snippets, little its and bits, nice thoughts for the day, but nothing, or practically nothing, from which bones and spiritual tissue can be built.'[11]

He quotes John Donne 'if there be discounting or slackening of Preaching, there is the danger of losing Christ'.[12]

Another writer with a long-term view is T.H.L. Parker. In 1947 he wrote a book called *The Oracles of God: An introduction to the Preaching of John Calvin*, and in 1992 produced the book *Calvin's Preaching*. The earlier book, *The Oracles of God*, included in its final chapter an appeal to the Church of England to be recalled to its

---

8. John Stott, *The Contemporary Christian*, I.V.P., Leicester, 1992
9. Stott, *op. cit.*, p.172
10. Donald Coggan, *On Preaching*, S.P.C.K., London, 1978
11. Coggan, *op. cit.*, p.9
12. Coggan, *op. cit.*, p.13

fundamental commitment to Preaching. This appeal is omitted in the later book, but not as Parker makes clear, because the appeal is not still appropriate. He writes:

'a word or two of explanation may not come amiss on why the final chapter of *The Oracles of God* is now omitted. It is most assuredly not because I consider that the churches in this country no longer need to be recalled to fundamentals. On the contrary, it appears to me that the Church of England (for I have no right to speak of others) is, in almost every respect that is worthwhile, in a far worse state now than it was in the 1940's. Doctrinally, morally, and in the understanding of its task as the Church of England, the failure has been disastrous. What wonder that a Church which picks and chooses what it wants out of the Bible should become confused in its theology, flabby in its morals, and with little to state but the worldly obvious – the day after worldly liberals have stated it more convincingly?'[13]

This general move away from the Bible and from Preaching perhaps reflects our contemporary commitment to an Enlightenment stance, which gives a distrust of external authorities, and the search for individuals to come to their own understanding of the truth. This preoccupation is represented in that close triangle of theologies which tend to concentrate on personal and internal revelation within the individual rather than objective revelation in the history or in the Bible: this triangle includes traditions which may on the surface appear to be poles apart but in practice are close together: the Charismatic emphasis on the immediate inspiration of the Holy Spirit, the Liberal emphasis on the authority of the individual's reason (nowadays tinged with emotion), and the Quaker emphasis on the immediacy of God speaking to the soul.

It is customary now to blame theological education for the decline in Preaching. A cluster of influences may have had a bad effect, including the move away from 'confessional theology' to 'university theology', treating the Old Testament as if it were not part of the Christian Bible, uncertainty in the area of Revelation; and perhaps the pastoral theology departments of our colleges have placed more emphasis on various pastoral ministries and neglected Preaching as a primary focus of pastoral ministry. Or is it that our theology has changed, that the loss of the pastoral epistles (1 & 2 Timothy and Titus) from our usable Canon has meant a change in our theology of ministry? But

---

13. T.H.L. Parker, *Calvin's Preaching,* T, & T. Clark, Edinburgh, p.x

perhaps it is just that we are reflecting more general changes in the churches and in the world.

In the context of our changing world Neil Postman in his book *Amusing Ourselves to Death*[14] comments on the radical changes in our society in terms of communication. He looks at the television age and the ability to turn everything into entertainment and amusement. It is fascinating to notice that he describes the age that is past as the age of Exposition. 'Exposition is a mode of thought, a method of learning, and a means of expression.'[15] He further characterizes Exposition as 'the sophisticated ability to think conceptually, deductively, and sequentially; a high valuation of reason and order; an abhorrence of contradiction; a large capacity for detachment and objectivity; and a tolerance for delayed response.'[16] He further describes Jonathan Edwards sermons as 'tightly knit and closely reasoned expositions of theological doctrine.'[17] Postman also notes that the age of Exposition has now been replaced by the Age of Show Business.[18]

Of course Postman is not concerned with the Preaching and teaching of the Bible yet it is interesting to notice that he uses the word 'exposition' which is commonly used in our Christian circles to refer to the 'exposition' of the text of the Bible. If in Postman's word the age of Exposition has been replaced by the Age of Show Business then in ecclesiastical circles perhaps the age of the Exposition of Holy Scripture has been replaced by less systematic and intentional use of Scripture as a basis for public teaching and Preaching.

When James Smart wrote of the 'Strange Silence of the Bible in the Church'[19] he opened a debate which has not yet been answered or resolved in the wider churches, and is I think also an issue for Evangelicals. So it seems that Evangelicals have lost their way in the area of Preaching, and that this confusion reflects the Church of England, the wider churches and the world in which we live. If it is an irony that an age which has seen so much biblical scholarship should not have produced Preachers and teachers of the Bible, it is also an irony that the age which has seen such an explosion in the translation and production

---

14. Neil Postman, *Amusing Ourselves to Death*, Methuen, London, 1985
15. Postman, *op. cit.*, p.64
16. Postman, *op. cit.*, p.64
17. Postman, *op. cit.*, p.55
18. Postman, *op. cit.*, p.64
19. James D. Smart, *Strange Silence of the Bible in the Church*, London, S.C.M., 1970

of the Bible should also have produced a generation who are unused to its teaching,

Can we reclaim Preaching?

1. An appeal for the ministry of the Word in Pastoral Ministry

The life of the people of God in every age is characterized by the presence of the words of God. Adam is addressed by the Lord God, Abraham received the promise, and Moses is called by God and brings the words of God to the people of Israel. The prophets speak the words of God, Jesus speaks as the Father directs him, and the apostles make known the word of truth, the gospel. If the life of the people of God is characterized by the presence of the words of God, so too it is characterized, at least from the time of Moses, by the Ministry of the Word, as prophets, prophetesses, wise men and women, disciples, apostles and their fellow workers exercise a many-faceted Ministry of the Word among the people of God.

So we see, for example, in Paul's letter to the Colossians many aspects of the Ministry of the Word. The Colossians have heard and understood 'God's grace and all its truth' (1:16) and they learnt it first from Epaphras whom Paul describes as 'our dear fellow servant, who is a faithful minister of Christ on our behalf' (1:7). If the church of God at Colossae has been founded by the ministry of Epaphras then Paul in his letter is continuing that ministry and what we now call the Epistle to the Colossians is an example of Paul's written Ministry of the Word. And as the Colossians are to pass on their letter to the church of the Laodiceans, so too they are to read the letter from Laodicea (4:16). So reading is also the Ministry of the Word. The Colossians are also to be those who engage in Ministry of the Word. 'Let the word of Christ dwell in you richly as you teach and admonish one another with all wisdom, and as you sing psalms, hymns and spiritual songs with gratitude in your hearts to God' (3:16).And their ministry to outsiders is also a Ministry of the Word. 'Let your conversation be always full of grace, seasoned with salt, so that you may know how to answer everyone' (4:6).

This same diverse Ministry of the Word is found in the life of our congregations today where in private conversation, in counselling, in one-to-one evangelism, in the public reading of the Bible, in teaching and Preaching the Scriptures, in public evangelism, in small group training, and in home Bible studies we are exercising many different forms of the Ministry of the Word.

We do so confident of the power and usefulness of the Word of God. Paul characterises the Holy Scriptures as 'able to make you wise for salvation through faith in Christ Jesus' (2 Timothy 3:15). And he further describes the effectiveness of Scripture as 'useful for teaching, rebuking, correcting and training in righteousness.' If Scripture is thus useful for changing character, its use also results in God's people being 'thoroughly equipped for every good work' (2 Timothy 3:16, 17). Or in Ephesians we discover that without speaking the truth in love the congregation may be described as 'infants tossed back and forth by the waves, and blown here and there by every wind of teaching and by the cunning and craftiness of men in their deceitful scheming' (Ephesians 4:14). Rather when the people of God engage in the ministry of speaking the truth in love Paul says they 'will in all things grow up into him who is the head, that is Christ' (Colossians 4:15).

While my main subject is a particular form of the Ministry of the Word which we call Preaching, my aim is not to promote Preaching while ignoring other important Ministries of the Word. Indeed in my opinion, if we try and make Preaching do all the work of the many different Ministries of the Word, we will certainly fail. By neglecting other important ministries we put too much pressure on public Preaching and teaching. Thus the broad base of my appeal is for the Ministry of the Word in pastoral ministry. That is, that in many different ways we allow God to teach us through his Word, conveyed to us through the men and women of faith.

While I want to encourage every form of the Ministry of the Word, I want to focus on Preaching in particular for the following reasons:

(1). Preaching is addressed to the body of believers, the church, and so it can help corporate maturity, and not just individual edification.

(2). Preaching to the assembled church reflects the nature of the Bible, which is in the most part addressed to the community, not to individuals. The best way to hear the Bible is in the congregation.

(3). The public Preacher and teacher provides a powerful public model of interpreting, using and obeying Scripture.

(4). It is essential that the Bible speaks clearly to the corporate culture of the congregation, and forms its vision and ministry.

2. An appeal for the Ministry of the Word in pastoral ministry, especially in Biblical Preaching

Donald Coggan makes the point that a 'healthy doctrine of Preaching springs from a healthy theology .... Begin with an inadequate or feeble doctrine of God's Word and the pulpit utterance will be feeble.' Coggan characterises a healthy theology of Preaching as deriving from the belief that God is a God who speaks: 'ours is not a silent God, a God who sits, sphinx-like, looking out unblinking on a world in agony.'[20] God is also a God who sends and as Coggan points out 'there is an unbroken chain from the creative word in Genesis 1 to those who Preach Sunday by Sunday.'[21] Finally this God who speaks and the God who sends is the God who feeds his people and this includes God's ministry from the pulpit 'where minds are stimulated, wills are touched, souls are nourished through the Ministry of the Word.'[22]

What then is Biblical Preaching? Biblical Preaching must be concerned with conveying the truth and its impact on the life of the congregation. For Preaching to be truly Biblical it must derive its message from some part or the whole of the Bible.

There are three ways in which Preachers today engage in Preaching which is not biblical.

(1). Treating a text as a pretext. We can all think of countless examples where the Preacher has already decided what he or she is going to say and the text is merely a pretext to get going. There may be some verbal connection or even theological connection between the text and the sermon, but in fact the substance of the sermon does not derive in any significant way from the text.

(2). Preaching a theological framework rather than the text. Again we know Preachers who have five or six sermons which convey their theological framework, and a function of the text of Scripture is to spark off a memory of the theological framework which the Preacher wants to convey yet again.

(3). Preaching between texts. This usually takes place when the Preacher reconstructs a Bible story or argument with a vivid use of imagination and the sermon derives its power and impetus from the gaps between the text which have been supplied by the Preacher's imagination. This is common in Preaching biblical stories by imagining the responses of various participants, in more traditional sermons this is marked by the

20. Donald Coggan, *Sacrament of the Word*, London, Collins, 1987, p.31
21. Coggan, *op. cit.*, p.32. 22. Coggan, *op. cit.*, p.32

classical phrase of Liberal Anglicanism – 'I like to think...'

Is it possible to engage in topical biblical Preaching? The best way to answer this questions is in terms of the following diagrams. In the usual form of an expository sermon we move from the text to the application.

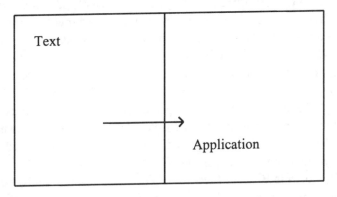

It is of course equally valid to begin with a topic and then to move from the text of Scripture to find a biblical view of the subject and then move to the application.

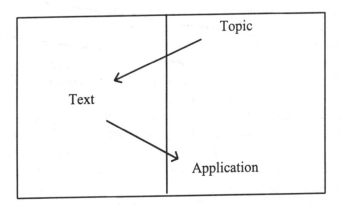

In fact with a topical sermon the sermon as heard looks as if it begins with the topic; but in terms of the Preacher's preparation his or her thinking about the topic will be informed by the Bible. So the preparation and the sermon can be characterised by the following diagram.

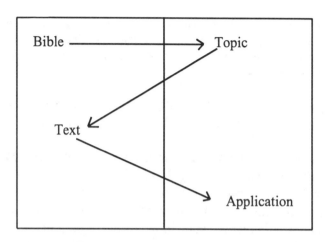

So Biblical Preaching can be *straightforwardly expository* where we begin with a text of Scripture and then explain it and apply it to the life of the congregation and to individuals to whom we're Preaching, or it may be topical in that we can begin the sermon with a topic. As I have shown we will still be doing biblical Preaching, in that our aim must be to apply what God has said in the Bible about the topic to the life of the congregation.

In my experience topical Preaching is very difficult and requires a lot more work than straightforward expository Preaching. The work involved is in thinking clearly about the topic in terms of our modern culture and then even more work in deciding what the Bible as a whole says about the topic. But good topical preaching is always exegetical, if not expository.

My appeal for Biblical Preaching is, of course, an appeal for a particular model of ministry. The model of the minister as student and teacher of the Word of God has now largely been replaced by the manager, the facilitator or the president, the social worker, the counsellor or the presenter of liturgy. I want to recall us to a model of ministry which has, I think, all but disappeared. John Stott describes Simeon's ministry in these terms:

> 'His over-riding concern was so to expound Scripture that his congregation would receive it undiluted and uncontaminated by worldly wisdom. To him "Biblical exposition" meant opening up some part of Scripture so that the people could feed upon it. "My endeavour," he wrote to his publisher, "is to bring out of Scripture what is there, and not to thrust in what I think might be there. I have a great jealousy on this head: never to speak more or less

than I believe to be the mind of the Spirit in the passage I am expounding." Those words seem to me to be the clearest statement ever made of the expositor's goal. Would that more Preachers could wholeheartedly echo and endorse it today!'[23]

My appeal is for such a Ministry of the Word especially in Biblical Preaching. We can further extend the appeal as follows.

3. An appeal for the Ministry of the Word in Pastoral Ministry, especially in *expository* Biblical Preaching

Haddon Robinson says 'expository Preaching is the communication of a Biblical concept derived from and transmitted through a historical, grammatical and literary study of a passage in its context, which the Holy Spirit first applies to the personality and experience of the Preacher, then through him to his hearers.'[24]

Or John Stott has recently described Preaching as 'to Preach is to open up the inspired text with such faithfulness and sensitivity that God's voice is heard and God's people obey him.'[25]

As we have seen, Preaching which in its presentation begins with a text of Scripture can be described as Biblical Preaching. So can Preaching which begins with a contemporary topic, as long as the Preacher's statement of the topic, treatment of the topic, and application of the Bible's teaching on the topic is faithful not only to the parts of Scripture but also to the whole. So my broad commitment is to Biblical Preaching. What then are the arguments for *expository* Biblical Preaching? That is, Preaching which in shape and substance *and in appearance* begins with a text of the Bible?

The motto of those who engage in expository Biblical Preaching must be 'let the Bible speak, let God speak'!

The best argument for expository Biblical Preaching, that is Preaching our way through a chapter of a book of the Bible or a whole book of the Bible, is that it allows us to take seriously the context of the passage on which we're Preaching. While it is perfectly possible to choose a passage from anywhere in the Bible and Preach on it, if we are to do the passage or text justice we must explain its context. The advantage of

---

23. *Evangelical Preaching: An anthology of sermons by Charles Simeon,* an introduction by John R.W. Stott, Multnomah Press, Portland, Oregon, 1986, p.xxxiii
24. Haddon W. Robinson, *Expository Preaching,* I.V.P., Leicester, 1986, p.20
25. John Stott, *The Contemporary Christian,* I.V.P., Leicester, 1992, p.208

expository Preaching is that there is some continuity of context, and people in our congregation can learn the salutary discipline of treating every text in its context.

Here context, of course, means historical context, theological context (the movement of salvation history), literary context, cultural context and intellectual context. One of the great features of the Bible is that we can see how much God respected the human authors in that he caused them to speak and write in a way which perfectly reflected their human, cultural and theological context, though they were not restricted by it. I believe that in our use of the Bible, especially in our public teaching of it, we ought to imitate God's respect for the human authors and not arbitrarily remove them from their context.

Another argument for expository Preaching is that it allows God to set the agenda for us. For the danger with topical Preaching is that we assume that our current issues are the real agenda.

It must be very confusing for newcomers to church services, who haven't been culturally conditioned to our way of doing things, to meet two, three or four readings from the Scripture which appear to be plucked at random from various pages of the Bible. It must be as disturbing as it would be for the average church-goer to attend the theatre for an evening of Shakespeare and hear a couple of lines from Hamlet, a scene from Richard III and a few helpful thoughts from Julius Caesar. The idea that we can take two, three or four readings from different parts of the Bible and stick them together is a form of liturgical fundamentalism in which we pay appropriate respect to the unity of Scripture deriving from the one mind of God, but fail to take note of the diversity of Scripture and God's respect for the different human authors and different contexts. One of the ironies of our lectionaries is that the more sophisticated and carefully thought-out the lectionary, the more dislocating they are to the average parishioner. If we are to have two of three readings in our services, I think the best lectionary form is one where there is not attempt to make any connection between them, but rather to work our way through different books of the Bible. My suspicion is that today it is probably more helpful to choose one book of the Bible and to try and take it seriously in the context of public Preaching and teaching.

Expository Biblical Preaching was found amongst the best Preachers of the early church – we can still read expository sermons of Augustine and Chrysostom. It is instructive to notice the reasons why expository Preaching died out after the time of Augustine and Chrysostom. Thomas K. Carroll characterises the changes in Preaching in the early church and, in particular, the move away from the expository Preaching of the Bible as occurring for the following reasons.

(1). Theological controversy meant that the sermon often became contentious doctrinal, point-scoring Preaching rather than the straightforward exposition of Scripture;

(2). The presence of the catechumenate, those being instructed in the faith, meant that Preaching often became more simple;

(3). The liturgical development in the early church meant that pressure built up to have thematic Preaching in liturgical seasons and also the greater liturgical complexity meant that there was less time for Preaching;

(4). The lowering standards of education among the clergy meant that many of them were unable to prepare biblical sermons.[26]

Are we suffering the same pressures today?

One of the great rediscoveries of the Reformation was of the importance of expository biblical Preaching, and Luther and Calvin both provided fine models for the Preachers of their own and subsequent generations.

In my opinion expository biblical Preaching ought to be the main pattern for church life. My own plan is to Preach on one Old Testament book, one Gospel and one Epistle each year. My longest series was on Hebrews which took me nine months, though I hasten to add that I Preached my way through Hebrews in three 3-month segments with a break before the second and third segment. It is also my rule to Preach on one difficult book of the Bible each year, because if we Preachers don't tackle difficult books in our Preaching, then it is very unlikely that our congregation will tackle them in their own Bible reading or home Bible studies.

One reason why I think that it is important for us to engage in the public expository Preaching ministry is because we want to model a good use of the Bible for our people, for one of our tasks as Preachers is to model good hermeneutics. If we want to encourage our people to read verses and chapters of the Bible in context then the best way to do that is to model it in our own Preaching.

However, I also try to make sure that I Preach one topical series each

26. Thomas K. Carroll, *Preaching the Word*, Michael Glazier, Wilmington, 1984, pp.63, 197, 206, 220

year ('Christians at Work', 'Current day issues') because, although we encourage our lay people to be able to read their Bibles intelligently and consecutively, it is also true that they need training in moving from an issue which they meet in daily life to the Bible and finding out the Bible's teaching on the subject. So the argument for Preaching a topical series is not only to demonstrate that the Preacher does live in the twentieth century, but also to model how lay people can move from a topic of everyday life to the Bible and find an answer to their dilemmas.

4. An appeal for the Ministry of the Word in Pastoral Ministry, especially in *applied* expository Preaching

Many people today react against expository Biblical Preaching because the model of expository Preaching which they have heard is little more than a theological lecture on a chapter in the Bible, a model of Preaching which never moves beyond the world of the Bible writers, a style in which there is so much attention to the text that there is no time to attend to the contemporary world. This is not the model of expository Biblical Preaching for which I am appealing.

I notice, for example, that when Paul has explained in 2 Timothy 3 the power and usefulness of Scripture in making us wise for salvation and for teaching, rebuking, correcting, and training in righteousness, the application that he makes of this doctrine is 'Preach the Word; be prepared in season and out of season; correct, rebuke and encourage – with great patience and careful instruction' (2 Timothy 4:2). That is, the use which Timothy is to make of Scripture is to apply it to the people in his care. He is to use it to correct, to rebuke and to encourage; and this will require both great patience and careful instruction.

There are, I think, three reasons why expository preachers don't engage in the task of applying the message of the Bible to their congregations.

The first is that people who are committed to Preaching and teaching the Word of God find that they spend so much time in understanding the text that they run out of time in working on the application for their hearers. Whenever I end a sermon with the immortal line 'and may God show us how to put this into practice in our lives', I know that I am admitting publicly that I haven't had the time to work out the implications of the text for the life of the congregation. The model which I recommend to others (though don't employ myself!) is to spend half my preparation time on the meaning of the text, understanding it clearly, and the other half in working out how it applies to the congregation. A good direction if not always a successful discipline!

The second reason why people don't apply the text is that they have the belief that the Bible is self-explanatory and contains its own application. Thus the argument runs that we have no need to attempt to apply the Bible to the congregation, since it is to attempt to do what has already been done by the Holy Spirit.

In thinking about this I have found Calvin's teaching on the significance of Christian ministry very helpful at this point. In his sermon on 2 Timothy 4:1, 2, Calvin writes:

> 'but yet God did not content himself to put forth the Holy Scripture that every man might study it, but he devised of his infinite goodness a second means to instruct us: and it is he would have the doctrine that is therein contained Preached and expounded to us: and for this end and purpose he hath appointed shepherds in his church which have the office in charge of teaching. This aid God thought good to add because of our rudeness (stupidity). It was already very much that he had given us his word and caused it to be written that everyone of us might read it and learn it. God showed himself herein very liberal toward us. But when we see he deals with us after our weakness and chews the morsels for us that we might digest them the better: to be short in that he feeds us as little children; we see thereby that we shall never be able to excuse ourselves unless we profit in his school. We might allege that the Holy Scripture is too hard for us if there were not some to expound it to us: but when God has given us both the means to which we might both read and hear, that every man may search and enquire of the truth as it is contained in the law and in the gospel: and moreover seeing we have messengers beside this which come and show us things at more large, and seeing God shows himself more familiar to us, ought not this break our hearts?'[27]

So Calvin sees that the task of the Preacher or teacher of the Bible is to explain it and apply it and encourage the hearers to receive it and obey it. Through the Preacher God accommodates himself to our weakness and humanity.

The third reason why people are reluctant to apply the Bible today is a growing assumption that the Bible is an ancient text and that to apply it to the twentieth Century is to engage in an impossible exercise. It is probably helpful to remember the phrase which so perfectly summa-

---

27. My modernised version of John Calvin's, *Sermons on Timothy & Titus*, facsimile 1579 edition, Banner of Truth Trust, Edinburgh, 1983, p.945

rises the way in which God addresses us in the Bible. The Bible is, as has been said, addressed *to them, for us*.

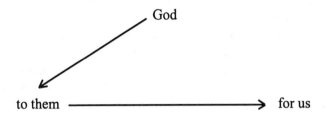

This double nature of the Bible is very important to keep in mind. Many people make the mistake of assuming the Bible is addressed directly to us and forget the need to understand it in its theological and historical context, that is it was written first of all *to them*.

On the other hand many today fall into the opposite trap and regard it as primarily *to them* and not written down *for us*. Paul describes the *to them, for us* link in these words, 'these things happened to them as examples and were written down as warnings for us on whom the fulfilment of the ages has come' (1 Corinthians 10:11). And as we have seen, he expects Timothy's ministry to consist in large part in rebuking and exhorting his hearers on the basis of the Word he has received.

The mood in many Anglican circles today is to accentuate 'the pastness of the past' and to see the Scriptures as documents of that past and to imply that the task of applying them to a modern congregation is not only inappropriate but also impossible. However it is important to identify the nature of the gap between the people of Bible times and ourselves. There is, of course, a gap in background information. We find it hard to understand what was happening at Corinth because we're listening to one part of a two way conversation. But a Christian at Rome would have had the same trouble. It is not an insurmountable barrier. We are also aware of the cultural and theological gap that exists between the assumptions of our own civilisation and culture, and the reality of that gap needs no underlining. However a similar, if not greater, gap existed between the Gentile polytheist and the world of the Old Testament monotheist Scriptures.

While I do not want to underplay the difficulties in applying the Scripture my assumptions are the following:

(1). Our main difficulty in applying Scripture is understanding how a particular text relates to the rest of the Bible, and this issue doesn't derive from a particular historical gap but from our need of a biblical theology, an overview of the whole counsel of God, as the context for our understanding Scripture.[28]

(2). The Bible's assumption is that we are in the same theological age as the Christians of the New Testament, we are those upon whom 'the fulfilment of the ages has come', we are in the 'last days'. Whereas people in the Old Testament were addressed in many and various ways by the prophets, in these 'last days' God has spoken to us by his Son. If the event of the Incarnation has been the decisive event of salvation history for the past 2,000 years, then that speaking of God about his Son also remains decisive.

(3). We are part of the historic people of God, called in Abraham, inheritors of the promises, a covenant people. There is a theological, historical and organic unity experienced by the people of God in every age, Jew and Gentile alike, and part of our shared inheritance is the Bible through which God addresses us all.[29]

My assumption then is that the Scripture was spoken by God *to them*, *for us*. My assumption must be that it does apply to the congregation, and that my task as a Preacher is to tease out that application and bring it with fervour and enthusiasm to the attention of the congregation so that they will respond with faith, repentance and obedience.

J.L. Packer in his excellent chapter Puritan Preaching[30] has indicated what a rich heritage evangelicals have in the Puritan tradition in its attention not only to the meaning of the text but also to its application, and he outlines many useful lessons on the way in which we might work on our application to our hearers. Packer comments:

'the Preacher's supreme concern was to bring men to know God. Their Preaching was avowedly "practical" and concerned with experience of God. Sin, the cross, Christ's heavenly ministry, the Holy Spirit, faith and hypocrisy, assurance and the lack of it, prayer, meditation, temptation, mortification, growth in grave, death, heaven, were their constant themes

28. see, for example, Graeme Goldsworthy, *According to Plan*, I.V.P./Lancer, Leicester, 1991
29. a useful practical guide to using the Bible is Andrew Reid, *Postcards from Palestine*, St. Matthias Press, Kingsford, N.S.W., 1989
30. J.I. Packer, *A Quest for Godliness: The Puritan vision of the Christian life*, Crossway Books, Wheaton, Illinois, 1990, ch.17

... Puritan Preaching was piercing in its applications. Over and above applicatory generalisations, the Preachers trained their homiletical search-lights on specific states of spiritual needs and spoke to these in a precise and detailed way.'[31]

In my plea for expository Preaching I am not appealing for Preaching which is removed from the life of the congregation and from their daily concerns, rather I am appealing for Preaching which under the sovereign hand of God brings the word of God to ordinary people in their ordinary lives.

An appeal for the Ministry of the Word in Pastoral Ministry especially in *passionately* applied expository Biblical Preaching
One of the common assumptions of our age is that intellect and emotion lie far apart within human personality and within human discourse.

I don't know how this assumed opposition has arisen but it has been powerfully effective within the Christian faith, particularly in our own century. The assumption is that intellectual argument must always be cold, rational and unemotional, and that to be emotional is to have left behind intellectual argument. A moment's reflection will help us to realise the falsehood of this assumption, for God is passionately concerned with the truth and is a passionate communicator of the truth as we can see on page after page of the Bible.

Expository Preaching has developed a tradition of being intellectual and therefore not emotional, and it is this tradition which I want to attack. I am trying to commend a kind of Preaching which is intellectual, that is concerned with ideas and the explanation of ideas and response to those ideas, but also Preaching which is passionate and emotional in its presentation.

The idea that we must separate intellect and emotion is a new one. I was very struck by reading again Hugh Evan Hopkin's biography of Charles Simeon to learn what a passionate Preacher Simeon was. Charles Simeon was Vicar of Holy Trinity Cambridge from 1782-1836 and most influential in the model of Preaching which he exemplified in his Sunday ministry and also which he taught through his voluminous writings. Simeon was an expository Preacher and his 26 volumes of expository outlines on the whole Bible indicate his commitment to the whole of Scripture. But he was also a passionate Preacher. The little

---

31. J.I Packer, *op.cit.*, p.286-7

girl's question, 'Oh Mamma, what is the gentleman in a passion about?' was a question about Charles Simeon in his Preaching.[32] We also read of an extraordinary beginning to one of Simeon's sermon. 'Once his text was "will a man rob God" (Malachi 3:8). With much deliberation he repeated it. Then looking around on the congregation he said, in tones that only Simeon could muster, "You have all robbed him" and pointing with his finger in various directions said "You! and you! and you!"'[33] If the Preacher's task is to communicate not only the theological content but also the style of the Bible, then the Preacher must be passionate.

In terms of the opposition which we assume between intellect and emotion we often solve the problem by attempting to meet in the middle, by being half intellectual and half emotional. I believe that the way forward is to be both intellectual and emotional in our Preaching. That is, to preach with a firm conviction about the truth and explanation of the truth and also to be passionate in our presentation of it.

As Martyn Lloyd-Jones wrote over 20 years ago:

'What is Preaching? Logic on fire. Eloquent reason ... a theology which does not take fire I maintain is a defective theology ... Preaching is theology coming through a man who is on fire. A true understanding and experience of the truth must lead to this. I say again that a man who can speak about these things dispassionately has no right whatever to be in a pulpit: and should never be allowed to enter one.'[34]

Discussions about Preaching often fall into the trap of when a cerebral and intellectual Preacher whose sermons are full of biblical content is told by a more emotional member of the congregation that his Preaching should be more emotional. He immediately interprets this as the statement that it should be more emotional and therefore have less cognitive content. He does not want to lost the content of his Preaching, so refuses to listen to the request. Or the emotional Preacher, who is challenged to have more Bible in his sermons, takes this as a request that he be less emotional and so will not accede to the request. I believe that Preaching can be both passionately applied, expository and biblical.

As the truth that we Preach comes from God, so the emotion and

32. Hugh Evan Hopkins, *Charles Simeon of Cambridge*, Hodder & Stoughton, London, 1977, p.65
33. Hopkins, op.cit., p.63
34. D. Martyn Lloyd-Jones, *Preaching and Preachers*, Hodder & Stoughton, 1985, p.97

passion that we convey in our Preaching also comes from God.

> 'It is within the church, as the pastor fulfils his holy ministry in word and sacrament, that God draws near to us as he did to them. "God himself appears ... and required his presence to be recognised in our midst." Even though such a treasure is given to us in "earthen vessels" nevertheless in the hearing of the Preached word within the church we hear the same voice as they heard. We "listen not only to his minister speaking but to himself." So real and personal is his presence in such an encounter today that to deny or resit it would be like blotting out the face of God which indeed shines through such teaching.'[35]

God is present in his truth and power and we poor Preachers must do our best not to stand in the way of the God who is present and addresses his people through our mouths.

In this chapter I have drawn attention to current difficulties in the area of Preaching and made an appeal for the Ministry of the Word in parish ministry, especially in passionately applied expository Biblical Preaching.

Let me repeat John Stott's appeal:

> 'Where are the Timothy's of the next generation? Where are the young evangelical men and women, who are determined by God's grace to stand firm in the Scripture, refusing to be swept off their feet by the prevailing winds of fashion, who are resolved to continue in it and live by it, relating the words to the world in order to obey it, and who are committed to passing it on, as they give themselves to the ministry of conscientious exposition.'[36]

Or, how are we teaching, training, encouraging, and nurturing faithful preachers and teachers who will be able to teach others also? (2 Timothy 2:2)[37]

---

35. Ronald S. Wallace, *Calvin's approach to theology*, in Nigel M.deS. Cameron, editor, The Challenge of Evangelical Theology, Rutherford House Books, Edinburgh, 1987, p.125
36. John Stott, *The Contemporary Christian*, op. cit., p.172
37. I am grateful to Janis Lampard and John Altmann for help in writing this chapter.

9

Lay Administration of the Lord's Supper:
A change to stay the same[1]
John Woodhouse

Evangelicals must be committed to practising what they preach. We cannot be content with practices which obscure or distort the gospel. This is why many Anglican evangelicals today are urging the removal of the prohibition which restricts the administration of the Lord's Supper to ordained priests.

The prohibition has no basis in Scripture. Indeed it is remarkable that a role which is not even mentioned in the New Testament should have become so important in the minds of many. There are some who suggest that a change in this matter, on which Scripture is completely silent, is more radical than any of the changes in church belief and practice over the last 400 years. Article VI brings a truer perspective:

> Holy Scripture containeth all things necessary to salvation: so that whatsoever is not read therein, nor may be proved thereby, is not required of any man, that it should be believed as an article of the Faith, or be thought requisite or necessary to salvation.

The problem perceived by many evangelicals is that the prohibition of lay persons from ever administering the Lord's Supper suggests to many in our churches (and to many outside our churches) that:

(a) there is something about an ordained priest that gives him/her the power to pray the prayer of consecration – a power which a lay person cannot have;

(b) higher qualifications are needed for the administration of the Lord's Supper than for preaching the Word of God – lay persons can often do the latter, but never the former;

(c) the validity of the Supper depends somehow on the person

---

1. This paper is a revision and expansion of a speech given to the Synod of the Diocese of Sydney in October, 1994 moving the second reading of a bill for an ordinance enabling lay persons and deacons to be authorised to administer the Lord's Supper. Readers will note that aspects of the original genre have not been entirely eliminated!

administering it – a priest (*any* priest) is needed to make the occasion authentic;

(d) ordination has more to do with the Sacrament than with preaching – a priest can share his preaching ministry with competent lay persons, but not his ministry of administering the Lord's Supper; and

(e) a priest is *essential* to the conduct of the Lord's Supper – though not essential for any other event in church life.

In each of these ways the practise of absolutely prohibiting a non-priest from administering the Lord's Supper contradicts, or at the very least obscures, the gospel we preach.

A change to stay the same
There are times when you have to change in order to stay the same. In order to remain true to fundamental principles there are times when the forms which express those fundamentals must change. Forms which performed one function at one time and in one context must be open to change if that same function is not to be obscured and hampered at another time and in another context.

The Book of Common Prayer itself insists that forms should change 'according to the various exigencies of times and occasions'[2]:

'There was never any thing by the wit of man so well devised, or so sure established, which in continuance of time hath not been corrupted.'[3]

The Book of Common Prayer recognises that there are things that 'at the first were of godly intent and purpose devised, and yet at length turned to vanity and superstition'[4].

It is the contention of this paper that the absolute prohibition of any person who is not an ordained priest from administering the Lord's Supper was 'at the first of godly intent and purpose devised', but 'yet at length (has) turned to vanity and superstition'.

It is helpful to distinguish the prohibition itself (which I will call a 'form') from its effects ('function'). The function of the prohibition today is very different from its function in the 16th and 17th centuries.

Consider the restrictions that surrounded public ministry in 1662. The Book of Common Prayer envisaged no lay ministry of the Word or the Lord's Supper. However

2. From The Preface.
3. From Concerning the Service of the Church.
4. From Of Ceremonies: why some be abolished, and some retained.

It appertaineth to the office of a Deacon ... to assist the Priest in Divine
Service, and specially when he ministereth the holy Communion, and to
help him in the distribution thereof, and to read holy Scriptures and
Homilies in the Church ... and to preach if he be admitted thereto by the
Bishop.[5]

It is not clear how extensive the involvement of the deacon in the
Lord's Supper might have been. The rubrics of the Order for the
Administration of the Lord's Supper specifically indicate that it was to
be the priest who said/read:

The Lord's Prayer
The Collect
The Ten Commandments
The Collect for the Queen
The Epistle
The Gospel
The Offertory Sentence(s)
The general Prayer for 'the whole state of Christ's Church militant
here in earth'
The Exhortation (at the time of the celebration of the Communion)
The call to repentance
The Absolution (said by the Bishop, if present)
The comfortable words
'It is meet, right, and our bounded duty ...'
The prayer of humble access
The Prayer of Consecration
The Lord's Prayer
The Blessing (said by the Bishop, if present)

It is particularly interesting to note that the Prayer of Consecration
is one of many items which, according to the rubrics, are to be said by
the priest. The 1662 Act of Uniformity made it clear that only those who
had been episcopally ordained priest may 'consecrate and administer
the holy sacrament of the Lord's Supper'. However, it is now commonly
accepted in many parts of the Anglican Communion that a person other
than the priest (a deacon or an authorised lay person) may say/read
several of the above items, but never the Prayer of Consecration. It is not

5. From The Form and Manner of Making of Deacons.

clear why the rubric to that prayer has popularly been given more weight than the others. Restricting that prayer to the priest, except on the same grounds that virtually the whole liturgy is restricted to him, has no basis in The Book of Common Prayer.

In 1662 the prohibition against non-priests from administering the Lord's Supper, expressed in the Act of Uniformity, was part and parcel of the restriction of all public ministry to the clergy. Only clergy had any part in the public ministry of the Word of God and the Sacrament of the Lord's Supper. There is no concept in the Book of Common Prayer of a lay person ever taking any part in the public liturgy of the church. Those who appeal to 'Anglican Order' must be very clear that in 1662 'Anglican Order' excluded lay persons from any part in public ministry. Certainly they were excluded from preaching, but also from leading Morning or Evening Prayer, reading the Scriptures in church, and so on.

In 1662 there was a hedge around *all* public ministry of Word and Sacrament. It was a big hedge. And it would be appropriate to describe this as a form with a 'godly intent and purpose'. In a day of widespread illiteracy, limited theological understanding – certainly among the laity – and a recently reformed church, the purpose and function of this restriction was to guard the public ministry of the gospel from corruption. It was a kind of quality control.

It is important to understand that in the 16th and 17th centuries in the Church of England, the fact that only priests could administer the Lord's Supper was not based on the idea that only priests, by virtue of their episcopal ordination, had the power to administer the Supper. Even a casual reading of Thomas Cranmer on the Lord's Supper will dispel that idea. Neither was it some concept of the 'president of the community' who was the right person to 'preside' at the Lord's Supper. That is a novel idea in Anglicanism, and has never been the practice. It is not that the Rector (or equivalent) must do it. There has never been an objection to assistant priests, or visiting priests administering the Sacrament. The issue in the 16th and 17th centuries was quality control. Only priests could do it. But not necessarily the Rector. And the same rule applied to *all* public ministry in church.

Canon 56 of the Canons of 1603 illustrates this last point. This canon envisages a minister who has 'cure and charge of souls', and who may 'chiefly attend to preaching', having 'a Curate under him to execute the other duties which are to be performed for him in the Church'. These duties included the administration of the Lord's Supper. The canon prescribes that such a minister must himself read the Divine Service and administer the Lord's Supper at least twice a year! On all other occasions 'the Curate under him' may perform this duty for him. There is no suggestion that the Lord's Supper should normally be administered by the minister 'that hath cure and charge of souls'.

Too much of the modern debate has departed far from a reformed understanding of ministry and sacraments. Thomas Cranmer discussed the distinction between priests and lay people in relation to the Lord's Supper in terms that are relevant to the present debate:

> Therefore Christ made no such difference between the priest and the layman, that the priest should make oblation and sacrifice of Christ for the layman, and eat the Lord's Supper from him, all alone and distribute and apply it as him liketh. Christ made no such difference; but the difference that is between the priest and the layman in this matter is only in the ministration; that the priest, as a common minister (i.e. servant) of the Church, doth minister and distribute the Lord's Supper unto other, and other receive it at his hands. ... As in a prince's house the officers and ministers (i.e. servants) prepare the table, and yet other, as well as they, eat the meat and drink the drink; so do the priests and ministers prepare the Lord's Supper, read the Gospel, and rehearse Christ's words; but *all the people* say thereto, Amen; *all* remember Christ's death, *all* give thanks to God, *all* repent and offer themselves an oblation to Christ, *all* take him for their Lord and Saviour, and spiritually feed upon him; and in token thereof, they eat the bread and drink the wine in his mystical (i.e. symbolic) Supper.[6]

Cranmer went to great lengths to play down the significance of the role of the priest at the Supper, and to emphasise that all that matters as we eat and drink together in remembrance of Christ's death, we all do together. The priest, like a servant in a king's house, prepares the Supper, and serves both the Word and the symbol of the Word. It is clear that Cranmer not only never did, but he never would call the priest's role in the Lord's Supper 'presidency'!

However, for the purpose of guarding the public ministry of Word and sacrament, it was *all* restricted to the clergy: essentially to priests, with some assistance from deacons.

While that wide restriction in the 16th and 17th centuries can be regarded as 'of godly intent and purpose devised', that does not mean

---

6. A Defence of the True and Catholick Doctrine of the Sacrament, Book V, chapter XI ('The difference between the priest and the layman'). Emphases added.

that it can or should be retained at the end of the 20th century. Today we are blessed with many gifted and highly educated, theologically qualified lay people. While oversight of congregations is still rightly entrusted to fully trained and recognised ordained persons, competent lay persons now share in the public ministry of the Word, and of prayer, and indeed often play some public role in the ministry of the Lord's Supper (such as assisting in distribution, or leading some of the prayers). This development has been largely uncontroversial and beneficial to us all.

Therefore the form ('Anglican order' if you like) has already changed radically, for the very good reason that today to restrict all public ministry to the clergy only would be to rob the church of much quality ministry. To insist that this further change is objectionable, because it is 'contrary to Anglican order' fails to appreciate the enormous changes that have already (and properly) taken place.

However a remnant of the old general prohibition remains. One aspect of public ministry still has that hedge about it. The hedge made sense when it surrounded all public ministry and, so to speak, protected it from ignorant and incompetent lay persons. But the hedge makes no sense when it is left around only one aspect of public ministry, and protects it from highly competent and knowledgable lay persons who share in church leadership in every other conceivable way under the oversight of the Rector.

Today the prohibition no longer serves its original function, and indeed works against the very theology which gave rise to it. It has, in the words of the Book of Common Prayer, 'at length turned to vanity and superstition'. Go back to the Reformation, and you will not find the ministry of the sacrament separated off from the ministry of the Word like this, as though a higher qualification is needed for administering the Lord's Supper than for preaching. Indeed, if anything, you will only find the reverse. Martin Luther wrote 'the man to whom has been committed the office of preaching has committed to him the highest office in the Christian Church. He may also baptise, say mass ...'[7]

To remove the absolute prohibition that has become part of Anglican church life would be to express an understanding of both ministry and the sacraments that is closer to our Anglican formularies. This is one of those times when it is important to change in order to stay the same.

---

7. 'The Right and Power of a Christian Congregation or Community to Judge all Teaching and to call, appoint, and dismiss Teachers, established and proved from Scripture' (1523) in The Works of Martin Luther, volume 4 (Philadelphia, 1931), p.84.

Not 'presidency'

Some confusion has come into the discussion of lay involvement with the Sacrament of the Lord's Supper, by the use of the term 'presidency'. The word is unhelpful for a number of reasons.

Firstly, 'president' is not a term found in the New Testament or The Book of Common Prayer, and its first known relevant use (by Justin Martyr in his *First Apology*) seems to be a reference to the regular head of the congregation in terms that would be understood by outsiders.[8] The Book of Common Prayer speaks of 'ministering' or 'administering' the Sacrament, a rather different concept.

Secondly, it has become usual to see the term 'president' to refer to the person who leads the people on a particular liturgical occasion (such as the Lord's Supper). The confusion arises because others (probably including Justin Martyr) refer to the 'president of the community', an ongoing role, not restricted to any particular occasion. The matter under consideration has been whether the only person who can 'preside' (in the former sense) is the 'president of the community'. Some have suggested that any 'presidency' exercised by a lay person will undermine the 'presidency' of the priest. This can be more clearly considered if different terms are used for the two concepts.

Thirdly, it is worth noting that even now a lay person can (and probably does occasionally) 'preside' (in an ordinary sense of the word) at the Lord's Supper quite legally, and without controversy. If, say, in the absence of the Rector, a lay person welcomes the congregation, and leads them in the first part of the liturgy (the 'Ante-Communion'), but invites a visiting priest to say the Prayer of Consecration, and to distribute the elements with the lay person's help, many would regard the lay person as the 'president' of that gathering on that occasion.

Fourthly, lay administration of the Lord's Supper should acknowledge the oversight that rightly belongs to the priest to whose 'cure and charge' the people have been committed. The Rector remains the 'president' of the congregation, but the particular service, at the 'president's' direction, is carried out by a lay person. Like all lay (and diaconal) ministry, this ministry would be 'assisting the priest'. The term 'presidency' for 'administration' tends to obscure this fact.

Fifthly, in the administration of the Lord's Supper the focus is not on the minister, but (as Cranmer emphasised) on the corporate act of

---

8. I owe this observation to D.W.B. Robinson in an unpublished paper 'Presidency and Assistance in Ministering Word and Sacrament: A Note'.

remembering the Lord's death through the total activity of the thanks-giving, distributing and eating together. The term 'presidency' tends to give too much weight to the role of the minister.

What about our 'order'?
Some who agree that there are no theological objections to lay admin-istration of the Lord's Supper, nevertheless object that such a 'novelty' would be contrary to Anglican 'order'. 'Order' is a word used in a number of different ways in this debate.

Sometimes 'order' means 'order' as opposed to chaos! What would the proposed change do to our relationships with other Anglicans, and to our relationships with other denominations, particularly the Roman Catholics?

It should be remembered that the Anglican Communion already lives with considerable diversity of opinion and practice. With good will and respect for sincerely held convictions, there is no reason for this change to be of greater concern than other differences. Indeed to suggest that this is the change which we *cannot* make would imply that what binds Anglicans together is some common sacramental theology – and that a theology which few evangelicals could endorse. These remarks apply with even more force to our relationships with the Roman Catholic denomination.

By 'order' others mean the ordering of ministry in the Anglican Church. Specifically there is commitment to the three 'orders' of bishop, priest, and deacon.

To think that lay administration of the Lord's Supper will be more damaging to these orders than lay preaching has been, suggests that ordination is more about the Sacraments than it is about preaching. This view cannot be supported from either the New Testament or The Book of Common Prayer.

In The Book of Common Prayer ordination to the priesthood authorises a person to oversee a congregation: 'how great a treasure (the sheep of Christ) is *committed to your charge*', 'the people *committed to your charge*', 'the people *committed to your cure and charge*', 'them that are or shall be *committed to your charge*'. This oversight is certainly exercised through preaching the Word of God and ministering the Sacraments, but just as a person may be competent to preach sermons from time to time, without all the training and gifts necessary for full time pastoral oversight of the congregation, so such a person may be fully competent to administer the Lord's Supper from time to time, without either being ready to be ordained, or threatening the significance of ordination.

Still others use 'order' as a way of referring to custom. Some feel that it is just too great a change from the way in which Anglicans have always done things and the practice which The Book of Common Prayer prescribes. Some may like to call such custom 'tradition'. This is misleading. Theologically the 'tradition' of the Christian Church is the Scriptures. Custom, however ancient, must never be elevated to the level of 'tradition'.

Quite clearly what is being proposed is a change in our customary ways. It is yet another change from the ways prescribed in The Book of Common Prayer. However to object to this charge, but to accept lay preaching and many other changes to the ways of the church in the 16th and 17th centuries is arbitrary and unjustified.

So long as there are sound theological objections to our present 'order', appeals to maintain that 'order' (in any of these senses) are not compelling, and amount to merely unprincipled conservatism.

The place of the Lord's Supper in church life
The Lord's Supper is an important occasion to which 'all such as shall be religiously and devoutly disposed'[9] should come, and 'the people negligent to come'[10] should be exhorted 'that ye will not refuse to come thereto, being so lovingly called and bidden by God himself.'[11] The reasons given in the second Exhortation in the Order for the Administration of the Lord's Supper are that to refuse to come when God himself has bidden you is shameful, and a neglect of duty. 'Sore punishments hang over your heads for the same; when ye wilfully abstain from the Lord's Table, and separate from your brethren ...'

The proposal to allow persons other than a priest to administer the Lord's Supper has led some to reconsider the place of the Sacrament in the life of the church. Some have found support for the present prohibition in a notion that the Lord's Supper is a complete occasion in which the whole community is involved, and where the appropriate 'president' must be the one with pastoral oversight (the priest). This reasoning rests on two fictions.

---

9. From the first Exhortation in The Order for the Administration of the Lord's Supper.
10. From the rubric preceding the second Exhortation.
11. From the second Exhortation.

Fiction 1: that the administration of the Lord's Supper is restricted to the one with pastoral oversight. This (as was pointed out earlier) is not, and has never been, the case. An assistant minister, who is a priest, or a visiting priest can and frequently administer the Sacrament. An assistant minister who is a deacon or a lay person cannot.

Fiction 2: that the Lord's Supper is the essential expression of the whole community's life. This, too, seems to be a novel invention to support a custom that has arisen without any such rationale. The Book of Common Prayer has no such notion. 'Every parishioner shall communicate at least three times in the year.'[12] Only three persons need to be present. If a sick person 'be not able to come to the Church'[13] the Lord's Supper can be administered in the sick man's house. In special circumstances a minister may communicate with a sick person with no one else present. The Book of Common Prayer does not suggest that the Lord's Supper is *the* expression of the community life.

Of course there are occasions where it is most appropriate for the one entrusted with the 'cure of souls' in that place to administer the Sacrament, just as there are occasions when it is most appropriate for the Rector to preach. However to extend the argument to say that the Lord's Supper is *always* such an occasion cannot be sustained.

Conclusion

Change is always difficult, particularly significant change. Change will nearly always be resisted. Change causes unease among some. So we need to take great care with change. But because change will often feel uncomfortable at the start, even change that is called for by sound principles requires a bit of courage. I have tried to work out why some people are uneasy about *this* change.

I have a theory. When you are clear about why you do what you do, then you can be relaxed about changing the forms when this is necessary and helpful.

For example: evangelicals are generally pretty clear about the purpose of preaching in church. The sermon serves the function of teaching or proclaiming the Word of God, of enabling God's people (and others) to hear God's Word. Since we are clear about the function of preaching, we have had little difficulty coping with a radical change to the form, namely allowing certain lay persons to preach. We can see

---

12. From the rubrics at the end of The Order for the Administration of the Lord's Supper.
13. From the rubric at the beginning of The Communion of the Sick.

nowadays that it does not necessarily damage the purpose of preaching. Because we understand the *purpose* clearly, we have no difficulty accepting proper changes to the *form*, so that it can function even better. Indeed I think that most of us can see that to insist that today's preaching be surrounded by the same restrictions, and take the same form as in the Church of England in the 16th and 17th centuries would, be to hinder the very purpose for which preaching was shaped in the 16th century.

However when you are less clear about why you do what you do, you can find yourself focusing on the form, and thinking that the form matters *in itself*. I take it that that is why we hear people saying 'It's against Anglican *order*.' But it can only be 'against' Anglican order if you think that the form is unchangeable. Then lay preaching would be against Anglican order. Lay persons reading Morning Prayer would be against Anglican order. Lay persons taking any part whatsoever in public liturgy would be against Anglican order. But The Book of Common Prayer rejects the notion that forms are unchangeable.

I believe that because we are much less clear about the *function* of administering the Lord's Supper than we are about the function of preaching, we feel that this is a more dramatic change in our way of doing things than allowing lay preachers was.

But we are less clear for good reason. The role of the priest in the Lord's Supper, as Cranmer insisted, is not itself important. Of all the ministries mentioned in the New Testament, there is not a word about who should take the leading role at the Lord's Supper, not a word to elders or anyone else that they should do it. That role is relatively unimportant since the focus is not on what that person does, but on the corporate act of remembering the Lord's death together.

Once that is clear, I believe we can see that the change in form will be good and will help people to understand the gospel better. The prohibition as it stands is one of those things that, in the words of the Book of Common Prayer, 'at the first was of godly intent and purpose devised, and yet at length has turned to vanity and superstition.' If that is so it *must* be removed, for the sake of the gospel.

I suspect that it will turn out to be a bit like a church I attended in the 1960's, where the priest did *everything* except take up the collection. And that was only done by the wardens. It was unthinkable that anyone else would take up the collection, or that a lay person would read the lesson. We probably thought it was illegal, or at least contrary to church 'order'. Gradually people came to accept that it was not only *legal*, but it was *good* for unnecessary and theologically groundless taboos to be removed from our church life. It helped us (and, importantly, others) to understand the truth of the gospel better. So will the removal of this one.

A bibliography

Adams, W.S. 'The Eucharistic Assembly: Who Presides?', *Anglican Theological Review*, 1982.

Beckwith, R.T. 'Lay Celebration of Communion' (Latimer Comment 49, 1994?)

Beckwith, R.T. *Priesthood and Sacraments*, Latimer Monograph 1, (Appleford, 1964)

Boff, L. 'The Lay Coordinator and the Celebration of the Lord's Supper', *Ecclesiogenesis,* 1986.

Bradshaw, P. *Liturgical Presidency in the Early Church* (Bamcote, Notts., 1983)

Bromiley, G.W. *Sacramental Teaching and Practice in the Reformed Churches* (Grand Rapids, 1957)

Chadwick, H. 'Church Leadership in History and Theology' in *Senior Church Appointments* (Church House Publishing, London, 1992)

Chadwick, H. 'Some Theological and Historical Consideration' in *Senior Church Appointments* (Church House Publishing, London, 1992)

Chapman, J. 'Lay Presidency at the Holy Communion' in *Agenda for a Biblical Church II* (Sydney, 1982)

Cocksworth, C.J. *Evangelical Eucharistic Thought in the Church of England* (Cambridge, 1993)

Cranmer, T. *A Defence of the True and Catholick Doctrine of the Sacrament.*

Hargrave, A. *But who will preside?* (Bamcote, Notts., 1990)

Harvey, A.E. *Priest or President* (London, 1975)

Legrand, H.M. 'The Presidency of the Eucharist According to the Ancient Tradition', *Worship,* 1979

Lloyd, T. *Lay Presidency at the Eucharist?* (Bamcote, Notts., 1977)

Pryor, J. 'Lay Presidency and Ordained Ministry Today', *St Mark's Review*, 138 (1989)

Roffey, J. 'The theology and Practice of Lay Ministry', *St Mark's Review,* 138 (1989)

Schillebeeckx, E. 'The Christian Community and its Office Bearers', *Concilium,* 1980

Speagle, H.L. *The Culture of Change* (Brunswick, 1993)

Sykes, S & Booty, J. *The Study of Anglicanism* (London, 1988)

10

THE WORD IN THE AGE OF THE IMAGE
THE CHALLENGE TO EVANGELICALS

Os Guinness[1]

Introduction

President Lyndon B Johnson, who was not exactly the most spiritual of the USA presidents, used to tell an amazing number of preacher stories. One of them was of a Baptist minister who, having prepared an elaborate sermon for church one Sunday, dropped his notes on the way to the service only to have them eaten by a passing dog. On entering the pulpit he turned to his congregation and confessed: 'I am sorry, but I have no sermon today. I will have to speak as the Spirit directs, but I promise to do better next week'!

Sadly, that is a situation not so far removed from the reality that happens in a good many places Sunday by Sunday. After several years in the United States, I would have to say that I have never known an English-speaking country where the churches are so full and the sermons are, by and large, so empty. Furthermore, as I survey the British scene, one of my sorrows as an Englishman is to see the missing generation of preachers coming after the John Stotts, the Dick Lucases and the Martyn Lloyd-Joneses of this world. I would wish to add my voice as a layman to the many others who have a deep hunger and burning desire for a better proclamation of the Word of God in our time. However, if evangelicals are to see this happen, then it is important that we understand what are some of the surrounding cultural influences which have led to the general malaise in present day western preaching. That is the burden of this chapter.

Just over a hundred years ago, in one of his first novels entitled *White Jacket*, Herman Melville wrote of a ships' surgeon by the name of Dr Cuticle. In the story, one of the sailors was struck by acute appendicitis which was seen by the surgeon to be something of a gift to him, causing him great delight that he had something more challeng-

---

1. Originally given as a lecture at the 1988 Evangelical Ministry Assembly.

ing to attend to other than blisters. And so with the help of the other sailors, Dr Cuticle stretched out his patient and began to perform the elaborate operation. As he did so, he explained point by point what he was doing thus suitably impressing his captivated audience, except that when he had finished, his patient was dead – and he had not even noticed.

At roughly the same time, Edgar Alan Poe wrote a story about an artist who was so obsessed with the quest of capturing life in his canvases that he took from his mistress's body the colour and all he needed for his painting. In his enthusiasm he failed to notice that by his actions he was draining the very life out of her until eventually he came to the end of his great painting and triumphantly declared, 'Ah, life itself.' As he turned to his mistress, she died.

Those are just two writers of the nineteenth century who began to see something devastating starting to take place little more than a hundred years ago. What they were observing and, in their own way commentating on, could be applied to biblical exposition. We know far more Hebrew than Jerome, much more historical-critical methodology than Augustine, much deeper background of culture than Calvin. We can brandish our Greek and Hebrew and wield our sophisticated 'hermeneutics', but, at the end of the day, the subject of our attention is, largely in the modern church, lifeless and might just as well be a corpse.

While that is true, there is a much wider application of what the artists of the nineteenth century were trying to capture. It was the premonition that at the heart of what people saw as the Industrial Revolution there was a part of it of immense significance. It was what was later to be known as the 'Graphics Revolution'. It is this revolution which through technology allows us to proliferate images of all kinds and has recently been described as 'the greatest mutation in human experience since the Stone Age'. Of course, we now live at the end of it when the revolution is almost complete. We are part of the generation in which the image has triumphed over the word, when the visual is dominant over the verbal and where entertainment drowns out exposition. We may go so far as to claim that we live in the age of the image which is also the age of the anti-word and which potentially is the age of the lie.

Jacques Ellul writes that 'Anyone today wishing to save humanity must first of all save the word'. That is true, but it also applies on smaller levels too, to democracy and supremely to the church. Anyone today wishing to save the church must first of all save the word. The crisis of the word is not simply a theological crisis, it is a crisis facing Western civilisation in general and must be viewed within its broadest context.

In this chapter we shall be examining the nature of this 'word crisis' flowing out of the graphics revolution. In so doing special attention will be paid to the shift that has taken place, the significance it occasions and what the shape of our response might be.

The shift from word to image
The shift in the graphics revolution is not a matter of philosophy, theology, ideas or choice. It is a matter of technology.

Let us think back to the pre-modern age. Of course images existed then. Evidence the cave paintings of southern France, the stain glass windows of the European cathedrals and the myriad of sculptures around the world. But to most pre-modern people the main image was nature. But even then nature was not an image in our sense of the word because it wasn't a mere spectacle. The people knew it to be source of their life as well as potential threat to their existence. Therefore, although nature was the main image in the pre-modern world it was never reduced to a mere object, a sort of visual muzak of the eyes. For most people images were very rare for there were no reproductions or photographs. Indeed, until very late there were no museums, so whatever images there were (and there were some connected with worship in the churches or in the houses of the wealthy) they were a rarity. Accordingly, it was an easy world for the word to prosper; story, dialogue and conversation were dominant in an age before the printing press.

All that is now a thing of the past. The world of fields, hedges, woods and rivers has been replaced by a world of a million images which are so normal and familiar to us that we don't realise how revolutionary the revolution has been. Consider: photographs, reproductions, signs, billboards, bumper stickers, comic books, charts, diagrams, labels, logos, ads, trade marks, computer print outs – every day we live with this constant diet – a bombardment of millions upon millions of images.

The two strongest examples come from advertising and television, but it is important to stress that these are only the two most prominent of what is all around us functioning on many levels. Consider advertising.

A century or so ago, there was almost no advertising. And the advertising which did exist was produced by the retailers, not the producers, and was factual and brief – a little like the classified ads of today. Suddenly, through the technological revolution and the creation of the age of abundance, everything was transformed. Ads changed their appearance from a few lines to half pages, even full pages. Black and white turned to colour and suddenly millions upon millions of pounds was being spent on advertising because no longer was supply coupled with demand, one could now *create* a demand to equal the new supply. Advertising was the natural response to the age of abundance. But as advertising grows, as we see especially in the highly developed commercial countries like the USA, it become one of the primary institutions of society. So while one may have the church, the university, the army and other primary institutions, advertising takes its place alongside them all but ranks as the *key shaping* institution in the western world. And yet it is the only one with no social purpose or moral responsibility. The others may betray their ideals but a least they have them, whereas advertising has only one basic demand – to get people to consume.

The very shaping of advertising has actually changed the nature of our discourses and perceptions in a variety of subtle ways. Take the way it has changed our thinking.

At the turn of the century it was pointed out that if you wanted to advertise to a whole nation then you had to take symbols and uncouple them from thinking and use them to drive emotions. In other words, there are three simple maxims underlying advertising:

1. Simplify thought
2. Intensify emotions
3. Magnify symbols.

By doing this one can go wide and deep, but also the logic and language of advertising militates against any thinking in a way that is rational and critical. When the early advertising came it was said: 'It no longer engages the mind, it merely fixes the attention'. This was quite deliberate. The aim was not to find an audience to hear the message but to find a message that would hold the audience.

Television is almost too easy as a bogeyman to attack today, but one can see in its forerunners how it has the same effect.

The two forerunners of television are the telegraph and the photograph. The essence of the telegraph can be summarised as 'the instant', and the essence of the photograph is 'the image' and both were very fateful switches.

With the advent of the telegraph we have the instant which meant that for the very first time there was no link between transportation and communication. No one had to run, no horses had to gallop, no pigeon had to fly – the message was instantly transmitted and instantly received. Consequently, it created the potential to have accumulation of knowledge without assessment.

Equally with the photograph, the switch from the word to the image took us away from the world of the abstract into the world of the concrete. Matters are not usually debated in the concrete world, they are simply documented. Things are not necessarily understood, they are just recognised.

The television can therefore be conceived as a blending of the 'instant' to the 'image' in the most powerful technology we now know. But again an extraordinary shaping of the way things are perceived takes place.

Many of our best British television producers have wrestled with the fact that television because of its nature as a medium, allows the viewer no context. It is fast, superficial and arresting. But without context there is no wisdom or deep understanding. When we come to the high influence of the commercial on television it becomes even more incoherent. In other words, in just one hundred years we have moved from a world where the word was largely dominant and images comparatively few, to a world where the image is dominant and the word has changed from being an authority to an accessory – an accessory to the image. That is the enormity of the shift in the graphics revolution.

The significance

It is self-evident that words and images, sight and sound are inseparable and complementary. But nonetheless there are differences and any culture that stresses the one at the expense of the other is bound to have certain detrimental results in the long run. Here are Ellul's view of the differences.

First, sight is largely intentional while sound is largely involuntary. Think of sight. We have to open our eyes, but we can shut them too. We turn our heads or we turn away. We direct our gaze or we don't bother. In other words, in seeing we are the subject, the ones in control, those at the centre of our own universe.

That is not the way it happens with sound. Sound *comes* to us and we receive it immediately. We are the ones *addressed* whether we like it or not. We may be aware of our ability or willingness to respond or not to what we hear, but the experience casts us back in a very different sense of who we are as human agents in the world.

Secondly, sight largely deals with the space, while sound essentially deals with time. We see an image, we see a picture, we see something on television and it is all there *now*. We can ask: 'What is just over the horizon?' but that type of question comes as a secondary extra thought, it is not a natural one inherent to the phenomena of seeing. Our mind is immediately taken up with what we see.

This is not so with sound.

If someone is speaking to us and they stop mid-sentence, we say 'What next?' 'Go on', because underlying the meaning of sound is the fact that words flow in time. It is a sequential, directional movement.

Thirdly, sights are largely effortless whereas sounds are often demanding. We can study a painting or a photograph, but very few of us do. We tend to take them in at a glance with an almost intuitive comprehensiveness that is effortless and which seems so certain. Seeing, we are told, is believing. But sound, because it comes in sequence, has to be at a certain speed or we cannot take it in and it demands that we stand back and listen to it. Monologues, dialogues, conversations are more demanding and those who do not think so are often shallow.

Fourthly, sights and images are more to do with appearances while sound and words take us into meaning. This is not say that sights are lies and words are always truth, but it is to maintain that the world of sight, the world of the eye, cannot take us *beyond* what is shown. It takes words to tease out meanings that go beyond the immediate, the apparent, or the demonstrable. Indeed, we may think of this in terms of the biblical distinction between manifestation (*phaneróo* – what is seen) and proclamation (*kérussó* – what is announced). Because sight can only go so far, it takes words and thought to give the real truth and meaning behind what is seen.

Finally, sight in many ways is common to all animals, whereas language and the ability to communicate in this specialised way is one of the distinctive features of human beings.

Simply by reflecting on these differences the amazing paradox about words and images becomes clear. Sight appears to be so certain. Here is the world we can see, touch, measure and yet strangely enough modern physics informs us that if we could see things as they really are it would be but the dance of atoms. Reality is elusive. The paradox is that sight which we think is so certain is far less certain than we realise, whereas words with all their mystery, irony and ambiguity, appearing to be fragile and fleeting, are the primary means whereby we can deal with things that are true and sure.

These differences are purely phenomenological, but they do corroborate differences which Scripture puts before us, Scripture in which the primacy of the word is constant and complete.

Martin Buber tells the story of a rabbi whose reading of the Scriptures never gets beyond Genesis 1:2, 'And God said'. The marvel of a God who speaks and whose Word was the heart of who he is was too much for him to contemplate. He who is our Lord not only lives, but speaks! What is more, the Word is the way he creates, redeems, rules and relates to us.

Also, we are made in his image as word-speaking creatures who live between his first Word of creation and his last Word of judgement. We as responsible agents are made answerable to his words as we live out our words.

When placed within this theological framework we soon discover that the modern crisis of the word is not modern at all. It is just one more critical moment in the long drama of words and images that we see in the Scriptures and throughout history. It started when through sin a rupture took place between the word and vision. Only in the person of Christ is there a reconciliation of word and vision, and for us that reconciliation will only be complete when he returns again.

We thus live at this crucial moment, but it is not a unique moment, it is simply a highly developed moment when the rupture has become so important to the whole culture because of its extreme exaggeration, but it is nothing new. The rupture has already taken place and we will not heal it, that has to wait until the final reconciliation in Christ.

In Scripture the evidence of this rupture is seen in the declaration that God is unapproachable by sight (1 Timothy 6:16). In the Old Testament it was the common sense of many that to see God was tantamount to a death sentence. Even Moses who came closer to seeing all that could be seen of the unseeable is told, 'You cannot see my face, for no man shall see me and live' (Exodus 33:20).

A second stress in Scripture is the linking of sight with sin – the 'lust of the eyes' as John puts it (1 John 2:16). One can almost see the contrast between Adam and Eve who rebelled against the Word because they followed sight and what they saw tempted them leading them astray, and Jesus Christ who we are told in Philippians 2:6 'though being in very nature God, did not consider equality with God something to be grasped'. Adam and Eve rejecting the command, saw the fruit, grasped and took. Theirs was the way of disobedience, Christ's was the way of obedience to his Father's word leading to the cross. Sight is linked with sin.

Thirdly, sight is linked to idolatry. It has been pointed out by several commentators that in the episode of the Golden Calf in Exodus 32 when the people say 'We will make gods that we can *see* to go before us', the irony is that they took their earrings, objects which honour the ear to make something which honours the eye, this being almost symbolic of the change from worshipping the true God who could not be seen, but who could be heard to false gods which could be seen but were dumb. In other words, the appeal of idols is that they are objectified to the eyes. The idol is permanent, controllable, accessible, but that which is of the essence of the visible is the heart of idolatry. Even those things which are good, like the bronze serpent of Moses, and performed a specific function can be turned into an idol if they are used in ways beyond that which they were intended for.

Fourthly, in Scripture this rupture may be conceived in terms of the dichotomy that we walk by faith and not be sight. This is beautifully expressed in the Fourth Gospel which includes in its opening section 'No one has ever seen God' (1:18) and ends with the great sentence 'Blessed are those who have not seen and yet believe' (20:29). The backdrop to the Gospel is the first sin through which the first rupture came between word and vision, and only through Christ is the rupture overcome in time in the incarnation (No one has ever seen God, but God the one and only, who is at the Father's side has made him known, literally 'exegeted him' – 1:18). He is the only image of the Father (14:9 – Anyone who has seen me has seen the Father), so when he is present we have the only time when the Word can be seen, when sight can be believed; but nonetheless what is true for him is transient and when he left to return to be with his Father (17:5) that truth will not occur again until he returns. In the between time (die mitte der Zeit), belief and making contact with God occurs through believing and receiving the apostolic message – 17:20 – 'I pray for those who will believe in me through their message'. Thus, there is a blasphemy and a folly in anticipating the end times by bringing the visual forward to where it does not belong.

I must stress that the Bible is not anti-visual. Word and vision are inseparable and complementary in human experience. Nonetheless, the Scriptures insist that sight is only proper in its place. Images are legitimate only when they deal with that which can be seen and shown. This gives ground for a Christian view of art. Scriptures also insists that while hearing is never superior to sight, nevertheless it is sufficient and necessary until the time comes when we attain that state of holiness without which no one shall see God.

There are certain consequences of the shift that has taken place through the graphics revolution.

As we live in a society where words are subservient to images, there are certain inevitable biases. First, our perceptions and expressions are image dominated, 'seeing is believing'; 'a picture is worth a thousand words'; 'a photo is worth a thousand witnesses'; 'what you see is evidence' – all truisms today. Consequently, what you say verbally is less certain. Images are reality to the modern person in arguable form and so all reality, if it is to be true to the modern person, must be put in visual form. And yet, as we have seen, from a biblical standpoint this is utterly wrong. A picture is not worth a thousand words, seeing is not believing. To make such statements today marks one out as an iconoclast, but to be true to the Bible the Christian must be an iconoclast.

A second by-product is the reinforcing of individualism and narcissism. Since a word addresses *us* it is more difficult to foster the illusion 'I am and who but I?' as the Old Testament puts it. But seeing allows you to do just that. As I see and look around I survey my horizons, indeed, I become the centre of the world. 'I am and who but I?' This mentality is then magnified by our modern images which in many ways are not images of reality, but merely reflections of *our* hopes and dreams, aspirations and fears, coming back to us in what the ad-makers tell us is good or bad, constructing a huge Vanity Fair. Daily, we are walking through a huge hall of mirrors and looking at ourselves in order to foster this great sense of the importance of our own being.

A third by-product of the shift is the generating of irrationality. The claim is not being made that in the past everyone was rational and analytical, but rather that just as the whole notion of speaking, reading and hearing has a pace that is moderate to slow, an order that is sequential and thus as an activity is quite demanding, so it favours critical thinking and analysis. Naturally, it gives a high place to truth, reason and argument. This stands in contrast to the day of the image. In the day of the image everything happens so fast, you glimpse something and it is gone, replaced by another image, and then another and so on. You see things in undemanding ways, in ways which are more intuitive than analytical. There is no standing back and exercising critical thought, indeed there is no need if something is considered to be obvious. So, many people today move in their minds not by analysis but by association. The word is an accessory not an authority. Emotion ('How do you feel about that?') and not reason ('What did you think about that?') dominates. The result is an intensity of convictions and incoherence in arguments. Consequently, on the one hand we have higher, wider pretensions to thinking; yet on the other hand the thinking we do is a passionate kind of reason because it often by-passes the brain. And far from being really critical we are more conformist than ever, because we are taken over much more easily by slogans and stereotypes. Without criticism even the 'thinkers' simply fit into being shaped by what everyone else is thinking.

For example, in university circles it is not uncommon for a student having heard a powerful speaker to react by saying 'Oh that was very good and no doubt he is right, but I feel differently about it'. There is a deeper irrationality in our modern discourse despite the fact of higher pretensions to thinking.

Take our fourth by-product – incoherence. As we have seen, words and stories give a context and wholeness to meaning, but modern images are fleeting and fragmentary and thus foster incoherence. This can be seen most clearly in television which is highly commercialised producing what one American critic has described as the 'Now this generation'. To a certain extent one has to see American TV to fully appreciate what this means, but segments of TV are being reduced in length and then suddenly a switch occurs – 'And now this ...' and an ad appears. The net effect is that you cannot have any world issue so titanic or murder so brutal that within forty five seconds you are then switched to an advert for, say, Burger King. If that was in the art world you would call it Dada. If it was psychology it would be labelled schizophrenia. If it was in philosophy one would call it nihilism. Yet we have it daily on television and think nothing of it because there is a basic incoherence of the world and information and images that flows on us without any wisdom or context, truth or understanding.

The fifth by-product is irresponsibility. A world where images are predominant reduces us largely to being spectators, consumers and passive recorders without much responsibility and power. Of all the news we may have heard this morning, how much could we do about it? There are few things we can do on hearing news. It is ironic that we who know more than any previous generation can do far less with what we know than used to be the case. News used to be related to what you could do about it, whereas today it becomes part of what is called the 'great loop of impotence'. It has been said that the next to last refuge is voting and the last refuge of all is giving your opinion to the pollster. And then your opinion comes back to you again as one more public opinion about which you can do nothing except give your opinion.

A sixth by-product is immediacy. Words with their sense of story give you a sense of history – the present with a past and a future. But images which are fast, fragmented and fleeting give you a sense of being preoccupied only with the present. It has been shown that many people who watch television know everything about the last twenty four hours but known next to nothing about the last twenty four years, let alone the last twenty four centuries. Yet, as we turn to Scripture we see something quite different; we see that with the people of God, faith and remembering are closely tied together because God moves in history and remembering is the way of keeping faith fresh in terms of the past and the future as we ourselves move with God in history. But so many Christians today dominated by images have become preoccupied with the immediate and so have lost their sense of history and the sovereignty of God.

The seventh by-product of the predominance of the image is a bias in religious appetite. In English society, Protestantism, with its high view of the Word is at a discount. Why? It is because with the shift from proclamation to manifestation there has been a shift from meaning to a hunger for effectiveness. There has been a move from listening to words to looking at signs and this has made a great crucial shift across the western world which explains much of the religious appetites of our generation. So there are people who look to the East in order to get away from wordy preaching to find something we can see and contemplate. Hunger for icons is creeping in as an acceptable part of 'evangelical' spirituality. We also see this in the present fascination with signs and wonders. The hunger is in direct proportion to the context. We are not in a day of the Word, but a day of the eye. The sight and manifestation seem more certain than mere words and so there is lust from the manifest, the spectacular.

All of this surely adds up to the final by-product which is idolatry because the image has a double action in confusing. First, an image confuses because what is artificial (the image) is taken from the real, and second, the image which is only part of the huge reality of things is taken as symbolic of the whole and is seen *as* the whole. The symbol *becomes* the reality. The created thing becomes the creator and is worshipped whether it be an idol, sign and wonder or whatever – the inversion takes place and idolatry is complete. Almost everything in our culture at the visual level dominates the word and encourages idolatry.

Our response
Evangelicals are people of the Word. There is both a negative and positive aspect to this.

Negatively, the people of the Word in a visual culture are unashamedly iconoclasts. This does not mean that we exclude the image and humiliate the image in an act of revenge. Rather, we give the image its proper place, recognising its value and legitimacy when dealing with what can be shown, but rejecting the image wherever it has been made idolatrous. Protestantism in general and evangelicalism in particular are in danger of following the corruption of Eastern Orthodoxy in the fifth century and Roman Catholicism in the fourteenth century. The preachers and the friars of the fourteenth century maintained that a shift from the Word to the image would be an effective way of bringing the Word and Sacrament to everyone. The result was in fact the massive corruption of the church. However, at least they had two enormous advantages over us: when the shift occurred, the symbols were largely Christian used from spiritual instruction and they were created by the church in a most innovative way. The church was following no-one. Our tragedy today is that the church is following the world at the level of insipid imitation and often ending up with things which are not Christian at all. These differences not withstanding the developments in the fourteenth century still resulted in corruption. The statues, the stain glass windows, the relics, the liturgies with their ornaments, vestments and gestures led to a repression of the Word and such a shift in mystical theology that it ushered in the corruption which came prior to the Reformation. The point which must be stressed is this: the same will happen to evangelicalism unless it escapes its captivity to an image-dominated society.

Here are just a few areas that evangelicals have to think through as iconoclasts.

Christian iconoclasm and our own cultural diet

Studies have shown that citizens of a democracy who get their news from the press are much more critical than those who simply get their news from television. This is not surprising given the nature of discourse in the two mediums. Yet it is disturbing to see how many Christians have a cultural diet which is hardly shaped by the word at all. Their dependency on the television news, their skimming of the popular press and dependency upon diagrams, and audio-visuals is actually leading them on at the general cultural level to be uncritical, unimaginative and uninventive. Christians must start with their own cultural diet.

Christian iconoclasm and chatter

Ingmar Bergman once remarked that when God dies in a culture the church chatters. You can see this in the day of the image, words mean little and they commit people to hardly anything. But traditionally Christians commitment to God's Word imbibed them with a due sense of seriousness, so that our 'yes's' mean yes and our 'no's' mean no. The Lord is in heaven and our words should be few and we shall be judged or justified according to our words. There should be a clarity, cogency and comprehensiveness about our use of the word which is remarkable in a day which is careless in its talk.

Interestingly enough, Paul who spoke freely in tongues, in 1 Corinthians 14, uses as his argument against speaking in tongues the love of neighbour – what will edify. And one can see that the reason why there is so much spiritual chatter in the church is because of a loss of love for neighbour. Much of the jargon used today within evangelicalism would have to go if we simply put it to the test by asking 'Does it mean anything?' to anyone who does not appreciate our subculture.

Christian iconoclasm and religious films and television

Again and again one can see that reliance upon the visual to communicate the spiritual is disappointed because spiritual reality is not contained by films, video or television. At best it is inadequate because all that you are filming is the surface appearance, religion as behaviour, worship as a rite, but never conveying the holiness and grace of God. As worship it is idolatrous because the concentration on the human which so many TV programmes do to some extent becomes so successful that they close off the divine. Studies show that one of the worst effects of the electronic church in the United States is that it leaves its viewers with no sense of the Lord at all, but a very strong sense of the celebrity preacher who is the whole concentration of the visual medium.

Christian iconoclasm and our dependence upon audio-visual techniques.

It is constantly being claimed that such techniques used in Christian meeting are an improvement because they marry image and word so effectively so they can communicate more effectively. That is not what studies show. The evidence is that the image becomes the king and the word loses its authority. So we can move people more, and gather them more, but at the end of the day we have not conveyed to them the truth of Christ. Much of the present crisis of preaching in Britain can be traced back to this turning towards a greater use of audio-visual techniques resulting in weaker preaching and not as promised, better preaching.

Hope for people of the Word in a non-word culture.

More positively we need to ask: What prevents evangelicals committed to the Word lapsing into despair or romantic antiquarianism?

The answer came to me one day in Oxford after attending a seminar which was being given by a specialist on Marxism before the fall of the Soviet Union. In the course of his address he remarked on the difference between Marxism and ideology going moribund and the church which was culturally captive and yet always had the seeds of its own renewal. Why? Because, he said, the church had two things which Marxism and no other religion had. First, the church has in the Word of God a judgement that transcends history. In other words, we sadly do fall captive to this generation, that class or this culture and philosophy, but when the Word itself speaks, nothing can hold it down. The church may go captive, but never the Word. Secondly, the church has uniquely a doctrine of its own failure. The first Christian right is the right to be wrong! Did we not come to Christ because we sinned and needed a

Saviour, having a faith which involves a confession of failure? We continually need to face up to this possibility and in some cases, actuality, of being wrong and so coming to Christ in repentance to be forgiven and renewed.

The church does have within itself the seeds of its own renewal. As G K Chesterton once put it, five times the church went to the dogs but each time it was the dog that died.

If those are our two grounds of confidence, that in the Word there is a judgement which transcends history and in the Word there is a doctrine of our own failure and renewal, then there are two prerequisites for preaching in evangelicalism.

Firstly, transcendence is the source of all true proclamation. What did Jeremiah say of the false prophets? 'Which of them has stood in the presence of the Lord?' The Word is transcendent and those who bear the message of the Word must come from there.

When I was a boy being brought up in evangelicalism, you could see from the very demeanour of the preacher coming into the pulpit where he had just come from. I don't often see that now amongst modern evangelical preachers, the sense of awe at having received a message from the King of Kings and which is about to be delivered to the people.

Secondly, tension is the secret of penetration in preaching. Studies have shown that it is not preaching which is simply correct theologically which transforms churches and communities. One ingredient makes a crucial difference, it is when you have as it were correct doctrine married to cultural diagnosis. That is, what the Word says is consciously brought in tension with what the world is doing, and that contradiction is the springboard of obedience. On several occasions now in the States I have heard sermons on the Beatitudes. Some of these have been magnificent, exegetically. But they have all been remarkably remote for a simple reason: they were never related to modern America. 'Blessed are the poor in spirit', in a culture which believes 'Blessed is number one'. The two need to be related in tension caused by the fundamental contradiction that inherently exists between the values of the Word of God and the values of a world in opposition to God. Then penetration occurs, for the Word in confrontation demands a response.

Nietzche remarked that when God dies culture becomes weightless. That is so true, and that word is very biblical. The opposite of the glory of God is the hollowness of all that lacks his glory. Glory at its deepest is not solely radiance, it is reality. That which stands in contrast to the glory, reality and weight of God is the emptiness of idolatry. Indeed, the term idol in Scripture literally means an 'empty thing'. The sad truth is that cultures which fall prey to the image become as hollow and empty as the image itself.

We who want reality in our own lives, our churches and in God's world will only find it in the Word and glory of God.

11

HOMOSEXUAL RELATIONSHIPS AND THE BIBLE

David Field

Introduction

Discussing homosexuality today is like fitting a plug to the lead of a lamp without being able to turn the current off first. Without knowledge, skill and enormous care the risks of disaster are high. All too often, more heat is generated than light.

I know this from painful personal experience. Within the space of a few weeks I spoke to two quite different audiences on this theme, using the same set of notes. On the first occasion, I was branded as a reactionary bigot; someone in the second row actually tore up a Bible, screwed the pages into paper balls and threw the lot at me during my talk. On the second, my approach was considered far too liberal by an outraged Anglican churchwarden who threatened, in his anger, to push me through the wall of his church hall.

Why should homosexuality be such an emotive subject? There are many reasons, some of them quite complex. At the root of them all is the fact that every human is a sexual being. Sexuality is not just about what we may or may not do; it is part of the way we are. If we belong to the heterosexual majority, the thought of same-sex genital contact probably nauseates us. It strikes at the heart of our personal being. And there, of course, we have to pause, because emotional disgust must not be muddled with moral outrage. The sight of a child swallowing raw bacon rinds may make me feel sick, but my feelings do not automatically brand the action itself as wrong.

Significant shifts in public opinion – and the heated debates which follow – also muddy the waters. Less than thirty years ago, all homosexual acts between consenting males were illegal in the United Kingdom (the British law has always ignored the existence of lesbianism). Nowadays, the debate has moved on to consider the age of homosexual consent, and opposition to homosexual behaviour is bracketed with racism, sexism, ageism and everything else that is politically incorrect. The social climate is certainly not conducive to cool ethical discussion.

The ecclesiastical climate has changed, too. If this book had been written fifty years ago, a chapter on homosexuality would never have been included. The morality of same-sex behaviour needed no discussing because its wrongness was self-evident to everyone – especially to those who engaged in it on the quiet.

Jack Spong, the American Bishop whose writings on this subject are always controversial, helpfully plots the course of change in the way some denominations have approached homosexuality.

First, he says, came the recognition that the subject merited serious discussion. Then came the distinction between the person and the act (we must hate the sin but love the sinner). Next was a sharpened awareness of injustice – whatever their *moral* judgement, Christians must raise their voices in protest whenever homosexual people are denied their civil rights and treated unjustly. Fourthly, claims that homosexuals cannot be blamed for their orientation (because they do not choose it) were taken on board by the church. Next the assumption that homosexual people should remain celibate was questioned – why should anyone be required to repress the way he is through no fault of his own? And finally the church shifted its ground to suggest ways in which homosexuals can be encouraged to lead responsible active sexual lives.

This is the social and ecclesiastical air that we breathe as late twentieth-century Christians. Whether we inhale deeply or fit ourselves up with masks to filter out the spirit of the age, we must not ignore its existence. It inevitably affects the way we approach homosexuals and homosexuality (the people as well the thing) and it charges our emotions (whether for or against the people or the practice).

More seriously, in a book of this kind, the climate in which we live can deeply affect the way we use the Scriptures as Christians. If you feel your blood pressure rising as you read on through the rest of this chapter, it may be worth revisiting these first few paragraphs and asking yourself the question, 'Why?'

What the Bible means

I am assuming (as I could not in another kind of book) that we are agreed on our starting-point as we explore the Bible's teaching on homosexuality. We believe in the inspiration and authority of Scripture. We accept the New Testament's declaration that 'all Scripture is God-breathed and is useful for teaching, rebuking, correcting and training in righteousness' (2 Timothy 3:16). If the Bible clearly teaches that homosexual behaviour is wrong, we will not dispute that. The reverse must also apply, of course. And we must be careful not to fill in the gaps which Scripture leaves with our own dogmatic opinions.

We have two main tasks ahead of us. In this section of the chapter we will do our best to discover what the Bible *means* in the relatively few passages where it deals with homosexuality directly. We must go about that job as dispassionately as we can, distinguishing what the Bible writers actually meant from what we would very much like them to have meant – whether they did so or not. That will involve us in a close study of key words, as well as in a careful recognition of the contexts in which the relevant passages occur.

Our second task is to work out how the Bible's teaching *applies*. The Scriptures were written to real people in real situations. Those people lived in cultures which are alien to ours. The situations they faced are in many ways different to those that confront us now. In building bridges between their times and ours we need to take great care, if our applications of biblical teaching are to be correct. That will be the theme of the next section.

So where do we start?

The obvious place to begin a Bible search is with the story of Sodom in Genesis 19, if only because the word 'sodomy' has passed into the English language from this passage of Scripture. What does the account of Lot's confrontation with the two heavenly messengers tell us about God's attitude to homosexuality?

The story is familiar. 'Where are the men who came to you tonight?', screams the mob outside Lot's door. 'Bring them out to us so that we can have sex with them' (verse 5). It is only his guests' powerful intervention which saves Lot's skin, and Sodom's destruction follows almost immediately. No sex act took place, but Christians have long assumed that God's judgement on the city reflects his extreme displeasure with homosexual intercourse – or even the threat of it.

But is that what the story means? Forty years ago, Derek Sherwin Bailey pointed out that the Hebrew expression translated 'have sex with' in verse 5 is the ordinary word for 'know'. The men of Sodom's sin, he suggested, had nothing to do with sex at all. It was xenophobia – hostility towards strangers – and that is something which the Bible consistently condemns.

Bailey's case is weak. The Hebrew word in question recurs three verses later when – amazingly – Lot offers the aggressive crowd his two virgin daughters if they will spare his male guests. The sexual connotation there is plain enough. Moreover, in a similar incident in the town of Gibeah described in Judges 19, the word 'know' obviously means 'have sex with'. It is a fundamental rule of biblical exegesis that you fix a word's meaning, where possible, from its context. In that light, as Derek Kidner wisely comments, 'the doubt created by Dr Bailey has travelled more widely than the reasons he produces for it.'

It is clear enough that the male mob's intention in Sodom was to have homosexual intercourse. But does God's judgement on those men clearly prove that he condemns all same-sex behaviour?

The biblical text falls a long way short of proving that. Sodom's threatened sin was gang rape. It comes as no surprise to anybody to find that God condemns this kind of behaviour. Modern homosexuals do not plead for the legalising of sexual assault. The loving, consenting relationships they want society to affirm are as distinct from rape as chalk is from cheese. And Genesis 19 has nothing to say about homosexuality of that sort.

So here is the first note of biblical caution we need to hear. Whether we like it or not, the story of Sodom is almost totally irrelevant to our modern debate about the rights and wrongs of homosexual relationships.

Turning over a few more pages of the Old Testament, we find two unequivocal condemnations of homosexual behaviour in the Levitical law (Leviticus 18:22 and 20:13). Same-sex intercourse is described there as 'detestable' and the death penalty is laid down for those who are caught in the act.

If we are looking for plain biblical guidance, these two verses certainly seem to provide it. There are no overtones of rape to complicate matters, as there are in the story of the threatened assault of Sodom. But we still need to be absolutely sure what these laws *mean* and – equally important – how we should *apply* them. To work at the meaning and application of Scripture is not to split hairs but to be faithful to the God who has provided his special revelation for our instruction.

We must leave the question of application until later, because it raises the bigger issue of how Christians are meant to use the Old Testament law. As far as the *meaning* of these two verses in Leviticus is concerned, the only question that needs concern us is the sense of the word translated 'detestable'.

Some Old Testament scholars claim that this word is a cultic term.

It is associated only (they say) with idolatry. So what the law is actually condemning here, when it labels homosexual intercourse as 'detestable', is cultic prostitution. Leviticus has nothing to say to a homosexual couple who have intercourse in order to express their love, not to worship false gods.

If we are to take the meaning of Scriptures seriously, as we must, this is an interpretation well worth investigating. It is certainly not far-fetched. We know that male prostitutes had a high profile in pagan rituals during Old Testament times (see, for example, 1 Kings 14:24, 15:12 and 22:46).

Nevertheless, those who maintain that the word in question *never* occurs outside a cultic context in the Old Testament are claiming too much. It is used several times in Proverbs, for example, in passages where moral, not religious, offences are highlighted.

The most important thing to work out is the meaning of this word in its context in Leviticus 18-29 (the only place where it is found in this book). Is the setting here cultic or moral? If the former, we must pause before taking it as God's veto on all homosexual intercourse. If this latter, we can apply it more widely to situations which do not involve the worship of idols.

It would be nice if we could be absolutely certain. Unfortunately we cannot. What we can say with confidence, however, is that though there are cultic overtones here and there in Leviticus 18-29 (such as the sacrifice of children to Molech in 20:21 and the defiling of the land in the following verse), it is moral issues which predominate. Homosexual behaviour is condemned in the same breath as adultery and incest. A fair, balanced study of the context in which homosexual intercourse is condemned as 'detestable' does not bear out the argument that these laws are *only* targeted at cultic prostitution.

What about the New Testament's teaching on homosexuality? Apart from allusions to Sodom in 2 Peter and Jude, there are just three explicit references to homosexual behaviour – all of them in Paul's letters.

Some would add to that short list Jesus' comment about eunuchs: 'for some are eunuchs because they were born that way' (Matthew 19:12). It is more natural, however, to understand this saying as a reference to those who are incapable of having sexual intercourse of any kind, not to congenital homosexuals specifically.

In Romans 1, Paul uses homosexual behaviour to illustrate the way God judges sinners by abandoning them to the destructive power of the lifestyles they themselves have chosen. Lesbians come under his hammer as well as men who practise gay sex. So do idolaters and the greedy, the envious and the arrogant. There is no league table of wickedness; all these sins illustrate the outworking of 'a depraved mind' (Romans 1:18-32).

We find a similar list in 1 Corinthians 6:9-11. Among the 'wicked' who 'will not inherit the Kingdom of God' are 'male prostitutes' and 'homosexual offenders' – along (note) with drunkards, swindlers and other people whose lifestyles are incompatible with God's rule in their lives. As in Romans 1, homosexual offences are not singled out as sins in a league of their own, nevertheless, they are decisively condemned.

Finally, in 1 Timothy 1:18-10, 'perverts' (the NIV's translation of the same word Paul uses in 1 Corinthians 6:9) feature in yet another list – of 'lawbreakers and rebels' this time, men and women whose behaviour (sexual or otherwise) 'is contrary to the sound doctrine that conforms to the glorious gospel of the blessed God'.

In spite of their scattered and illustrative nature, these New Testament verses seem to point clearly to just one conclusion: a homosexual lifestyle is against God's will and subject to his judgement. Some biblical scholars, however, seriously question whether this is what Paul actually meant. And if we genuinely want to let Scriptures say what it means (and are not just after textual ammunition to fire at opponents), we must listen carefully to their arguments.

In Romans 1, they maintain, Paul targets men and women who 'abandon natural relations'. Natural to whom? Well, natural to *them*, of course! He is aiming his guns at heterosexuals who act unnaturally by having homosexual intercourse. Indeed, he seems to assume that anyone who has intercourse with someone of the same sex is a heterosexual gone wrong. We cannot blame Paul for that assumption (the argument goes) because it is only recently that the experts have revealed the existence to a fixed homosexual orientation. Nevertheless, we cannot extend his condemnation of unnatural sexual behaviour to cover people who accept same-sex intercourse as the most natural thing in the world – for them.

In 1 Corinthians 6, the same scholars point out that Paul's negative reference to 'homosexual offenders' comes in the context of an extended passage about prostitution. When trying to discover the meaning of a biblical verse, we know how important it is to read the words in their wider context. So is Paul's real target here *promiscuity* – straight

or gay? If he only means to condemn those who treat intercourse as a
recreational release from a demanding physical appetite, homosexual
couples who intend to live in an exclusive, lifelong relationship do not
come into the picture here at all. All Paul is condemning is the one
night stand.

There is also a serious problem in understanding the meaning of the
words Paul uses in 1 Corinthians 6. The expression translated 'male
prostitutes' (*malakoi*) in verse 9 is the ordinary Greek word for 'soft'.
Some writers in New Testament times used it to describe boy prostitutes. Given that restricted meaning, might not the next word
(*arsenokoitai*, translated 'homosexual offenders') logically have a cultic significance, too? After all, this letter was addressed to a bustling
city port where sailors and traders were encouraged to let off their
sexual steam in the name of religion by buying the services of temple
prostitutes. If that was what Paul had in mind, we are quite wrong to
translate either expression as though he meant it to apply to two homosexual people in love.

Finally, argue some scholars, the context of 1 Timothy 1:10 highlights wrecked relationships. 'Perverts' come in the same category as
those who ruin other people's lives by killing, stealing and telling lies.
But two homosexual people who have intercourse to seal their love and
cement their relationship are not wreckers at all. It is surely quite wrong
to use Paul's words to condemn something that never even entered his
mind.

Quite deliberately, I have set out the exegetical case against the popular understanding of these New Testament passages without hinting at
any counter-arguments. The scholars whose position I have summarised demand our serious attention simply because they highlight two
vital principles of biblical interpretation. If we have a high view of the
Bible's verbal inspiration, we must take great pains to discover what
biblical words actually mean. And if we believe that Scripture retains
its authority today, we must pay special attention to the original contexts to which its teaching was directed. If those exercises torpedo
some of our most cherished ideas about Christian beliefs and behaviour – so be it.

There *are* counter-arguments, of course. Most of them bridge the
gap between the *meaning* of Scripture and its *use* – the two main sec-
tions of this chapter. For that reason, I will not set them out quite yet.
But we can at least deal briefly at this point with the linguistic doubts

raised by the two key words Paul uses in 1 Corinthians 6:9.

The problem, you will remember, is whether the words *malakoi* (translated 'male prostitutes') and *arsenokoitai* ('homosexual offenders') are just religious words in Paul's vocabulary. Do they refer to religious prostitution – and nothing else?

As far as *arsenokoitai* is concerned, the case for giving the word such a restricted meaning is very weak indeed. This expression is, in fact, two Greek words rolled into one. Put together, they mean 'male intercourse'. There is no evidence that this expression was ever used in a specialised religious way. It simply refers to men who have sexual intercourse – for whatever reason – with other men.

The case for limiting the meaning of *malakoi* to religious prostitution is a little stronger, but by no means conclusive. Outside the Bible it occasionally has this restricted sense, but there is no other example of its use in Scripture to encourage us to endorse the NIV's narrow translation. The word itself simply means 'soft'. Many commentators – and they are as likely to be right as the scholars who disagree with them – think that Paul is referring to the 'soft' or submissive partner in a homosexual relationship here.

Linguistically, it is fair to say that a shadow of doubt may remain. But the weight of the evidence suggests that Paul has all kinds of homosexual behaviour in mind, not only male prostitution, just as he intends to make no distinctions later on in his list between different kinds of greed and slander.

How the Bible's teaching applies

So far, we have identified the few passages in Scripture which refer to homosexuality explicitly, and we have struggled with different interpretations of the biblical text. Now we move on to the next stage.

When we are reasonably sure what the biblical writers meant to say, only half the exercise has been completed.

That is not to disparage what we have been doing up to this point in the chapter. All too often church leaders who claim to teach biblically, especially on a subject as emotive as homosexuality, twist the meaning of Scripture to prop up their own pre-set conclusions – rather like a secretary who drafts the minute of the meeting before it has happened. That is very tempting, but very wrong. Discovering what the text of Scripture means is the foundation on which accurate application of its teaching rests.

Nevertheless, we must not muddle the two exercises. Biblical builders have not finished their task when they have laid the foundation. Discovering how the Bible's teaching applies across the culture gap between then and now is not something which comes automatically once the meaning of Scripture has been worked out. Building sensible applications calls for even more careful work.

Do not be put off by that thought – the rewards are exciting!

The idea of a 'culture gap' is a helpful starting point. It is worth repeating that the biblical writers did not aim their words into a cultural vacuum. They spoke to real people living in real places over the course of several centuries of real time. The political, economic and religious conditions in which those people lived were – by and large – quite different from ours. It should not surprise us, therefore, to find the Bible addressing issues that make us either smile or scratch our heads. Nor should we be puzzled when Scripture says nothing about issues which (to us) cry out for clear teaching – like nuclear war and organ transplants. There *is* a culture gap to be bridged.

In thinking about homosexuality, we have already glimpsed the breadth of this gap. If the Old Testament law has ritual prostitution in its sights when it targets homosexual intercourse, how can we apply that teaching to today's world where most prostitutes do not sell their bodies in the name of religion? If Paul did not understand about a fixed homosexual orientation, how can we apply what he says about 'unnatural' sex to modern situations? How *do* we build bridges across the culture gap between biblical times and our own?

The most important thing to do in this bridge building exercise is to recognise the difference between lasting principles and specific rules in Scripture. To take just one straight forward example (and one which has nothing to do with sex), the Old Testament law tells householders to build parapets round their roofs. That was a specific rule aimed at people who lived in houses with flat roofs on which they often entertained their guests. As a law, its *wording* does not apply to most twentieth-century Christian householders living in the United Kingdom. Our homes are not usually built that way. But the *principle* this Old Testament law expresses – that God's people are under a moral obligation to make sure that visitors to their homes are safe – is one that crosses every culture gap. And it would, of course, be very easy to re-translate it into specifically modern guidelines (referring, perhaps, to slippery floors or exposed electrical wiring).

Forgive me if that sounds trivial. At a deeper theological level, a search for lasting principles will take us straight to the fundamental truths of our faith – truths that transcend all human differences, like *the nature of God* (which ultimately defines the difference between right and wrong), *his creation scheme* for all mankind, and *his kingdom lifestyle* for those who submit to his rule.

Yes, the water is getting deeper! But we must plunge in, if we are to apply the Bible's teaching about homosexuality to modern society with any confidence. And once we have identified the lasting principle which underlies a specific biblical rule or veto, its application usually becomes clear and compelling.

It is time to re-visit the key New Testament passages about homosexuality. What are the lasting principles which underlie Paul's highly specific vetoes on homosexual behaviour when he writes to Christians living in first-century Rome and Corinth, and to Timothy in Ephesus.

In Romans 1, Paul's theme is *God's creation scheme*. His aim is to show how mankind has made a bad exchange, both spiritually and morally, from the Creator's plan for human life. The word 'exchange' holds his argument together in the second half of the chapter. Men and women were created to glorify God, he writes, but they 'exchange the glory of the immortal God for images .... They exchanged the truth of God for a lie, and worshipped and served created things rather than the Creator' (verses 19-25). And that bad spiritual exchange was matched morally, as 'their women exchanged natural relations for unnatural ones. In the same way the men also abandoned natural relations with women and were inflamed with lust for one another' (verses 26-27).

Here, in a nutshell, is the great, lasting principle which underlies Paul's distinction between 'natural' and 'homosexual' sexual behaviour. He may have had promiscuous heterosexuals at the front of his mind when he wrote his letter to the Christians in Rome – men and women in Roman society who were sacrificing their sexual integrity by experimenting with same-sex intercourse. He may even have been ignorant of the existence of people with a fixed homosexual orientation – though personally I doubt it. These just may have been the specific cultural conditions in which Paul's readers at Rome lived out their sexual lives. But the lasting principle he invokes to condemn the specific kind of homosexual behaviour they knew builds a solid bridge across the gap between their culture and ours.

In writing about 'natural relations' within the context of God's creation scheme, Paul is not referring to individual men and women as they were and are. By 'unnatural', he does not mean 'what seems unnatural to me as a homosexual or heterosexual person'. His canvas is much broader than that. He is taking the argument back, far more radically, to man and woman as the Creator made them. And when we follow his lead and look back to what we are told about the beginnings of human sexuality in the Book of Genesis, we find that sexual intercourse was intended to be the seal on a faithful, loving, exclusive *hetero*sexual relationship. As God created man and woman together in his image, 'becoming one flesh' in heterosexual intercourse is not just a union but a reunion – and a homosexual relationship is in effect a denial of that awesome divine arrangement.

Putting it all together, Paul is arguing that homosexual behaviour is as much the outcome of mankind's rebellion against God as idolatry – or (as he goes on to say) greed, envy and gossip. The bad 'exchange' he highlights is not just the capricious sex-swapping of a heterosexual person searching for a fresh physical stimulus but the divergence all homosexual behaviour represents from God's creation scheme. When seen in the light of that lasting principle, every homosexual act is 'unnatural'.

If Paul's argument in Romans 1 moves against the backdrop of creation, the doctrine of *the Kingdom of God* provides the setting for his veto on homosexual behaviour in 1 Corinthians 6. Certain kinds of behaviour, he warns his readers, are incompatible with life in God's Kingdom. That is the principle at stake. And among those behaviour patterns (which include, please notice, greed and slander) is a homosexual lifestyle. People who acknowledge God's rule must turn their back on these things. And the good news is that our situation is never hopeless, however ingrained the bad habits may be. Change in the power of God's Spirit is always possible. No doubt Paul had particular individuals in his mind's eye as he concluded in triumph, ' And that is what some of you *were*' (verse 11).

Once again, it is recognition of the principle behind the rule which builds the necessary bridge across the culture gap between New Testament times and our own. Paul certainly had prostitution at the front of his mind when he wrote this chapter, but he gives his veto on homosexual behaviour (as well as on the other attitudes and activities in his list) far wider currency by rooting his rules for Christian living firmly in the doctrine of the Kingdom. The Bible tells us that God's Kingdom will fully come when his will is perfectly done. And in that eschato-logical scenario there is no place for homosexual behaviour.

What, then, of Paul's third list of banned activities in 1 Timothy 1? In some ways, this is the most compelling of them all.

Paul is writing about the lasting relevance of *God's law*. The wording of the Ten Commandments is, in fact, only just below the surface of his list of banned activities in verses 9 and 10. He does not quote the Old Testament's wording exactly because he is keen to do exactly what we are trying to achieve in this chapter. His aim is to apply God's Word across the culture gap which separated Old Testament times from his own.

So he takes the principles behind the commandments and re-clothes them in contemporary language. 'You shall not murder' is sharpened to include 'those who kill their fathers and mothers' – a practice all too well known in the sub-culture of the pagan city where Timothy worked. And 'You shall not steal' is aimed at slave traders – because there was a thriving black market in kidnapped slaves at Ephesus.

It is all the more interesting, therefore, to find that Paul's condemnation of 'adulterers and perverts' (or 'male homosexuals' – the second word translates *arsenokoitai*, which we have looked at already) is his updated version of the seventh commandment – 'You shall not commit adultery'. He obviously believed that homosexual behaviour betrays the principle behind this commandment as blatantly as heterosexual unfaithfulness. The parallel is incredibly striking.

We are now in a position to sum up. The three New Testament references to homosexuality which we have been examining are not three isolated passages from letters written to long-forgotten early Christian communities. Once we expose the lasting principles behind the specific prohibitions, we find that we are handling three links in a very impressive doctrinal chain.

All three references are to do with God's will – something that crosses every culture gap. Romans 1 sets out his will as *Creator*. 1 Corinthians 6 explores his will as *King*. And 1 Timothy 1 illustrates his will as *law-giver*. We can draw a straight theological line from God's creation plan (when his will was perfectly done) through to the coming of his Kingdom (when it will be perfectly done once more). And the biblical link between the two is the Ten Commandments – God's law which reflects his creation plan for human behaviour and anticipates his Kingdom lifestyle.

The conclusion is surely inescapable. In God's scheme for man-kind, from the beginning of creation to the coming of his Kingdom, homosexual behaviour has no place.

And yet we have not quite reached the end of the biblical road.

Towards the beginning of this section I forecast that a search for lasting principles would take us straight to the fundamental truths of our faith. I mentioned three in particular. We have already found our way to two of them – the great doctrines of Creation and of God's Kingdom. What about the third?

The third, if you remember, is *the nature of God himself*. And fun-damental to the Lord's nature, according to Scripture, is the quality of *love* (see 1 John 4:16).

Here we have to move with great care. For one thing, 'love' is such a slippery word. If we want to use it biblically, we must make sure it is packed with its biblical meaning (*agape* is the New Testament word). And in the second place we must not be taken in by the false reasoning that tries to persuade us that any action – even one that breaks God's law – is justified if it is done lovingly. Jesus never taught that. He told his followers that love is law's headline (Matthew 22:37-40). He never suggested that it is the Heavenly Editor's blue pencil which puts a line through the small print underneath (see, for example, Matthew 5:17-20).

Nevertheless, Christians who uphold the Bible's condemnation of homosexual behaviour with great relish, but without a glimmer of love for homosexual people, earn Mark Twain's caustic description of being 'good people in the worst sense of the word'. Homophobia – a fear of homosexuals which leads to rejection – should not be on any church's agenda.

To explore the ways in which God's *agape* standard can be applied would need another chapter. Let me conclude this one by making just two suggestions.

The first is that Christians should be in the forefront of those who protest when homosexuals are treated unjustly. That is because love and injustice are incompatible. Whenever homosexual people are the object of snide humour on the television screen or harsh penalties in the law-courts, genuinely loving Christian people ought to be the first to stand up in their support. Any minority group which suffers dis-crimination should have full Christian backing in a struggle for their legal and moral rights.

My second suggestion is also a requirement, if biblical standards are to be kept. Those who accept the Bible's veto on homosexual *behaviour* must go out of their way to express genuine love for homosexual *people*.

At least two important distinctions underlie this essential Christian requirement. In the first place, temptation is not the same as sin. Even if homosexual acts are wrong to God's eyes, it is not sinful to be tempted to make love to someone of your own sex – unless, of course, you go on to perform the act mentally (see Matthew 5:27-28 where Jesus has heterosexual in his sights). Heterosexual Christians who ostracise their homosexual neighbours simply because of the pattern of temptations they experience are very confused and very wrong.

12

Evangelical Social Action Today:
Road to Recovery or Road to Ruin?

Rachel Tingle

Since the first National Evangelical Anglican Congress (NEAC) at Keele in 1967, and more particularly since the 1977 NEAC at Nottingham, Anglican evangelicals have shown a much increased interest in social ethics. This is not a particularly Anglican phenomenon – rather it is a trend common to evangelicals in other denominations in Britain and elsewhere. As Dr Nigel Biggar has noted, whilst 'it is perfectly possible to speak ... of an evangelical contribution to social ethics in the Anglican church ... it is much less possible to speak of an Anglican evangelical contribution, because what evangelicals have written about social ethics has seldom been distinctively Anglican'.[1] Indeed, as this chapter will show, Anglican evangelicals active in the field of social ethics have largely been adopting positions developed within an international melting pot of ideas – few, if any, of their ideas or approaches are either distinctively British or Anglican. More importantly, but perhaps more controversially, it will attempt to show that few of their ideas are distinctively evangelical.

Although this increased interest in social ethics has been accompanied by a great deal of debate, the majority of the books and papers which have appeared on the subject have welcomed it as a return to evangelicalism's historic roots – a reversal of the 'great reversal', as it has been called, whereby the socially-concerned and active evangelicals of the nineteenth century apparently retreated during the early years of this century until the 1960s into a pietistic, individualistic form of Christianity.[2]

---

1. Nigel Biggar, 'Evangelicalism and Social Ethics' in R.T. France and A.E. McGrath (ed.), *Evangelical Anglicans: Their Role and Influence in the Church Today* (SPCK, 1993).
2. The term 'great reversal' was first coined by the American church historian, Timothy L. Smith, but was popularised by an American sociologist, Dr. David Moburg, in his influential book, *The Great Reversal: Evangelism versus Social Concern* (Scripture Union, 1972).

John Stott, for instance, in *Issues Facing Christians Today,* has described the process as 'the recovery of our temporarily mislaid social conscience' after 'the half-century of neglect',[3] whilst a leading Baptist, Derek Tidball, has said in his recent book entitled *Who Are The Evangelicals?* that as far as social action is concerned 'evangelicals, betrayed their heritage' but are now 'on the road to recovery'.[4]

Stott and Tidball also present this development as having been initiated largely from within evangelicalism itself – prompted initially by calls from prominent and influential evangelicals like Carl Henry (founding editor of *Christianity Today*) in America; and Oliver Barclay (writing as A.N. Triton), Sir Frederick Catherwood, and Sir Norman Anderson in Britain.[5]

Is this an accurate interpretation of events? Few people would deny that British evangelicals – as responsible citizens in a free democracy, if nothing else – should take an informed and active interest in public affairs. As befits those who are trying to live their lives after the example of Jesus Christ, moreover, their public policy preferences, as well as the action of their individual and corporate church lives, should show a loving concern for the most vulnerable members of our society – the poor, the sick, and the prisoners of Galatians 6:10, for example. Few, too, would deny that nineteenth-century evangelicals showed such a concern to a remarkable degree. The efforts of people like William Wilberforce, Lord Shaftesbury, Elizabeth Fry, John Venn, and George Müller in securing anti-slavery legislation, the factory acts, penal reform, educational provision, care for orphans, and so on have been well document,[6] as have those of Theodore Weld, Albert Simpson, Jerry

3. John Stott, *Issues Facing Christians Today* (Marshalls, 1984), p. xi.
4. Derek J. Tidball, *Who are the Evangelicals?* (Marshall Pickering, 1994), pp. 188, 194. See also Timothy Chester, *Awakening to a World of Need* (Inter-Varsity Press, 1993) and Donald Dayton, *Discovering an Evangelical Heritage* (New York: Harper and Row, 1976).
5. Carl Henry, *The Uneasy Conscience of Modern Fundamentalism* (Grand Rapids, USA: Eerdmans, 1947); Carl Henry, Aspects of Christian Social Ethics (Grand Rapids, USA: Eerdmans, 1964); A.N.Triton, Whose World? (IVP, 1970); J.N.D. Anderson, *Into the World: The Needs and Limits of Christian Involvement* (Falcon Books, 1968); Sir Frederick Catherwood, *The Christian in Industrial Society* (Tyndale Press, 1974). A summary of the theological approach of these British contributions is given by Derek Tidball, in *Contemporary Evangelical Social Thinking – A Review* (Shaftesbury Project Publications, 1977).
6. Kathleen Heasman, *Evangelicals in Action: An Appraisal of their Social Work in the Victorian Era* (Geoffrey Bles, 1962); Ernest Howse, *Saints in Politics: The Clapham Sect and the Growth of Freedom* (Allen and Unwin, 1953).

McAuley and others in securing similar reforms in the USA.[7]

But whilst it may be agreed that evangelicals ought to show a social concern, and that in the nineteenth and early twentieth century they did so to such a degree that they brought about massive improvements in society, can it also be agreed that the renewed evangelical social activism we are seeing today is a welcome return to this heritage?

Strikingly, the very people pointed to by Stott and Tidball as being amongst the first to call for renewed evangelical social activism after the neglect earlier this century have recently expressed concern about the course it has been taking in practice. In an essay written in 1987, for example, Carl Henry compared what has actually happened with what he had hoped when he wrote his influential call to action, *The Uneasy Conscience of Modern Fundamentalism,* forty years earlier. He concluded that 'having emerged from their subcultural cocoon, evangelicals now are often politically and culturally engaged in ways no less troublesome than their earlier disengagement'.[8] He noted the prayerlessness, lack of concern for mission, and tensions over Biblical authority in American evangelicalism, as well as disagreements over the nature and direction of social activism and the lack of a precise philosophy of cultural engagement. He lamented that American evangelicalism is 'swamped by the very culture that it sought to alter' observing that 'some young evangelicals now define sin almost entirely in terms of social injustice. Premarital sex is common. Church discipline is lax or nonexistent. Divorce and remarriage snares even the clergy.' 'Meanwhile,' he said, 'the surrounding culture is collapsing from humanism into paganism.'[9]

Similarly in Britain, Sir Norman Anderson[10] and Oliver Barclay[11] have both expressed concern about the theological underpinning which has been developed for much of today's evangelical social action, whilst

---

7. Earle Cairns, *Saints and Society* (Chicago: Moody Press, 1960); Timothy L. Smith, *Revivalism and Social Reform* (Nashville: Abingdon Press, 1957); Timothy L. Smith, *Called Unto Holiness: The Story of the Nazarenes* (Kansas City, Mo.: Nazarene Publishing House, 1962).

8. Carl Henry, 'The Uneasy Conscience Revisted' in *Twilight of a Great Civilization: The Drift Toward Neo-Paganism* (Westchester, Illinois: Crossway Books, 1987) p. 170.

9. *Ibid,* p. 172.

10. Private meeting with the author in Cambridge, July 1989.

11. Oliver Barclay, 'The Theology of Social Ethics: A Survey of Current Positions', *The Evangelical Quarterly,* January 1990; Chris Sugden and Oliver Barclay, *Kingdom and Creation in Social Ethics,* (Grove books, 1990).

in an article published in 1986, Sir Fred Catherwood, like Carl Henry, has bemoaned the way in which the world seems to be setting the agenda for evangelical social action. He stated:[12]

> 'In the sixties I wrote that we Evangelicals should come out of our pietistic ghetto and take part in the social debate as Christian citizens ... I and others in the movement won the argument ... But we also lost a vital part of the case we were making. We did not allow for the 'zeitgeist'. We argued that it was the task of the Christian church to bring the trends in public opinion to the standards of eternal truth and judge them by God's word. But that was not what happened. The Evangelicals joined the Liberals in a concern for social issues, but it was the world and not the church which set the agenda.'

The concerns expressed by Carl Henry and Sir Fred Catherwood point to the fact that the impulses – theological and practical – which motivate social action, indeed even what is meant by 'social action', are not necessarily the same at different periods of history. Whilst we can all agree that nineteenth century evangelical social action did much good, this is no guarantee of the benefits of today's efforts if the theological presuppositions, types of action, or aims of the action are different.

In considering nineteenth-century evangelical social action in Britain, the most obvious fact to bear in mind is that it had been preceded by widespread proclamation of the gospel and Biblical teaching which had resulted in the mass conversions of the Wesleyan revival. J. Wesley Bready has shown in his remarkable study of the conditions in England before and after Wesley, that much of the social improvement – for instance the tremendous decrease in alcoholism and prostitution; the reduction in cruelty to animals; even the increase in literacy and personal living standards – proceeded directly from changed lives which resulted from the response to the preaching of the gospel.[13] As historian of the period, Kathleen Heasman, has noted, these evangelicals 'were all agreed upon salvation by faith and the infallibility and overriding importance of the Scriptures'.[14] Added to this, as David Bebbington, another historian of the period, has pointed out 'nineteenth-century evangelicals insisted on the personal nature of sin and were

---

12. Sir Fred Catherwood, 'The Zeitgeist', *Transformation*, October/December 1986.
13. J. Wesley Bready, *England Before and After Wesley* (Hodder and Stoughton, 1939)
14. Heasman, *op. cit.*, p. 16.

reluctant outside the anti-slavery context to talk in terms of structural evil'.[15] Thus, nineteenth-century evangelical social action was preceded by a great spiritual revival and in the main was limited to what we today would call 'social welfare', or attempts to alleviate problems which had already arisen, rather than changing the whole structure of society – in other words, the evangelical activists of the nineteenth century were mainly reformers, not political radicals.

Bearing all this in mind, it is clear that the resurgence of evangelical social action since the 1960s is different from that of the last century in several respects. In the first place, and crucially, it has not been preceded by a widespread proclamation of the gospel or general revival. On the contrary, although there are obvious exceptions, the period since the 1960s has seen the leaders of the Church of England (including evangelicals) increasingly unsure of themselves in matters of faith and morality, giving a mixed and unclear message to the nation.[16] This has surely contributed to the fact that the last thirty years has witnessed a massive decline in personal morality and family breakdown. As a number of authors have recently pointed out, with an accumulating weight of evidence, this decline in personal morality and breakdown of the traditional family structure is itself leading to a self-perpetuating spiral of increasing social problems and criminality.[17] Against this background, much of today's increased concern for evangelical social action has appeared futile or even hypocritical since, it can be argued, the Church itself, by its accommodation of the 'new morality', is helping to create the very problems which it says it wants to correct.

Secondly, and paradoxically, although evangelical influence upon the nation is clearly weaker than during the last century, some who advocate social action today are much more ambitious in their aims: they talk of combating 'structural sin', 'transforming' society, and 'extending the Kingdom'. This, in turn, has led to strong and sometimes acrimonious disagreements between those social activists who advocate such a radical approach and those who speak in more reformist terms – evidenced, for example, at the 'Salt and Light' conferences on

15. D.W.Bebbington, 'Evangelicals and reform: an analysis of social and political action', *Third Way*, May 1983.

16. Rachel Tingle, *Another Gospel?* (Christian Studies Centre, 1988), pp. 10-14.

17. See, for instance, Norman Dennis and George Erdos, *Families Without Fatherhood* (Institute of Economic Affairs, 1993); Jon Davies (ed.) *The Family: Is it just another lifestyle choice?* (Institute of Economic Affairs, 1993); Charles Murray et. al, *The Emerging British Underclass* (Institute of Economic Affairs, 1990).

evangelical social action held at Swanwick in Autumn 1988 and in Oxford in September 1990.[18] The situation is the same in America, where although there is a consensus amongst evangelicals that they should be involved in public affairs, there is much disagreement over the substance of that involvement. This has been so bad that Ron Sider, himself a leading advocate of radical evangelical social action, has referred to a 'blaze of ferocious fratricide'.[19]

But if today's evangelical social action is different in such key respects from that of the nineteenth century, how did it come about, and what is its driving force? The answer to this is highly complex, but some of the reasons can be traced to the cause and the events following the 'great reversal' itself.

The term 'the great reversal' was originally used to describe the social disengagement of a large section of evangelicalism in America in the years around 1910-1920. (Similar tendencies were at work in Britain in a slightly earlier period).[20] As we shall see, this happened at least partly in response to the way in which the 'social gospel' movement had reduced Christianity to little more than a socio-political agenda.

The most influential thinker and spokesman for the social gospel movement was Walter Rauschenbusch, a Baptist minister and professor of church history at Rochester Seminary. Most accounts describe Rauschenbusch as starting his ministry with theologically orthodox views and then being 'converted' by his ten-year stint in a dreadful New York slum to 'liberal social Christianity'.[21] The American bishop, Bromley Oxnam, has stated however, that 'he had planned to go to India as a missionary for the American Baptist Mission Society, but his professor in Old Testament and Hebrew questioned his liberal views, and he was rejected'.[22] Rauschenbusch was a fierce critic of capital-

18. These conferences were sponsored jointly by Tear Fund, the Evangelical Alliance, and the Evangelical Missionary Alliance, and are described (somewhat inaccurately) by Chester, *op. cit.*, pp. 155-7.
19. Ronald Sider, 'A Plea for Conservative Radicals and Radical Conservatives', *The Christian Century,* 1st October 1986.
20. See Brian Stanley, 'Evangelical Social and Political Ethics: An Historical Perspective', *The Evangelical Quarterly*, January 1990.
21. See, for instance, John Atherton (ed.), *Social Christianity: A Reader* (SPCK, 1994), p. 171.
22. G. Bromley Oxnam, *Personalities in Social Reform* (New York: Abingdon-Cokebury Press, 1950), p. 58.

ism, which he blamed for the social evils around him, whilst his friend-
ship with leading New York socialists and contact with Sidney and
Beatrice Webb in England inspired him with an alternative political
vision for which he developed a theological justification. This was based
largely on a perspective of the Kingdom of God derived from the Ger-
man liberal theologian, Albrecht Ritschl.

Rejecting the possibility of any metaphysical knowledge of God
and stressing instead merely the ethical aspects of Christianity, Ritschl
had defined the Kingdom of God as the 'organisation of humanity
through action inspired by love'.[23] In *Christianity and the Social Crisis,* published in 1907, Rauschenbusch argued in similar terms. He rejected the 'old evangel of the saved soul' in favour of 'the new evangel
of the Kingdom of God'.[24] 'It is not a matter of getting individuals into
heaven,' he declared, 'but of transforming the life of earth into the
harmony of heaven.'[25] Thus he argued that the 'essential purpose of
Christianity' was 'to transform human society into the Kingdom of
God by regenerating all human relationships'.[26]

Five years later Rauschenbusch published his 400-page *Christianizing the Social Order.*[27] In this he saw sin as imbedded in social structures, and salvation as essentially liberation from capitalism. Regarding Jesus as 'a prophesy of the future glory of humanity, the type of
Man as he is to be', he developed his vision of a socialist system based
on ethical humanism.[28] Later, in his *A Theology for the Social Gospel,*
he made even clearer the subservience of his 'theology' to this political dream declaring that: 'We have a social gospel. We need a systematic theology large enough to match it and vital enough to back it', and
argued that 'a readjustment and expansion of theology' is necessary in
order to 'furnish an adequate intellectual basis for the social gospel'.[29]

Both Rauschenbusch and his colleague, the Congregationalist leader,
Walter Gladden, were seminal influences on the American Federal

---

23. J. Richmond, *Ritschl: A Reappraisal* (London: 1978).

24. Walter Rauschenbusch, *Christianity and the Social Crisis* (Macmillan, 1907), p.
357.

25. *Ibid.,* p. 65.

26. *Ibid.,* p. xiii.

27. Walter Rauschenbusch, *Christianizing the Social Order* (New York: Macmillan,
1912).

28. See extract in Atherton, *op. cit.,* pp. 173-181.

29. Walter Rauschenbusch, *A Theology for the Social Gospel* (New York: Macmillan,
1918), p. 1.

Council of Churches (FCC) which was launched in 1908. Thus the social gospel approach became embedded in the emerging ecumenical movement and influenced denominations affiliated to the FCC and its successor, the National Council of Churches.[30] Because of this, as Bishop Oxnam stated in 1950, 'the greatest single personal influence on the life and thought of the American Church in the last fifty years was exerted by Walter Rauschenbusch'.[31] It was the reaction against this social gospel, combined with the growing pessimism about the possibility of establishing anything approaching a perfect society on earth – engendered both by the experiences of World War 1 and the increasing adoption of premillenialist eschatology, which led many American evangelicals to shift their concern away from social action. The twelve-volume series, *The Fundamentals,* which appeared from 1909-1915, acted as a rallying point for such conservative evangelicals, and from this time on the American Church split into two broad camps – the liberalist FCC-affiliated denominations, and the 'fundamentalist' evangelicals who concentrated on evangelism, a defence of orthodox theology against modernism, and, to a varying degree, separation from the world.

Through the FCC and other channels the social gospel movement also took root in the World Council of Churches (WCC), established in 1948. As Harvey Hoekstra has described in detail, this eventually had enormous consequences for the way in which the role of the church in the world (its 'mission') came to be viewed.[32] In order to co-ordinate their efforts in world-wide evangelism, most of the world's leading missionary societies were united in 1921 under the umbrella of the International Missionary Council (IMC) and in 1961 the IMC became subsumed within the WCC as the Commission on World Mission and Evangelism (CWME). Gradually at first, but then more rapidly during the 1960s, first the IMC and then the CWME radically redefined the whole concept of 'mission'.

---

30. C. Gregg Singer, *The Unholy Alliance* (New Rochelle, New York: Arlington House, 1975) gives a detailed account of the theological liberalism and ambitious leftist political agenda of the Federal Council of Churches and its successor the National Council of Churches.

31. Oxnam, *op. cit.,* p. 73.

32. Harvey Hoekstra, *Evangelism in Eclipse* (Paternoster Press, 1979). See also Arthur Johnston, *The Battle for World Evangelism* (Wheaton, Illinois: Tyndale House Publishers, 1978), and Peter Beyerhaus, *Missions: Which Way?* (Grand Rapids, Michigan: Zondervan, 1974).

Such changes were crystallised in a report, accepted by the 1968 WCC General Assembly, which suggested that the focus of God's plan is the world, not the church; and which saw the goal and purpose of mission not as 'Christianization' – bring man to God through Christ – but rather 'humanization', defined as the creation of the 'true man'.[33] This process was continued at the 1973 CWME conference at Bangkok on the theme 'Salvation Today'. Here it was accepted that, like 'mission', 'salvation' should be seen as what we believe God is doing in today's world. Thus, it was argued, salvation is 'contextual', that is, it means different things in different contexts. Although in some contexts salvation might be viewed in traditional spiritual terms, in others it might be given a more materialistic or political interpretation. In a now infamous statement the CWME expressed this 'inclusivist' view of salvation like this:[34]

'it can be said, for example, that salvation is the peace of the people in Vietnam, independence in Angola, justice and reconciliation in Northern Ireland, and release from the captivity of power in the North Atlantic community, or personal conversion in the release of a submerged society into hope, or of new life-styles amidst corporate self-interest and lovelessness'.

It is important to understand the havoc to traditional missionary activity caused by such thinking. If the 'mission' of the church is to bring people to 'salvation', but 'salvation' may be understood in some contexts in purely socio-political terms, then it follows that *in those contexts the 'mission' of the church is socio-political action and nothing else.* This would mean that church resources – both financial and manpower – could legitimately be diverted to socio-political action. This change in thinking bore immediate practical consequences opening the way, for example, for the WCC's highly controversial policy of giving financial support to revolutionary African liberation movements.[35]

It is also important to note that these conceptual changes happening within the WCC were virtually identical to the development of liberation theology which was taking place in Catholic circles in Latin America at about the same time. As one writer from within the ecu-

33. *The Church for Others* (Geneva: World Council of Churches, 1967).
34. *Bangkok Assembly* (Geneva: World Council of Churches, 1973), p. 90.
35. Rachel Tingle, *Revolution or Reconciliation?* (Christian Studies Centre, 1992), pp. 29-52.

menical movement has stated, 'it was not until the 1970s that this theological movement became well-known but it was widespread in the
late 1960s and found in the World Council of Churches both a mouth-
piece and a target'.[36]

It was because they were so disturbed by these developments and
wanted to form some sort of united front against them that, in 1966,
two of the largest North American evangelical missionary societies
organised an international conference on the Church's Worldwide Mission at Wheaton College, Illinois. Wheaton did not overlook the importance of evangelical social concern and indeed confessed a failure
'to apply Scriptural principles to such problems as racism, war, popu-
lation explosion, family disintegration, social revolution, and commu-
nism'.[37] However, in the face of the confusion in terms engendered by
the WCC, the paper on social responsibility reaffirmed the traditional
evangelical view that the 'mission' of the church was evangelism (spoken proclamation of the gospel), and that social action was something
distinct. The four guidelines which emerged from this paper can be
summarised roughly as follows:[38]

– any program of social action must point men to the central message of redemption through the blood of Christ;

– any expression of social concern must provide, where possible,
for a spoken witness to Christ;

– any social action should make sure that it does not arouse ideal-
istic and unscriptural expectations about the possibility of creating a
perfect society on earth, which will only happen after the Second Coming of Christ;

– in engaging in social action, the church should not enter into
wasteful competition with secular agencies.

A similarly distinct approach from the WCC emerged from the more
ambitious World Congress on Evangelism, organised by *Christianity
Today* magazine, and held in Berlin later in 1966.[39] In his opening ad-

36. John Matthews, *The Unity Scene* (British Council of Churches, 1986), p. 50.
37. C. René Padilla, 'Evangelism and Social Responsibility: From Wheaton '66 to
Wheaton '83', *Transformation*, July/September 1985.
38. The conference papers were published in Harold Lindsell (ed.), *The Church's Worldwide Mission* (Waco, Texas: Word Publishing, 1966).
39. The conference papers were published in Carl Henry and Stanley Mooneyham
(eds.), *The Official Reference Volumes: One Race, One Gospel, One Task* (Minneapolis:
World Wide Publications, 1967). For a discussion of the conference, see Johnston, *op.
cit.*

dress, for example, American evangelist, Billy Graham, declared:[40]

'if the church went back to its main task of proclaiming the gospel and people converted to Christ, it would have a far greater impact on the social, moral and psychological needs of men than it could achieve through any other thing it could possibly do.'

John Stott also concluded from his three Bible studies on the 'Great Commission' as found in John, Matthew, and Luke that:[41]

'The commission of the church ... is not to reform society, but to preach the gospel. Certainly, Christ's disciples ... are to love and serve their generation, and play their part in the community as responsible Christian citizens. But the primary task of the members of Christ's church is to be gospel heralds, not social reformers.'

Up to the mid-1960s, then, there was a clear division in the approach to social action between the ecumenical movement on the one hand and evangelicalism on the other. In the years that followed, however, evangelical thought became subject to a number of complex and interrelated factors which shifted it much closer to the ecumenical position. These included: the growing influence of ecumenical theology on evangelicals within WCC-aligned denominations; the influence of liberation theology on young evangelical theologians in Latin America and Asia;[42] and the impact of the American 'radical evangelical movement', led by people like Jim Wallis and Ron Sider, which married the politics of 1960s radical protests with Christianity.[43] The follow-up conference to Berlin, the enormous congress on world evangelisation held in Lausanne in 1974, reflected all these factors and resulted in what can only be described as a paradigm shift in evangelical thinking.

Critical to this process was the role played by John Stott who openly shifted his position from that which he had taken at Berlin, concluding that whilst 'evangelism is part of God's mission', 'mission' is 'every-

40. 'Why the Berlin Congress', *Christianity Today*, 11th November 1966.

41. John Stott, 'The Great Commission' in Henry and Mooneyham, *op. cit.*

42. This was reflected in the Latin American and Asian regional follow-up conferences to Berlin. See Chester, *op. cit.*, pp. 31-32.

43. Jim Wallis's *The Post American* magazine (later *Sojourners*), founded in 1971, played a key role in establishing this 'radical evangelical' movement. See Chester, *op. cit.*, pp. 50-55 and Jim Wallis's autobiography, *The New Radical* (Lion, 1973).

thing the church is sent into the world to do'.[44] Hence he supported 'wholistic', or 'holistic' mission – that is, evangelism *and* social action. Two Latin Americans – C. René Padilla and Samuel Escobar – went further.[45] According to them, social action should not merely be elevated to a position of importance alongside evangelism; rather, the gospel proclamation itself should include a call for social justice and for repentance from social and structural sin. In other words, they called for 'wholistic' evangelism.[46]

A draft of the Lausanne Covenant containing an endorsement of social action had already been prepared before the congress. However, Escobar and Padilla received such an enthusiastic reception, particularly from the many Third World delegates, that the reference to social action was replaced by one to 'socio-political involvement' and additional direct references were made to alienation, oppression and discrimination. Thus article 5 of the Lausanne Covenant affirmed that:[47]

> 'evangelism and socio-political involvement are both part of our Christian duty. ... The message of salvation implies also a message of judgement upon every form of alienation, oppression and discrimination ... the salvation we claim should be transforming us in the totality of our personal and social responsibilities.'

It is probably fair to say that at the time it was formulated, this article did not represent the position of the vast majority of evangelicals around the world, as much as that of some of the more radical, articulate and well-organised elements. Timothy Chester, in his informative book on the recent history of evangelical social action has described how, in the run up to Lausanne, a group connected with Partnership in Mission (PIM) met regularly to discuss the things they wanted to see emerge. One member of the group was Vinay Samuel, who Ches-

---

44. See John Stott, 'The Biblical Basis for Evangelism' in J.A. Douglas (ed.), *Let the Earth Hear His Voice: International Congress on World Evangelism, Lausanne, Switzerland* (Minneapolis: World Wide Publications, 1975).
45. Chris Sugden has stated that 'the blue touch-paper for evangelical social responsibility this century was lit at the Lausanne Congress ... by René Padilla and Samuel Escobar'. See Chris Sugden, 'Evangelicals and Wholistic Evangelism' in Vinay Samuel and Albrecht Hauser (eds.), *Proclaiming Christ in Christ's Way* (Regnum, 1991).
46. See Samuel Escobar, 'Evangelism and Man's Search for Freedom, Justice and Fulfilment' and René Padilla, 'Evangelism and the World' in J.D. Douglas (ed.), *Let the Earth Hear His Voice* (Minneapolis: World Wide Publications, 1975).
47. The full text of article 5 is to be found in Douglas, *op. cit.*

ter quotes as saying, 'there was a definite attempt not to subvert, but an attempt to demonstrate there was another position (on social action).[48] At the congress itself the PIM group came together with a number of other delegates to form an ad hoc 'Radical Discipleship' group. For them even article 5 did not go far enough, and they drafted a statement – in some ways remarkably similar to the approach taken by the WCC at Bangkok the previous year – accepted as an addendum to the Covenant, which defined the gospel as the 'Good News of liberation, of restoration, of wholeness and of salvation that is personal, social, global, and cosmic.'[49]

Since this time a number of other international evangelical congresses have been held which have discussed these issues further. Although there were attempts at both the Consultation on World Evangelisation held in Pattaya, Thailand, in 1980, and at Lausanne 11 in Manila in 1989 (both organised by the Lausanne Committee for World Evangelisation), to emphasise the primacy in mission of traditional evangelism, as with Lausanne 1, a more radical group (in which representatives from Latin American and Asia again played a leading role) succeeded in injecting their views.[50] But their approach was most evident at the relatively small Consultation on the Church in Response to Human Need, held in Wheaton in 1983 and sponsored by the World Evangelical Fellowship. This declared that 'economic and political action is inseparable from evangelism' and coined a new term for the mission of the church – that of 'social transformation'.[51]

The influence of Lausanne on evangelicalism in Britain was immediate. The second NEAC conference at Nottingham in 1977, for instance, stressed not only that social action should be part of Christian mission but also that this should be taken further than social welfare, involving in addition a 'quest for better structures'. Thus it emphasised the importance of political action and saw 'an urgent need for the church to divert more of its time and resources to in-depth political education'.[52] Regular workshops on social action at big Christian conferences like *Greenbelt* and *Spring Harvest* have also been justified as part of the Lausanne mandate.

---

48. Chester, op. cit., pp. 80-1.
49. Padilla *op. cit.*
50. *Ibid.* and Chester, *op. cit.*
51. The full statement is published as 'Social Transformation: The Church in Response to Human Need', *Transformation*, January-March 1984.
52. *The Nottingham Statement* (Falcon, 1977), pp. 7,8,47.

Like the old social gospel, today's calls for radical social action have increasingly been made by reference to the perceived social implications of the kingdom of God. Reflecting the stance of some Third World theologians, American radical evangelicals,[53] and the Partnership in Mission group,[54] for instance, Wheaton '83 declared that the kingdom of God is 'both present and future, both societal and individual, both physical and spiritual'.[55] Amongst Anglican evangelicals who have most insistently adopted this approach are members of the Scripture Union offshoot, Frontier Youth Trust (FYT), and Chris Sugden, assistant editor of the journal *Transformation,* set up in direct response to Wheaton '83's call for 'social transformation'.

The kingdom approach to social action broadens the gospel from personal salvation through Christ's death on the Cross, to the advent of the kingdom – where the kingdom is understood in terms wider than the rule of Christ in the heart of the believer, to the present realisation in society of aspects of the coming eschatological kingdom. Thus Sugden, for instance, argues, like Rauschenbusch, that 'evangelism is making known the evangel, the good news of the kingdom of God' and describes the kingdom as a 'kingdom of right relationships' not just between 'God and man' but also between 'man and man and his environment'.[56] Elsewhere, like the liberation theologians, he has stated that 'the good news of the kingdom is described as good news to poor people'. According to Sugden 'the future kingdom of God determines the present attitudes and actions of the disciples'.[57] Thus, he argues, the task of Christians is 'not just to bring men into new relationships with God, but to bring all the new relationships that the kingdom brings ...The present order must be changed into ever increasing conformity

---

53. Jim Wallis has stated, for instance, 'Many evangelists must plead guilty to the charge of holding a low view of Christ in restricting the gospel to the personal, private, and "religious" issues of life. This sort of preaching offers salvation without "making disciples" who life in radical obedience to Christ as active agents of the kingdom of God ... We can no longer talk of people's need for salvation apart from our responsibility to give the kingdom of God a presence in our generation.' Jim Wallis, *Agenda for Biblical people* (New York: Harper and Row, 1976), pp. 32-33.
54. Chester, *op. cit.*, p. 80, has referred to the fact that Partnership in Mission was led by Steve Knapp who according to Vinay Samuel was 'ahead of almost everyone else in defining the gospel in terms of the kingdom of God.'
55. See 'Social Transformation: the Church in Response to Human Need', *op. cit.*
56. Christopher Sugden, *Radical Discipleship* (Marshall Morgan and Scott, 1981), p. 110.
57. Christopher Sugden, *Social Gospel or No Gospel?* (Grove Books, 1977), p. 12.

with that order which is God's will for it and that will one day super-sede it'.[58]

The consequences of this approach for social action are profound. We live in a fallen world so compared with the ideal kingdom which is to come virtually every aspect of even the best of our societies may be found wanting. Thus the kingdom model of social action has a built-in predisposition to socio-political change, possibly of the most radical kind. In an FYT publication entitled *Towards a New Social Revolution,* John Gladwin (now bishop of Guildford) has argued, for instance, that:

'Kingdom thinking is about more than simply following the example of Jesus in His acts of mercy for the needy ... it is concerned with the struc-tures of society, their inability to reform themselves and the need, there-fore, for confrontation with them and for radical change of them ... King-dom patterns remind the church that it is not only concerned with *preserv-ing* the social order, not even only with providing it with an *alternative,* but also that it is concerned with the radical *transformation* of social order.'

What is wholly missing from this approach (as indeed it has been from most of the discussion on social action at big international evan-gelical conferences), however, is any analysis of what may be socially, economically or politically possible; any consideration of what are appropriate means to use to effect change; or (as Carl Henry has pointed out with reference to recent evangelical social action in America)[59] any recognition or appreciation of the fact that in long-Christianised soci-eties like our own much of the present order is derived from Christian social activity in the past and based on Christian principles – as such it is worth protecting and defending from the humanistic onslaught of the present age.[60] Other evangelicals, aware of these considerations, have thus reacted with dismay to the implications of the kingdom ap-proach to social action which they consider to be either deeply naive or else, like Rauschenbusch's social gospel and much liberation theology, merely a method of advancing a prior commitment to a particular po-litical philosophy. This is one of the factors behind the fierce debate

58. *Ibid.,* pp. 13, 8.
59. Henry, *op. cit.,* p. 170.
60. For a further discussion of these points, see also Rachel Tingle, 'Evangelicals Embrace Liberation Theology', *Crossway,* Autumn 1986 and Rachel Tingle, 'Evan-gelicals and Liberation Theology: An answer to Chris Sugden', *Crossway,* Summer 1987.

within the ranks of socially-active evangelicals mentioned earlier.

Related to this, and more fundamentally, is the question of whether it is theologically correct to use the kingdom concept in this way. Many evangelicals feel it is more accurate to insist, as has John Stott, for instance, that 'the kingdom of God in the New Testament ... may be said to exist only where Jesus Christ is acknowledged as Lord'.[61] Or, as the Scottish Congregationalist theologian, P.T. Forsyth argued in 1915 when the kingdom model for social action was previously in vogue,[62]

'We get the idea by substituting for the word "kingdom" the word "sovereignty" or "lordship" .. We cease to think of an order of society giving effect to certain principles ... and we come to think of a state of things in which God actually, and consciously, and experimentally rules in each soul. The particular social organisation is a secondary affair ... the kingdom of God rising socially from this act of love is not a matter of organisation ... it is a matter of spiritual re-creation.'

If indeed it is the job of the church to help build the kingdom, but the kingdom is seen in the way defined by Forsyth, then we get back to the idea of the primacy of bringing men and women to spiritual new birth through Christ. In other words, the kingdom concept is the theological underpinning and spur for *evangelism* – not social action.[63] This does not, of course, mean that social action is not important, particularly as spiritually reborn men and women are duty bound to obey their Lord's command and love their neighbour as themselves. But social action should not usurp the gospel, or be presented as if it were the gospel.

From what we have seen, then, in this brief overview of immensely complex processes, the renewed concern for evangelical social action we are seeing in Britain today is only partly a return to the nineteenth century evangelical heritage. It is also partly a return to the old social gospel, recycled via the ecumenical movement and liberation theology, and now adopted with only minor modifications by a radical strand of evangelicalism. Because of this a divide has been opening up within

---

61. Ronald Sider and John Stott, *Evangelism, Salvation and Social Justice* (Grove Books, 1979).
62. P.T.Forsyth, *Theology in Church and State* (Hodder and Stoughton, 1915), p. 82.
63. See also John Woodhouse, 'Evangelism and Social Responsibility' in B.G.Webb (ed.), *Christianity and Society: Explorations 3* (Homebush West, Australia: Lancer Books, 1988).

world evangelicalism which over the past thirty years has been getting ever wider. Anglican evangelicals in Britain find themselves on both sides of this divide which the Anglo-Catholic theologian, Ken Leech, has referred to as a 'new reformation'. As he says, 'increasingly the real division within world Christianity does not run along historic denominational lines. It is a division between those who believe that the Kingdom of God involves the transformation of the world and its structures of injustice, and those who do not'.[64]

He might equally well have said that it is a division between those who see the gospel primarily in socio-political terms and those who do not. For this debate is only superficially about social action. It is fundamentally about the meaning of the gospel of Christ.

---

64. Ken Leech, *Marxism Today*, February 1986.

13

OBSERVATIONS OF A FRIEND

D. A. Carson

Introduction

Although I have lived in England for eight of the last twenty-three years, and although I have many friends and colleagues in the Anglican communion, I am neither English nor Anglican. But I am an evangelical, one who is close enough to many brothers and sisters within the Church of England who are going through the throes of recent tensions to agonize with them, yet far enough removed to attempt to offer the reflections of a little distance. I suppose that is why I have been invited to participate. In any case I am honoured, and I hope I have as many friends and colleagues in the Anglican communion when I have finished as I do now.

When the manuscript of this book arrived, I read it carefully, and then re-read with no less care a volume I had earlier skimmed, viz. the book edited by France and McGrath that analyses evangelical Anglicans from a somewhat different perspective.[1] The two books are so divergent that a complete outsider would find it hard to believe that they emerge from what is widely assumed to be more or less the same camp. Both claim to capture the best of the evangelical Anglican heritage, yet clearly they construe that heritage rather differently. So as not to prejudge the issue by appealing to labels some might find pejorative (e.g. 'moderates' vs. 'conservatives', or 'liberal evangelicals' vs. 'conservative evangelicals'), I shall refer to France/McGrath and to Tinker as names representative of the two books and the two constituencies they represent, whatever the overlap.

The Tinker volume is only occasionally a direct response to the France/McGrath volume (e.g. in Gerald Bray's comments on Scripture). Its primary purpose is to call English Anglicanism back to the

---

1. R. T. France and Alister E. McGrath, eds, *Evangelical Anglicans: Their Role and Influence in the Church Today* (London: SPCK, 1993).

theology and discipline represented by the Thirty-Nine Articles, the Ordinal, and the Book of Common Prayer.[2] The open aim is to reform the Church and motivate it to evangelize the country. By contrast, the France/McGrath contributors, though doubtless they share such aims, seem more intent on justifying the validity of (their brand of) evangelicalism within the Church of England.

It may help to organize what follows into six points.

A. Scripture, Truth, and Preaching

From the perspective of historic evangelicalism, from the perspective of the Bible itself, the Tinker group is much more serious about upholding what is not only the ancient position of the church on Scripture[3] but also the view set forth in the Church of England's foundational documents.[4] By contrast, although the contributors to the France/McGrath volume speak of the finality and authority of Scripture, at least some of them seem to be primarily intent on distancing themselves from the heritage from which they spring.[5] If the heritage is wrong, then of course it should be modified. But so long and stable is that tradition that only very powerful arguments and evidence should be allowed to overturn it. Their volume, however, is not the place where such arguments are marshalled. Indeed, it is somewhat disconcerting to be told that 'the methods [Christian scholars] adopt and the conclusions they reach in their studies . . . may even be justified theologically

---

2. Or at least to their theology, if not necessarily to their form: see, for example, the comments of David Holloway on on the Book of Common Prayer.

3. This point must be insisted upon against those who make a 'high' view of Scripture a fairly recent innovation. See especially the plethora of primary documentation treated by John D. Woodbridge, *Biblical Authority: A Critique of the Rogers/McKim Proposal* (Grand Rapids: Zondervan Publishing House, 1982).

4. See also the important work by Gerard Reedy, S.J., *The Bible and Reason: Anglicans and Scripture in Late Seventeenth-Century England* (Philadelphia: University of Pennsylvania Press, 1985), not least Appendix I (pp.145-155), which reprints a sermon of Bishop Stillingfleet responding to Spinoza and Richard Simon.

5. There is an unfortunate lapse in the quality of the argument when R. T. France writes, 'There was a time when the Pauline authorship of Hebrews would have been regarded as part of evangelical orthodoxy, but that time has long gone' ('Evangelicalism and Biblical Scholarship (2) The New Testament', in France and McGrath, eds., *Evangelical Anglicans*, p.51). The late patristic period witnessed a division of opinion between the eastern and western branches on this issue, but one does not normally deploy the label 'evangelical orthodoxy' to refer to the convictions of the western church. I am unaware of any period in Anglican history when this statement would have applied.

by appeal to the idea of the Christian's freedom in Christ',[6] as if any of
the 'freedom' passages in the Bible sanction any and every reading of
Scripture, provided it is scholarly. When the same author casts around
to find some sort of constraint on critical judgments that evangelicals
might enjoy that their more liberal colleagues have abandoned, the best
he can suggest is that 'evangelical biblical scholarship derives a certain sense of direction from its understanding of the Bible as the Word
of God'.[7] That, surely, is no constraint at all, for it is individualistically
interpreted[8] – even though, as McGrath and Wenham rightly point out
elsewhere in the same volume, *sola Scriptura* was never meant to authorize an individualistic reading of Scripture.[9]

The Tinker volume keeps returning to the primacy of Scripture, not
only in the classic categories of conservative/liberal debate (Gerald
Bray, Melvin Tinker) but also in terms of the importance of words and
truth in an age addicted to images (Os Guinness), and in the primacy of
expository preaching (Peter Adam). On the other hand, there is little
reflection, at least in this volume, of what the humanness of Scripture
does mean – e.g. in terms of witness, historical method, and so forth.
Nor is there any reflection (doubtless because it is not the primary
focus of interest) on the way evangelical scholars *ought* to interact with
others. Almost all the emphasis when this subject arises is on what the
humanness of Scripture *does not* mean. That is understandable as a
reaction, considering the emphasis on naturalism in the surrounding
culture. But it is not enough.

B. Hermeneutical Challenges
Both books sometimes display a regrettable lack of hermeneutical so-
phistication. Not without warrant, the Tinker group identifies hermeneutical abuses in the earlier volume. Thus Melvin Tinker rightly points
out that 'kingdom of God' in the New Testament does not normally
refer to the farthest reaches of God's sovereignty. His purpose, of course,
is to confute the view that the overthrow of, say, political or economic

6. Gordon McConville, 'Evangelicalism and Biblical Scholarship (1) The Old Testament', in France and McGrath, *Evangelical Anglicans*, p.39.
7. Ibid., p.42.
8. 'The central tenets of Christian faith, furthermore, do not *directly* require a particular view of any part of the Old Testament. ... The limits will be found in different places
by different scholars.'
9. Alister E. McGrath and David Wenham, 'Evangelicalism and Biblical Authority', in
France and McGrath, *Evangelical Anglicans*, p.29.

evil is 'kingdom' work in exactly the same sense that proclamation of 'the good news' is kingdom work. On the other hand, when David Holloway, in this volume, urges that what we need is 'common sense' exegesis (shades of Thomas Reid *redivivus*), while there is a certain pragmatic side of me that utters a loud 'Amen!', another side recognizes that in an age increasingly dominated by postmodernity something a little more rigorous will have to be advanced.

There is space for only three brief comments.

First, quite a number of arguments from the France/McGrath camp, not least those connected with women's ordination but certainly not only those, turn on perceived 'tensions' in Scripture that can be configured in different ways. Again, when Bishop Holloway (in the France/McGrath volume) blames evangelicals for making too much of the cross and of redemption, and too little of creation and incarnation, the assumption seems to be that these are more or less independent themes that can be juggled and configured in various ways, to the advantage of the particular confessional group.

What is lacking is the confidence that the Bible, however mediated by human authors, ultimately has one Mind behind it. It has a story line, a coherent plot. To interpret bits and pieces of that plot without reference to the entire plot is irresponsible, akin to reading *Romeo and Juliet* as a tract against suicide, or *The Lion, the Witch and the Wardrobe* as a book about the majesty of lions or the danger of the occult. If the Bible fits together – and one cannot abandon that conviction without ceasing to be an evangelical – then how does the story-line 'work'? What is the danger human beings face? How and why has God intervened? What has God disclosed of himself? How is he directing history, and where is that history taking us? What saves us? For what purpose? And who is rescued? How do Israel and the church relate to each other? How is this age tied to the next? Why do the four gospels drive toward the cross? What is the significance of the way the New Testament writers variously pick up themes like temple, sacrifice, priest, passover lamb, bread of God, exodus, and a host of others elaborated in the Old Testament, and tie them to Jesus and his work? Whether one agrees with every stroke in Spanner's essay, at least one admires his attempt to deal with 'the whole counsel of God' holistically. In the same way, Rachel Tingle is surely right to appeal to the Bible's central plot-line in order to constrain political discussion that appeals to the Scriptures.

Second, Gerald Bray has put his finger on a sore point when he insists that much (especially British) evangelical biblical scholarship is devoted to what he calls *sola exegesis* and not *sola Scriptura*. The endeavour becomes atomistic and arid, and turns out to be meaningless unless there is also a systematic theology. The problem can be put a slightly different way. One of the things that is needed is careful delineation of the relationships amongst exegesis, biblical theology, and systematic theology. Each of those terms cries out for definition, of course, a task I cannot undertake here. But even if one were to adopt some *ad hoc* definitions – e.g. biblical exegesis is the responsible reading of the biblical texts, biblical theology is an inductive discipline that attempts to synthesize the content of the biblical corpora while bearing in mind both their different literary genres and the sequential biblical plot-line, and systematic theology is the synthesis that results from asking atemporal questions of the text while remaining in full discussion with historical theology and contemporary culture – even, as I say, if one were to adopt some such *ad hoc* definitions, one would still be responsible to spell out how each of these disciplines ought (and ought not) to influence the others.

The problem is not exegesis over against Scripture/systematic theology, but bad exegesis. Exegesis that is in reality a devout and careful reading of the Word of God is surely entirely salutary. But in what ways should biblical and systematic theology exercise a restraining or guiding influence on exegesis? Conversely, how does exegesis properly inform and reform one's biblical and systematic theology? Some of these questions have recently been addressed by Kevin J. Vanhoozer;[10] there is a great deal more to be done. But because no exegesis is presuppositionless, our theology *does* constrain our exegesis. That is true of *all* exegesis. If much contemporary evangelical exegesis is atomistic, this reflects what those evangelical scholars think or do not think about Scripture. This does not mean that exegesis, which is one step closer to the actual text than the lofty syntheses theology constructs, should not itself reform theological syntheses. It means, rather, that if in exegesis after exegesis a reading is uncovered that no evangelical would have admitted three or four decades ago, then one's the-

10. 'From Canon to Concept': "Same" and "Other" in the Relation between Biblical and Systematic Theology', *Scottish Bulletin of Evangelical Theology* 12 (1994) 96-124. Cf. also D. A. Carson, 'Current Issues in Biblical Theology: A New Testament Perspective', *Bulletin for Biblical Research* (forthcoming).

ology has *already* changed, whether this is admitted or not.

Failure to recognize these realities lies, in part, behind France's response to James Barr. France has offered some of the most thoughtful interaction with the latter's (in)famous *Fundamentalism*.[11] But he seems to buy into Barr's association of 'fundamentalism' with those who hold to 'inerrancy, infallibility and the other accompanying features' he spells out, and who therefore seem unwilling to engage in critical study as Barr thinks of critical study. France writes:

> The question remains, however, how much of current evangelical biblical scholarship does in fact fall within Professor Barr's definition of 'fundamentalism', however much we might dislike the term – or at any rate how much residual 'fundamentalism' there is within the work of those of us who think of ourselves as evangelicals operating within the mainstream of critical scholarship rather than against it. Or, to put it the other way, how real is our commitment to critical study? Are we in fact willing to follow standard critical method only so far as our evangelical tradition, and the expectations of the evangelical constituency, will allow? Are we really playing the game by the accepted rules? Can we justly expect to be received as *bona fide* members of the scholarly guild?[12]

This is very unsatisfactory. Suppose our study of Scripture leads us to the conclusion that the long-established 'high' view of Scripture is correct: should we abandon it to be acceptable to the guild? Doesn't Barr's understanding of critical method assume a human autonomy that is foundationally at odds with the biblical outlook? Must we accept his view of 'critical method' – apparently having more to do with buying into a certain epistemological construct than with providing reasons for one's views? I was always taught that properly 'critical' views were those that were ably defended in the broadest arena, not those that follow the party line whether well-defended or not. If the guild decides that belief in, say, substitutionary atonement is naive and 'uncritical' (and much of the guild adopts just that stance), are we thereby warranted to jettison substitutionary atonement in order to play 'the game by the accepted rules'? Did Luther play by 'the accepted rules' in his day? Or Whitefield and Wesley in theirs? And in any case,

---

11. London: SCM Press, 1977.
12. R. T. France, 'Evangelicalism and Biblical Scholarship (2) The New Testament', pp.48-49.

isn't it fair to say that in the contemporary scholarly community, increasingly steeped in postmodernism, Barr's views on what can be achieved by critical method sound rather out of date anyway? Why must we be so easily intimidated? *Of course* my understanding of the nature of Scripture shapes the way I read it. The same is true of Barr, and his bluff should be called. But to tie his epistemological presuppositions to 'critical' and 'critical' to whatever is the opposite of 'fundamentalist' is not only a doubtful reading of the history of fundamentalism, but is theologically and epistemologically naive.

Third, by referring to postmodernism I have hinted a couple of times at our society's changing epistemology. The new hermeneutic, arising out of fundamental issues in interpretation, and radical hermeneutics, which traces its origin to developments in linguistics, have conceived and brought forth deconstruction. If no evangelical would like to buy into deconstruction's dogmatic insistence that the only heresy is that there is such a thing as heresy, many nevertheless want to face squarely the unvarnished fact that all expressions of truth, including this one, are framed by culture (not least owing to the fact that language itself, in this case the English language, is a cultural phenomenon). Many Western thinkers infer from this that all claims to objective, culture-transcending truth are chimerical: truth is tied to individuals or to an interpretive community or is a raw display of manipulative power (depending on whether one is reading Derrida, Rorty, or Foucault).

Elsewhere I have argued at some length that finite sinners can know truth truly even if not exhaustively or absolutely; that the existence of an omniscient God grounds the objectivity of knowledge; that all human knowing is necessarily culturally constrained, but that does not inhibit the possibility of communicating it to other human beings; that various models – the hermeneutical spiral, the fusion of horizons, the asymptotic approach – show the reasonableness of such a stance; that hard experience confutes the strongest forms of postmodernism (Have you ever met a deconstructionist who is pleased when his or her book is misunderstood by a reviewer? Isn't the deconstructionist thereby pragmatically committed to the primacy of authorial intent?). When I engage in university evangelism, I find the climate very different from what it was a quarter of a century ago. But I do not always sense that all the authors in this book have picked up on the changes. Thus, when in his second essay Melvin Tinker refers to Calvin's second mark of the church, viz. preaching the 'pure Word of God', he adds, 'unadulterated by human speculation or, as is more the case today, by liberal theology.' I think I understand what Melvin Tinker is affirming, and I, no less than he, want to insist that there is a gospel 'once for all entrusted to the saints', to use Jude's words. But greater awareness of the nature of the opposition would surely encourage him to state his case no less forcefully, but with clear evidence of greater reflection on the relation between the 'pure Word of God' and the theological syntheses that we evangelicals, too, bring to the table. In other words, it is not that I am disagreeing with his point: far from it, I endorse it enthusiastically. But I fear that some will not listen with the sympathy he deserves because he has not guarded himself against hermeneutical misunderstanding.

C. Different Readings of Anglican History
Reading Alister McGrath in the France/McGrath volume, and David Holloway and to some extent J. I. Packer in the Tinker volume, force upon me the recognition of how much each side is trying to lasso history in order to support a case.

Compare, for instance, what Alister McGrath and David Holloway say about the Thirty-Nine Articles (1571). Pointing out that the Articles 'are explicitly described as "for the avoiding of diversity of opinions and for the establishing of consent touching true religion",' McGrath concludes: 'They are not, and were never intended to be, a confession of faith.'[13] Isn't this a confusion of form and function? I have always thought that one of the functions of confessions was 'for the avoiding of diversity of opinions and for the establishing of consent touching true religion'. Besides, two pages later McGrath says that the Thirty-Nine Articles is 'the only document, apart from Scripture, the creeds[14] and the Prayer Book, regarded as *authoritative* [emphasis mine] for Anglicans.'[15] In what sense are articles shaped in the form of a creed and possessing the authority of the great ecumenical creeds and even (insofar as they reflect the Bible) the authority of Scripture itself, *not* a creed? I frankly do not understand what McGrath means when he says that the Articles were never intended to be a confession of faith. Does he make a distinction between 'creed' and 'confession of faith' that quite escapes me?

---

13. Alister E. McGrath, 'Evangelical Anglicanism: A Contradiction in Terms?', in France/McGrath, eds, *Evangelical Anglicans*, p.11.
14. Although McGrath does not specify, it is of course a commonplace among Anglicans to espouse the first four ecumenical creeds.
15. McGrath, 'Evangelical Anglicanism', p.13.

The purpose of this section of his work, however, is clear enough:

> Historically, Anglicanism has encompassed within its ample girth a variety of theological positions, regarding itself as possessed of a comprehensiveness which prevents the exclusion of demonstrably Christian positions. The latter was viewed as a sectarian tendency, inappropriate for a national established church. As a result, views which could be labelled 'evangelical', 'liberal', 'rationalist' or 'catholic' have been found throughout Anglican history. ... I have no intention of claiming that evangelicalism is the only authentic form of Anglicanism. My concern is simply to insist that evangelicalism is, historically and theologically, a legitimate and respectable option within Anglicanism.[16]

Of course, if the Articles are viewed as in any sense a confession, is not the Church bound *only* to evangelicalism? Is that why the denial that they constitute a confession so firm?

More fundamentally, does McGrath really think that classic liberalism is one of the 'demonstrably Christian positions'? Surely if liberalism adopts a position on, say, Christology that effectively relegates Nicaea and Chalcedon to an age of superstition, it cannot in any useful sense be thought of as a demonstrably Christian position. It is a 'Christian position' only in the dubious sense that many people espouse it, both within Anglicanism and without, and still think of themselves as Christians. If that is a valid use of 'demonstrably Christian position', it is difficult to see on what grounds the stances of Jehovah's Witnesses or the Mormons or the Moonies should not be acknowledged to be 'demonstrably Christian positions'. After all, if the Thirty-Nine Articles have never been a creed and cannot be used to reject classic liberalism, and if even the early ecumenical creeds have no power to expel 'liberal' views on Christology from the 'ample girth' of Anglicanism, why not embrace the Mormons and thus avoid the charge of sectarianism? On McGrath's reasoning, I cannot think of any *doctrinal* reason for not proceeding to accept Mormons into the Church of England. The only *real* reason, I suspect, is that in the 'accidents' of history the Mormons have not historically been part of the Anglican communion – and for that matter would not want to be part of it, because they are too doctrinally robust themselves (as are most cultists).

For David Holloway (in this volume), Anglican history teaches quite

---

16. Ibid., pp.12-13.

different lessons. The Thirty-Nine Articles, the Ordinal, and the Book
of Common Prayer were designed to be doctrinally binding. That was
what the English Reformation under Cranmer was all about. The parameters were sufficiently firm and comprehensive that the Church of
England properly belongs to the Reformation tradition, yet sufficiently
free from cluttered detail that Hooker could establish his principle:
where Scripture does not speak, the Church is free to establish patterns
that seem useful and beneficial. Holloway argues that historically the
prime dispute between the Church of England and the nonconformists
was not over the form of government (two offices or three?) but as to
whether or not there should be a *national* church.

My comments on this reading of Anglican history are three.

First, I suspect that Holloway's comments on the Thirty-Nine Articles and the Book of Common Prayer are right: they were designed to
shape the direction of the church, and bring about a doctrinal uniformity in line with the magisterial Reformation. But they were never sys-
tematically and effectively used to excise those elements that disagreed.
However much their most loyal adherents are right in thinking of them
as credal, they were not so deployed that those who choked over some
of the Articles were excommunicated forthwith. Doubtless Cranmer
was moving the Church toward a consistent Reformation stance. In
that sense, the Articles and Book of Common Prayer functioned as
agents of change within a Church that was now independent of Rome
for primarily pragmatic reasons: Henry VIII and his wives cannot be
completely ignored. If by 'confession' we understand an ecclesiastical
instrument of exclusion *not only in stated aim but also in practice*, the
Articles have never served very effectively as a confession. Is this what
McGrath means? If so, what McGrath sees to be a badge of honour
Holloway would, I suspect, take to be an unfortunate and regrettable
lapse.

Second, although the Hooker principle helped the Church wend its
way through the swamp of debates over vestments and other matters,
what is less clear – to me, at least, as an outsider – is precisely how that
principle squares with Article VI, on the sufficiency of Scripture. If the
Church has the right to *prescribe* on matters that are not clearly spelled
out, then where is the freedom of conscience for those who are in entire accord with the Scripture *and its sufficiency*, and who feel that the
doctrinal formulation accurately reflect what the Bible says, but who
are very uncomfortable with binding prescriptions about adiaphora? I

would very much like to see some intelligent debate between the most sympathetic reading of Hooker and the most sympathetic reading of the Presbyterian regulative principle. Perhaps that is to ask too much. What is clear, I think, is that Hooker did not intend to extend his flexibility to the doctrinal foundations.

Third, if Holloway is right about the fundamental divergence between the Church of England and the Nonconformists, and if others in this volume are right about the Church being primarily the local church, with dioceses and bishops being little more than useful organizational options (of the *bene esse* and not the *esse* of the church),[17] I remain unclear as to what exactly is meant by 'national church'. Suppose there were in England as many Baptist churches or Methodist churches as Anglican churches. Suppose they were organized into areas (dioceses?) and gently supervised, with the consent of the churches themselves, by district superintendents (bishops?). Would they constitute a national church? Why not? Certainly in some parts of the world that is exactly how the expression 'national church' is used. Yet here in England not only would most Anglo-Catholics tie the rubric to the three-fold office and to apostolic connections, but most Anglicans from all theological stripes connect it with establishment: the monarch is the head of the church, and Parliament directly regulates some of her affairs but not the affairs of any other church. David Holloway's attempt to be faithful to Scripture and to read the Church's foundational documents in an historically responsible way is entirely commendable. How then would he defend establishment biblically? Or does establishment, too, depend, rather anachronistically, on the Hooker principle? What a staggering thought.

However much an evangelical reading of the primacy of the local church can be justified after the fact (and theologically I am entirely sympathetic with that view), J. I. Packer's brief summary of the Eliza-

---

17. During a long walk with an Anglican Archbishop a few years ago, my learned interlocutor put forth the interesting argument that the only biblical defense for the office of bishop was the example of Timothy and Titus – not apostles, yet not exercising merely local ministry, but clearly sent to exercise a kind of general oversight over groups of churches. The question arises as to whether Timothy and Titus are best thought of as constituting a paradigm of a continued operational structure, or as an extension of the apostles themselves (or of a particular apostle). I incline toward the latter, which of course relegates bishops (and district superintendents) to the level of useful optional leaders who may serve well but who cannot under any circumstances be thought of as defining the church or as establishing continuity with the apostles. The arguments of Lightfoot, that noble Anglican, are still sound.

bethan settlement (in this volume) is surely an accurate reading of the arrangements that soon prevailed in the Church of England, regardless of the intent of the earliest Reformers. To which period of Anglican history should one refer to establish what is normative?

But Packer's essay offers a reading on another historical matter about which I am less than persuaded. Packer holds that the Thirty-Nine Articles and the Book of Common Prayer established catholicity and unity, a kind of bipolar arrangement that accepted evangelicals and Anglo-Catholics, but would surely have had little truck with liberals steeped in naturalism (this wording, of course, is mine, not his). This arrangement basically worked, with minor lapses in the seventeenth century when the Puritans were expelled and in the eighteenth century when Whitefield and the Wesleys were not in good odour. I doubt if either the Puritan pastors of the great ejection or the people who became known as Methodists would have viewed these events as 'minor lapses', but I shall let that point pass. According to Packer, the arrangement was threatened in the nineteenth century by the Tractarian charge that the Church of England exhibited 'defective catholicity because of what it jettisoned at the Reformation'.[18] Certainly that is one of the arguments that the Tractarians deployed. But hasn't it been well established that one of the primary motivating factors in Tractarian thought was the search for authority and finality at a time when the Broad Church was becoming more and more anaemic about almost everything?[19] I would have thought that this reflects an ongoing tension generated by the extraordinary diversity within the body of empirical Anglicanism rather than some radically new development.

In short, I cannot escape the feeling that J. I. Packer is reading history to support a kind of consensus of Christian theistic supernaturalism, whether evangelicalism or Anglo-Catholicism, over against liberalism and other forms of unbelief. True, the Thirty-Nine Articles cannot easily be understood to tolerate modern liberalism, which was of course virtually unknown when they were published. But it is less than clear to me that the Articles are quite so tolerant of Anglo-Catholicism as Packer suggests. The institutional Church was more tolerant than her founding documents.

---

18. So Packer in this volume.
19. See, for instance, David Newsome, *The Parting of Friends: The Wilberforces and Henry Manning* (Grand Rapids: William B. Eerdmans Publishing Company, 1993 [1966]), *passim*.

My point in going over this old ground again is that the Church of England has always been broader than its foundational documents.[20] Part of the reason is bound up with the peculiar circumstances by which she came into the Reformation camp. But the result, in the eyes of this outsider, is that different parties are reading that complex history in order to justify particular theological stances today. Theologically, I am entirely sympathetic with attempts not merely to win a place in the sun for the theology articulated in the Thirty-Nine Articles, but to ensure that it will prevail in the Church of England. But historical difficulties must be faced. I suspect these divergent readings of Anglican history say as much about modern evangelical Anglican thought as they do about the history itself. More serious yet, I suspect that in an age when postmodern assumptions control so much intellectual endeavour in the Western world, readings of Anglican history, no matter how cogent, will have little influence on the direction the Church of England actually takes today. The arguments serve, rather, to strengthen the hands of those already within this or that party, rather than to win people from one party to another.

D. Lloyd-Jones (1966), Keele (1967), and All That

The France/McGrath volume repeatedly and somewhat triumphalistically refers to Lloyd-Jones's call to evangelical Anglicans to come out from Anglicanism, and to John Stott's celebrated intervention. Triggered in part by this public difference of opinion, the National Evangelical Anglican Congress held at Keele University the next year crystallized the commitments of evangelical Anglicans to work within the framework of Anglicanism and to view themselves as part

---

20. This is quite another matter from the argument of Alister McGrath, 'Evangelical Anglicanism', in France and McGrath, eds, *Evangelical Anglicans*, p.19, that a 'separatist' view of the church 'carries with it the danger of imposing such doctrinal commitments upon church attendance that the mere attending of church can be seen as equivalent to a public Christian profession', while the Anglican tradition assumes 'that the congregation will include both believers and unbelievers, and that attendance at church does not necessarily signify any profession of Christian faith.' I am astonished by this judgment. Quite apart from the fact that believers in what he calls the 'separatist' tradition do not normally refer to themselves that way (they are 'nonconformists' or belong to 'free churches' or to 'the believers' church tradition'), I know very few congregations in that tradition that assume attendance signals doctrinal commitment or any profession of Christian faith. This is simply a caricature. In any case it is a separate issue from my observation that the doctrinal experience and range of (sometimes uneasily) tolerated opinion within the Church of England has always been broader than what one might have expected from its foundational documents.

of the Church of England's framework, rather than as a group of awkward outsiders who couldn't quite bring themselves to leave. This Congress, we are told, marked 'the beginning of the more positive role of evangelicalism within the Church of England, and the end of any serious "separationist" party within English evangelicalism.'[21] By contrast, the Tinker volume avoids Lloyd-Jones (Why?), but tends to view Keele as a sign of doctrinal declension.

The most trenchant assessment of the France/McGrath line on Keele is not found in the Tinker volume, but in a review:

> They all [i.e. the contributors to France/McGrath] seem committed to the myth of Keele. Before SEAC 1967 all was chaos and darkness; pietism, parochialism and isolation reigned unchallenged. Then a thousand evangelicals met, and there was light! They bathed the church, the world, cultures and structures with instant illumination.
>
> Like most myths, this cartoon has just enough truth to make it plausible. Writer after writer now passes it on, with no suggestion of anything lost in the process and no trace of the shudder among Free Church evangelicals. One day someone will write the story differently. My own vicar in 1967 was a first class scholar-pastor, absent from Keele since he was helping our bishop to run his diocese, up to his neck in those ecclesiastical structures whose existence, it is alleged, we never before suspected. Other clergy and laity have told similar stories.
>
> Up to then we had survived on Quiet Times, Prayer Meetings and Guest Services; Keele discovered politics, sacraments and the arts. But evangelicals were outside Aldermaston by 1960; Alan Stibbs on the Lord's Supper still looks radical today; and the tragi-comic side of post-Keele culture is the thirteen-hundred page slab of staleness called the 'Alternative Service Book of 1980'. If we are so newly literate, so culturally adult, why is it virtually impossible to find any senior literary figure of the late twentieth century who has a good word to say for it?[22]

I am not sure that any of the major figures in these defining moments of modern Anglican evangelicalism covered themselves with glory. Lloyd-Jones could have been clearer and more focused if he had not tied the primacy of the gospel to the call to abandon Anglicanism. Despite repeated assertions to the contrary, he did not invite evangeli-

21. 'Introduction', in France and McGrath, eds., *Evangelical Anglicans*, p.5.
22. Christopher Idle, review of France and McGrath, eds., *Evangelical Anglicans*, in *Churchman* 107 (1993) 279.

cal Anglicans to come out *and form a new denomination*: he was so little given to questions of strategic organization that it is far from certain he had a clear conception in his own mind as to what he was inviting them to.[23] But he did want evangelical Anglicans to leave the established church, primarily because he perceived that many were shifting from a view in which evangelicalism, at its best, is the locus of where the gospel is defended and proclaimed, to a view in which evangelicalism is one form of the gospel, within the cherished diversity of other equally valid forms expressed in the national church. What was at stake, for him, was the gospel. And I have to say that, however much I think his solution was misjudged, his reading of trends was both accurate and prophetic. One of the tragic ironies is that the form of his appeal probably hastened the developments he was trying to derail. Doubtless with the benefit of hindsight many wish he had focused his considerable energies, that evening of 18 October 1966, on the non-negotiability of the evangel, with clear warnings as to the drift he was seeing, without calling on evangelical Anglicans to leave the Church many were still committed to reforming (even if other evangelical Anglicans were less interested in reformation than in securing their place in the ecclesiastical sun). Doubtless with the benefit of hindsight many wish that John Stott, if he was going to step out of the chair in that unprecedented way, had spent less time blunting the unfortunate call to 'come out' and more time reinforcing the urgency of preserving the exclusiveness of the evangel among evangelical Anglicans he wanted to stay in. Had both these wishes been realized, perhaps English evangelicalism would today be far more robust, and unified, than it is. But if I continue in this vein I shall soon be in danger of drifting from hindsight to speculation.

The issue, surely, is the evangel, the gospel – what it is, and how it relates to what the church is. Melvin Tinker rather shrewdly comments that when evangelicals are patronizingly dismissed as having no ecclesiology, 'what critics often mean is that they do not like the ecclesiology evangelicals have'.[24] I wish there were space to address this complex question here, for clearly not all evangelical Anglicans share the ecclesiology articulated by David Holloway, Melvin Tinker and John Woodhouse.

---

23. Here, surely, Iain H. Murray is right: see his *David Martyn Lloyd-Jones: The Fight of Faith*, 1939-1981 (Edinburgh: The Banner of Truth Trust, 1990), *passim*.
24. 'Toward an Evangelical View of the Church', in this collection, p.95.

E. Ordination of Women to the Priesthood

It would be tiresome to summarize, even briefly, the divergent stances on this subject taken by the France/McGrath and the Tinker camps. Certainly there is no space here to evaluate the quality of the argumentation on the two sides, or to analyse the underlying hermeneutical issues. My own views are well enough known that it will surprise no one if I say that the best of the arguments in the Tinker camp on this issue are far more cogent, and their conclusions far more biblically aligned, than those of their counterparts. But perhaps four practical observations from an outsider will suffice for the moment and may be helpful to some.

First, it is mildly shocking that not one of the twelve bishops normally thought of as evangelical voted against the ordination of women to the priesthood. It is shocking not because it happened – frankly, there is little the House of Bishops does these days that strikes outsiders as particularly shocking – but because the convictions of tens of thousands of ordinary conservative evangelicals were entirely unrepresented in that House. One could draw numerous inferences, but I refrain, because I am not certain how many of them are valid.

Second, if left to stand unmodified, the decision of November 1992 does not bode well for the future of the Church of England. Regardless of what one thinks of the decision on exegetical and theological grounds, the distressing fact remains that not one mainline denomination anywhere in the world has taken this step, to the best of my knowledge, without accelerating the denomination's decline. Doubtless the reasons are complex. Moreover, if those who voted did so with reverent conviction that this was the wise and godly and biblically responsible thing to do, regardless of the outcome, then their courage should be applauded, whatever one thinks of their judgment. Nevertheless, though I am neither a prophet nor the son of a prophet, I predict accelerating decline in the Church of England unless this decision is reversed or substantially modified.

Third, although current incumbents who are doctrinally opposed to this step are not threatened by it, it is hard to see how a substantial number of new evangelicals of the Tinker stripe will manage to be ordained in the future. The odd one will slip through this cordon, of course: ABM may be asleep at the switch, or someone may change his mind after taking the ordination vows, or perhaps the occasional candidate will be ordained in Sydney before returning to England. But unless this step is reversed, the number and witness of conservative evangelicals is heading for precipitate decline. And since the witness of conservative evangelicals is quite commonly the most evangelistically fruitful in the church, the loss of such young men to the ministry, or at least to the Anglican ministry, will inevitably damage the Church of England.

Fourth, a substantial number of evangelicals associated with the Tinker group have pointed out that the hermeneutical and exegetical slippage that has sanctioned the ordination of women is indifferentiable from the arguments some now advance to champion the ordination of homosexuals. Others concede the point, but think it is strategically unwise to bring the matter up, as it unnecessarily alienates some who might otherwise help. I tended to agree with the latter camp, until the House of Bishops recently decided to validate lay homosexual relationships. If present trends continue, it is only a matter of time before the ordination of homosexuals comes up for a vote: three years? four years? Let the arguments begin, courteously and firmly: confessional believers will want to know if there are any lines the leadership of the Church will not cross, any at all. It is even conceivable that that issue will generate the schism that Lloyd-Jones called for. Conceivable, but unlikely: the habit of belonging is a hard one to break, regardless of whether belonging is a badge of honour, courage and loyalty, or a badge of shame, fear and compromise.

F. *Reform* and Miscellaneous Musings

There are several interesting papers in these two volumes on which I have said nothing or almost nothing – e.g. Oliver O'Donovan in the France/McGrath volume, and John Woodhouse in this one. In addition to their intrinsic value, the best of them show that both sides can make useful suggestions and advances in areas where they are not in dispute with each other. But in a paper already grown too long, I pass by the luxury of comment on these matters, and offer five final observations.

(1) One of the really attractive features of *Reform* is its attempt to influence the Church of England not simply on a single agenda item, but on a broad base that is passionately gospel-related, committed to evangelism, devoted to a return to doctrinal standards. What its prospects are I really cannot say; how wise or effective its tactics are I am too poorly positioned to judge. But I am encouraged by its published goals and articulate call, and pray that God will use this movement in

220 THE ANGLICAN EVANGELICAL CRISIS

surprising and fruitful ways. Whether it will prove to be nothing more than a spirited rearguard action in the context of an institutional church determined to go another way, or an agent of genuine reformation, is probably too early to say, even for those who have much closer access than I.

(2) A number of critics have pointed out that the only person in the France/McGrath volume to mention the importance of justification for evangelicals, or to reflect on how close to the centre of things substitutionary atonement is for them, is the liberal Anglo-Catholic bishop who wrote the last chapter. What is at stake is not, finally, the ordination of women or even the authority of the Bible, but the gospel. The Tinker volume makes more insistent reference to the gospel, and provides us with one essay to define it.[25] That essay is an important summary, even if at one point its content is debatable[26] and at a couple of points it ventures into critical terrain where one might wish, perhaps unreasonably, that it would argue its case instead of merely affirming it.[27]

(3) Insofar as Anglican evangelicalism is part of worldwide evangelicalism, it reflects some of the strengths and weaknesses of the broader movement. Because both books, for understandable reasons, focus so much attention on (if I may put it this way) *Anglican* evangelicals rather than on Anglican *evangelicals*, neither locates the parameters of the debate within the framework of worldwide evangelicalism, but within the framework of (English) Anglicanism. That means there is too little attention, especially in the France/McGrath volume, devoted to the critical issues that the broader movement is facing: novel

---

25. Viz., Mark Thompson, 'Saving the Heart of Evangelicalism'.

26. The sixth distinctive of evangelical theology, Thompson avers, is 'the imminent personal return of Jesus to judge: a distinctive view of universal history'. There is nothing in the following paragraphs to which thoughtful evangelicals would be likely to take exception. On the other hand, the word 'imminent' in the heading of that section (a word not developed within the section) is normally taken to refer, in evangelical theology, to the belief that Jesus could return at any time – and certainly some influential evangelicals have denied that belief. They have insisted that Jesus is coming at the end of the age, but insist that his return will not be before the gospel triumphs in glorious splendour around the world. Such postmillennialism, of course, was typical of the English Puritans, whom Thompson would surely not wish to exclude from his definition.

27. E.g. the current debates on justification, or the rising body of literature insisting that evangelicalism must be defined primarily in the categories of the social sciences, cry out for interaction.

definitions of justification; the drift to the peripheral at the expense of the central; a nervous, reactionary twitching in some parts of its constituency because of the pace of cultural change, and an infatuation with novelty in other parts of its constituency for exactly the same reason; secularizing trends in many sectors, and an ill-informed flirtation with forms of 'spirituality' divorced from the gospel in others; and so forth.

(4) The first of these two books has a title that is slightly misleading. It does not really attempt to assess the 'role and influence' of 'Evangelical Anglicans' in the Church of England today. For a start, it refuses to mention anyone to the 'right' of where its contributors are, no matter how influential (e.g. Dick Lucas), and it does not evaluate the extent and influence of evangelical movements, clergy, and institutions, however defined. For example, there is not a word about evangelical hymn-writers (e.g. Timothy Dudley-Smith and Michael Perry). Primarily it justifies the ways of (one subset of) evangelicalism to Anglicanism, and calls on evangelical Anglicans to be better Anglicans, not better evangelicals.

(5) Finally, although I have deployed two books as the foci for offering comments on evangelical Anglicans, I must conclude by confessing that this is in some measure artificial. There is a spectrum of views, and many who are perceived to be in the 'other' camp on some issues are clearly in 'our' camp on others. The France/McGrath contributors celebrate John Stott's leadership in 1966 and 1967, though I suspect that some of them would be very uncomfortable with many of the things he insists upon with respect to the Bible, the cross, and the gospel. Which contributor in the Tinker volume has not greatly benefited from Stott's writings and preaching, even if they might want to distance themselves from him here and there? A score of other examples come to mind.

* * * * *

Many of us nonconformist evangelicals feel we owe an incalculable debt of gratitude to many, many evangelical Anglicans in this country. We pray for you and agonize with you as you face a crisis in theology, leadership, and ecclesiastical direction of very considerable proportions. If we offer suggestions, do not always listen to us: we make our own share of mistakes and commit our own sins. But we beg of you to retain the integrity of the gospel, unflinching commitment to its finality, uncommon courtesy toward those who will disagree with you, a continuing zeal for a continuing reformation, and a clear-sighted ability to distinguish between what is of ultimate importance and what is a passing allegiance. May the Lord have mercy on us all.